FIRST RESPONDER

SELF-HELP

SOLUTIONS

PRACTICAL TOOLS TO BUILD MENTAL RESILIENCE, STRENGTHEN RELATIONSHIPS, AND THRIVE IN A HIGH-STRESS CAREER

JERRY VINSON, CRNA, CHAPLAIN, FF, LP

ISBN Paperback: 979-8-9989242-0-0
ISBN Hardback: 979-8-9989242-1-7
For inquiries, permission, or further information, please contact:
Email: support@livewealthyformula.com

CONTENTS

Introduction   7

1. FOUNDATIONS OF MENTAL RESILIENCE   17
   Understanding the First Responder Mindset   18
   The Science of Stress and Resilience   20
   Emotional Triggers and Response Mechanisms   22
   Grounding Techniques Focusing on Your Five
   Senses   24
   Emotional Regulation Strategies and Cognitive
   Reframing   26
   The Weight of the Badge: Balancing Duty and
   Vulnerability   30
   Building Blocks of Psychological Strength   32
   Body Scan Meditation   33

2. TECHNIQUES FOR STRESS MANAGEMENT   37
   Stress Management Tools at a Moment's
   Notice   37
   Encouraging Cognitive Flexibility   40
   Mindfulness on Duty: Staying Present in High-
   Stress Situations   42
   The Role of Physical Fitness in Mental Health   44
   Other Breathing Techniques for Instant Relief   46

3. OVERCOMING TRAUMA FROM CSI
   AND PTSD   49
   Defining Trauma and Its Impact on First
   Responders   50
   Trauma-Informed Care for Self and Others   55
   Self-Help Coping Mechanisms and Therapies   58
   Creating a Personal PTSD Management Plan   60

4. MENTAL HEALTH AWARENESS AND
   STIGMA REDUCTION   63
   Communicating Your Mental Health Concerns   64
   Stigma Busting: Changing Perceptions in the
   Workplace   66
   Encouragement of Open Dialogue: Communal
   Support   68
   Building a Culture of Mental Health Advocacy   70

5. CREATING A SUPPORT NETWORK   73
   Peer Networks: A Way Forward   74
   Engaging with Mental Health Professionals   76
   Strengthening Family Ties for Emotional
   Support   79
   Community Resources and How to
   Access Them   81

6. IMPROVING YOUR COMMUNICATION
   SKILLS   85
   Communication During Emergencies   85
   Working Through Difficult Conversations with
   Empathy   87
   Listening Skills: The Foundation of Strong
   Relationships   89
   Communicating Your Needs Clearly   92

7. BALANCING YOUR WORK AND PERSONAL
   LIVES   95
   Establishing A Routine   95
   Techniques for Detaching from Work Stress
   at Home   98
   Scheduling Self-Care into Busy Shifts   100
   Cultivating Hobbies and Interests Outside
   of Work   102

8. LEADERSHIP AND MENTORSHIP IN HIGH-
   STRESS CAREERS   107
   Leading by Example: Promoting Mental Health
   Awareness   108
   Leading with Empathy and Understanding   110
   Creating Supportive Environments: Policies
   and Practices   112

Encouraging Open Dialogue: Facilitating
Important Conversations   114
Mentorship in Mental Health: Guiding the
Next Generation   116
Building a Resilient Team Culture   118

9. PERSONAL GROWTH AND PROFESSIONAL
   DEVELOPMENT   121
   Goal-Setting for First Responders   121
   Embracing Change and Adaptability   123
   Continuous Learning: Staying Informed and
   Skilled   126
   Building Confidence and Self-Efficacy   128

10. SELF-CARE ROUTINES FOR FIRST
    RESPONDERS   131
    Your Personalized Self-Care Plan   131
    Nutrition: The First Pillar of Wellbeing   140
    Sleep: The Second Pillar of Wellbeing   143

11. FAMILY DYNAMICS AND IMPACT   147
    How Family Members Can Help You   148
    Involving Loved Ones in Your Healing Process 149
    Making A Family Support Plan   152
    Maintaining Strong Family Connections   156
    Supporting Children in First-Responder
    Families   157
    Conflict Resolution in High-Stress Marriages 159
    Working Through Relationship Challenges
    with Partners   161

12. LONG-TERM CAREER SUSTAINABILITY   165
    Preventing Burnout with a Supportive Work
    Environment   166
    Financial Planning for Long-Term Stability   167
    Planning for Career Transitions and
    Retirement   169
    Celebrating Achievements and Reflecting on
    Your Growth   171

Managing Reputation: Building a Legacy of
Integrity   173
Professional Networks: Building Community
Support   175

Conclusion   177
References   181

INTRODUCTION

As a seasoned healthcare provider, volunteer firefighter, licensed paramedic, and volunteer licensed Emergency Services Chaplain, I've witnessed firsthand the toll that the daily grind of emergency response can take on the hearts and minds of those who serve. I remember a day when a fellow firefighter, a friend I had known for years, confided in me about the weight of the trauma he carried with him. His eyes, once bright with purpose, now held a haunting emptiness. At that moment, I realized the true cost of our calling—and our community's desperate need for support and understanding.

First responders such as paramedics, firefighters, police officers, emergency medical technicians (EMTs), military personnel, and healthcare providers often face extremely stressful, traumatic, and high-pressure situations as part of their daily duties. While they are trained to respond to emergencies effectively, they can still develop poor coping mechanisms that affect their long-term mental and emotional wellbeing. These coping mechanisms can stem from the nature of the work itself, the lack of adequate emotional support, or systemic issues within their professions. These coping mechanisms take all sorts of forms:

- **Substance Abuse:** Many first responders turn to alcohol or drugs as a way to numb the emotional pain, stress, and trauma they experience. The desire to escape from vivid memories of traumatic events—accidents, deaths, violent situations, etc.—can lead to unhealthy patterns of substance use. One study showed that around up to 40 percent of first responders struggle with some form of substance abuse in order to deal with the stress of their jobs (Witkowski et al. 2024). Police officers, meanwhile, face substance abuse issues at a rate of two to three times higher than the general population (Ballenger et al. 2010).

- **Avoidance:** Some first responders avoid processing their emotions or confronting traumatic experiences. This generally involves keeping their feelings bottled up, not talking about their experiences, or avoiding discussions that trigger memories of traumatic events. Over time, this avoidance can lead to emotional numbness or an inability to effectively deal with stress—not to mention the potential for a catastrophic breakdown.

- **Hypervigilance:** First responders are constantly exposed to high-risk situations, and as a result, they often remain hyper-vigilant even outside of their work. They may have trouble relaxing, trusting others, or feeling safe in normal, everyday situations.

This prolonged state of alertness can cause chronic stress, anxiety, and burnout.

- **Isolation:** Feeling disconnected from friends and family or withdrawing from social interactions is another common response to the trauma first responders experience. They might feel misunderstood or unable to share their experiences with those who don't have similar jobs, leading to feelings of loneliness and isolation.

- **Overworking:** First responders sometimes cope with trauma by throwing themselves deeper into their work, working excessively to avoid confronting difficult emotions. This solution is often one of the quickest to cause issues, as it frequently exacerbates feelings of exhaustion, burnout, and emotional detachment.

- **Anger and Aggression:** Exposure to traumatic events coupled with a lack of adequate coping skills can lead to irritability, anger, or even heightened aggression. These emotions can be directed inward, leading to self-destructive behaviors, or outward, affecting relationships with colleagues, friends, and family members.

When poor coping mechanisms are not addressed, the long-term effects on first responders can be absolutely debilitating. We'll get into this a lot more over the course of this book, but for now, just know that some of the most common long-term effects include:

- **Post-Traumatic Stress Disorder (PTSD) and Cumulative Stress Injury (CSI):** PTSD and CSI are serious mental health conditions that can result from witnessing or experiencing traumatic events. Symptoms of these conditions can include flashbacks, nightmares, severe anxiety, and emotional numbness. First responders and healthcare providers are at a particularly high risk of developing PTSD and CSI due to their frequent exposure to traumatic incidents. Approximately 10 to 35 percent of first responders will experience symptoms of PTSD during their professional lives (Obuobi-Donkor et al. 2022)—a much higher number than the general population, where PTSD rates are around 2 to 6 percent (Schein et al. 2021).

- **Burnout:** Burnout is a state of emotional, physical, and mental exhaustion caused by prolonged exposure to stress, often resulting from overworking and a lack of self-care. Symptoms of burnout include feelings of detachment, reduced performance, fatigue, and a sense of ineffectiveness. It can also lead to reduced empathy toward those in need, which affects the quality of care they provide. Up to 60 percent of first responders experience some form of burnout, with paramedics and EMTs often at the highest risk due to the demanding nature of their work (Ryals 2024). Police officers report burnout rates of 12 to 35 percent, with a higher prevalence in departments with low morale or high call volumes (Oginska-Bulik and Juczynski 2021).

- **Depression and Anxiety:** The weight of constantly dealing with crises coupled with poor coping strategies among first responders can result in long-term mental health issues like depression and anxiety. These conditions can manifest as persistent sadness, hopelessness, irritability, and physical symptoms like fatigue, sleep disturbances, and digestive issues. Studies indicate that up to 30 percent of first responders suffer from depression or anxiety disorders. Research in the U.S. shows that around 37 percent of paramedics and EMTs report experiencing symptoms of depression (Huang et al. 2022), significantly higher than the general population's rate of depression of around 5 percent (Koskie and Raypole 2023).

- **Relationship Issues:** The emotional toll of being a first responder often spills over into personal relationships. Issues such as emotional unavailability, anger, and irritability can strain relationships with partners, family members, and friends. The isolation and detachment that many first responders experience can also lead to difficulties in maintaining healthy social connections. Research suggests that around 29 percent of first responders experience relationship difficulties, particularly stemming from emotional distance, hyper-vigilance, and irritability associated with trauma exposure (Sharp et al. 2022).

- **Physical Health Problems:** Chronic stress, poor sleep, and lack of self-care often result in physical health issues for first responders. These can include cardiovascular problems, weight gain or loss, high blood pressure, gastrointestinal issues, and chronic pain (Mariotti 2015). The physical and emotional toll of the job can also exacerbate existing conditions or lead to the development of new health problems. Stress-related illnesses are responsible for a higher incidence of disability among first responders than among the general populace (Obuobi-Donkor et al. 2022). A study on police officers, meanwhile, found that those suffering from PTSD were twice as likely to have a chronic illness or disability compared to those without PTSD (Sareen et al. 2007).

- **Underreporting Issues:** Despite the prevalence of mental health challenges, the stigma surrounding seeking help is a significant issue within first-responder communities. Surveys show that less than half of firefighters in need of professional help for mental health issues have actually sought it out, with many fearing that it will be seen as a weakness or jeopardize their careers. Many responders report being reluctant to seek treatment for mental health issues due to concerns about confidentiality or job repercussions (Wright et al. 2022).

- **Suicidal Thoughts and Behaviors:** Tragically, many first responders face an increased risk of suicide. That same stigma surrounding mental health in first responder cultures often prevents individuals from seeking help, which can further worsen their mental state. Firefighters, and particularly police officers, have suicide rates that are significantly higher than the national average (Carson et al. 2023). In 2021, the Firefighter Behavioral Health Alliance reported around a hundred firefighter suicides annually in the U.S., which is higher than the number of firefighter deaths from line-of-duty accidents (Roberts 2023). Research suggests that around 37 percent of EMTs and paramedics have considered suicide at some point in their careers, while 6.6 percent have actually attempted it (Columbia Lighthouse Project n.d.).

It's extremely important for first responders to have access to mental health support and develop healthy coping mechanisms rather than the unhealthy ones I've highlighted above. The statistics we just looked at paint a concerning picture of the mental and physical toll that poor coping mechanisms take on first responders. With high rates of PTSD, CSI, substance abuse, burnout, and suicides, there's a huge need for systemic change. Luckily, there's a pretty solid map for the process to follow. Steps to address poor coping strategies and the long-term effects of trauma include:

- **Mental Health Education and Support:** Regular training on mental health awareness and coping skills can help first responders recognize when they're struggling and seek help early. Peer support programs and counseling services can also provide a confidential space for them to share their experiences.
- **Promoting Work-Life Balance:** Encouraging a balance between work and personal life is extremely important for maintaining mental and physical well-being. It's particularly important to make sure there's plenty of time for rest and recovery mixed in to further reduce the risk of burnout.
- **Developing Healthy Coping Strategies:** Teaching first responders healthy ways to cope with stress—

mindfulness, physical exercise, hobbies, creative outlets, etc.—can help reduce reliance on unhealthy behaviors like substance use or avoidance.

• **Stigma Reduction:** Reducing the stigma surrounding mental health within first responder communities can help individuals feel more comfortable seeking help in the first place. One great way to reduce barriers to treatment, therefore, is normalizing mental health care and making it an integral part of the first responder workplace culture.

Poor coping mechanisms among first responders can have devastating long-term effects, affecting both their own well-being and the quality of care they provide to others. Addressing these issues through education, support systems, and proactive mental health care is extremely important for helping first responders cope with the challenges of their demanding and often traumatic roles.

This book is dedicated to the resilience and strength of first responders and healthcare workers who dedicate their lives to serving others. Whether you are in the military, a fire-fighter, police officer, EMT, paramedic, 911 dispatcher, or healthcare worker, this book is for you. My goal is to provide equal help to the newly minted recruit eager to make a difference and the seasoned veteran who is battle-worn but still standing strong. It's for families of first responders to help them understand why they may be seeing changes in their loved ones, for the leaders and supervisors responsible for guiding their teams through the storm, and for the mental health professionals who walk alongside us on the path to healing. Each of these roles is extremely important, and this book is a guide to help all of them work through the unique challenges first responders face in their service to others.

My personal path has not been easy. I have faced my share of dark days and inner demons, but through the support of my brothers and sisters in uniform, I have learned to find strength in my scars. This book is a culmination of the lessons I've learned, the wisdom shared by those who have walked this path before me, and the hope that together, we can create a culture of openness and understanding within our professions.

The need for this book has never been more urgent. The demands placed upon first responders and healthcare workers are immense, and they're not getting any easier on their own. We can no longer ignore the toll on our mental health; we must confront the reality that our jobs can both give us purpose and break us down, that we are not invincible, and that seeking help is a sign of strength rather than weakness. The urgency of this message calls for immediate action and highlights the importance of prioritizing our mental well-being.

As you turn these pages, I invite you to engage with the content, think about your own experiences, and start important conversations that can lead to healing and growth. This book is intended to help you overcome your fears and embrace your potential to make things better. Together, we can build a future where no first responder or healthcare worker feels alone in their struggle, where we can proudly wear our uniforms and carry out our duties while prioritizing our well-being. It's long past time we did something about the silent epidemic rampaging through the first responder community.

1

FOUNDATIONS OF MENTAL RESILIENCE

On a bitterly cold night, a call comes through the station. It's a situation that no amount of training could prepare you for—the kind where the outcome rests not just on your skill but on your mental fortitude to face what lies ahead. As you gear up, the adrenaline kicks in, a familiar yet jarring rush. Your mind sharpens, zoning in on the tasks like a well-oiled machine—yet an unspoken weight presses on your shoulders.

This moment, one of many similar instances in a first responder's life, exemplifies the need for mental resilience. It's the invisible armor that sustains you through the chaos, the strength you draw upon when the stakes are unimaginably high. Your ability to make split-second decisions can mean the difference between life and death for both you and the people in your care. This skill, honed over years of experience, is both a gift and a burden. It demands a level of focus and calm that few outside your world can comprehend—but such prowess comes with its own challenges, especially when coupled with the emotional detachment often required to cope with what you witness.

UNDERSTANDING THE FIRST RESPONDER MINDSET

The essence of being a first responder lies in an ever-present sense of duty. You are part of a select group chosen to act when others falter, to serve with an unwavering commitment. This calling is less a career than an identity that shapes your very thoughts and actions. The public often sees you as a hero, an archetype etched into the societal consciousness. This perception is a double-edged sword, carrying with it immense pressure while also reflecting the immense appreciation and value society places on your service. It's an expectation that you must always be strong and always in control. The reality, however, is far more complex—and your unique strength lies in your ability to face this complexity head-on.

Beneath the surface, you might grapple with the mental health challenges that come with chronic exposure to stress and trauma. Each call, each incident, leaves an indelible mark. The risk of CSI, PTSD, and anxiety looms large. It's a shadow that follows you home, intruding upon moments meant for peace, relaxation, and recovery. These experiences take a toll, which is often overlooked or underestimated. The culture of silence in our profession surrounding mental health, though, often leaves you to find a path through these waters alone. It's important to acknowledge these challenges and the strength it takes to face them.

Self-awareness is not simply a concept but an extremely important tool in understanding and managing your mindset. It involves peeling back the layers of your very self to reveal your strengths and vulnerabilities. Taking an honest appraisal of yourself allows you to identify your response patterns and develop strategies to manage them effectively. Personal reflection exercises can help you understand the triggers that lead to stress and the coping mechanisms you employ—and whether they're healthy or harmful. Recognizing these aspects allows you to harness your strengths and highlights the value of your self-awareness in your role as a first responder.

As we continue to explore the foundations of mental resilience, always hold that you are not alone somewhere close in your mind. Many have walked this path before you and found ways to thrive despite the challenges we face. Through the powerful tools of self-awareness and reflection, we can build the strength needed to face the demands of our roles as society's protectors.

Identifying Strengths and Weaknesses

Take a moment to think about a recent challenging incident. What were your immediate thoughts and emotions? How did you respond physically and mentally? Write down the strengths you demonstrated and the weaknesses you noticed. Your goal here is not judgment but understanding your motivations and responses in order to access your potential for growth and healing. Awareness is the first step toward resilience, and acknowledging what you do well and where you struggle lays the groundwork for a brighter future.

THE SCIENCE OF STRESS AND RESILIENCE

It's important to empower yourself by understanding the biological and psychological underpinnings of stress. This knowledge is especially vital for first responders, who frequently operate within high-pressure environments. The body's response to stress is often called the fight-or-flight response—a deeply ingrained survival mechanism. When faced with a perceived threat, your body releases stress hormones like cortisol and adrenaline. These hormones prepare you to either confront the danger or flee from it, increasing your heart rate and blood pressure, sharpening your focus, and tensing your muscles. While this response is an evolutionary coping mechanism that's had a major part in humanity's survival as a species, it's a bit less relevant to our everyday lives than it was in the thousands of years before recorded civilization. Moreover, chronic activation can lead to long-term health issues such as anxiety, depression, or cardiovascular problems. Understanding this process, however, gives you a greater amount of control over your body's reactions, even in the most challenging situations (Cherry 2024).

Resilience, meanwhile, is not a static trait but a process that can be cultivated over time through intentional practices. This adaptability is grounded in the concept of neuroplasticity, which refers to the brain's ability to reorganize itself by forming new neural connections (von Bernhardi, Eugenín-von Bernhardi, and Eugenín 2017). Mental training, such as mindfulness meditation and cognitive behavioral techniques, can improve our resilience by strengthening these neural pathways. Resilience can be further strengthened through the use of adaptive coping strategies like problem-solving and seeking social support, allowing you to work through stress with greater ease and efficiency. These practices serve as a buffer that instills hope and optimism by showing you that you can bounce back from adversity and maintain mental equilibrium.

Research in high-stress professions—including first responders—has identified several effective resilience-building techniques. These techniques are not just theoretical but have been proven to work. For example, studies have shown that stress inoculation training—where individuals are gradually exposed to stressors in a controlled setting—can significantly improve one's ability to handle real-world stress (Saunders et al. 1996). Evidence-based techniques like mindfulness and controlled breathing exercises have been found to reduce physiological stress markers, such as cortisol levels, and improve overall psychological well-being (Fincham et al. 2023). Knowing that these techniques are effective can give you the confidence to implement them in your daily life.

Effective stress management is closely linked to maintaining overall mental health. By actively managing stress, you can prevent the long-term mental health complications common to high-stress careers. Consistent resilience practices such as engaging in regular physical activity, maintaining a balanced diet, and prioritizing sleep all support mental wellness by stabilizing mood and improving cognitive function (Godos et al. 2021). Over time, these practices can lead to lasting improvements in mental health, reducing the risk of burnout, depression, and anxiety. When you incorporate all of these strategies into your daily routine, they eventually become second nature, providing a reliable foundation for dealing with the inherent challenges of your profession.

Understanding and applying the science of stress and resilience is absolutely necessary for first responders. These practices are your tools for maintaining both your personal well-being and your professional effectiveness, enabling you to continue serving your community with strength and dedication.

EMOTIONAL TRIGGERS AND RESPONSE MECHANISMS

Emotional triggers are an ever-present part of the whirlwind of first responder duties. When an EMT, paramedic, or firefighter arrives at the scene of a severe accident, they're likely to be bombarded with sights of trauma and violence. It's no surprise that these experiences leave a lasting imprint on the psyche. The unpredictability of each call and the relentless pressure to make swift, life-altering decisions can place an immense strain on mental well-being. The graphic nature of the scenes encountered is difficult enough to deal with, but the suddenness with which they occur brings it to a whole other level. This constant exposure to trauma can spark a cascade of emotional responses, challenging even the most seasoned professionals. The physiological response is imme-diate. Heart rates spiking, muscles tensing, and the body preparing for action—a vestige of that primal fight-or-flight instinct we talked about. This surge of adrenaline frequently equips responders with the focus and energy needed to act, but it also heightens emotional sensitivity. Some may experi-ence emotional numbing, a protective mechanism that allows them to perform their duties without becoming over-whelmed. Others might go the other direction and find themselves even more acutely aware of their emotional state, rendering them very susceptible to anxiety or sadness.

The relationship between trauma and memory is intricate. For many, repeated exposure to distressing events alters how memories are processed and stored. Flashbacks and intrusive thoughts can become uninvited guests, replaying traumatic scenes at particularly inopportune times (although, to be fair, there's really no such thing as a "good" time for a traumatic flashback). This can lead to difficulty regulating emotions, where even minor stressors trigger disproportionate emotional reactions. In its attempt to make sense of chaos, the brain may inadvertently reinforce these distressing memories, making them even more vivid and accessible.

The good news, though, is that there are effective strategies to manage and mitigate these reactions. Awareness of one's triggers is paramount; first responders can begin developing coping strategies by identifying situations or cues that provoke emotional responses. Mindfulness practices like focused breathing and meditation cultivate self-awareness and allow individuals to observe their thoughts and feelings without judgment. These practices create a mental buffer that can enable responders to approach their duties clearly and rationally.

Peer discussions and debriefings can offer another avenue for processing experiences. Sharing stories with colleagues who understand the unique challenges of the job encourages a sense of camaraderie and collective resilience. In these conversations, healing often begins with shared experiences being used to validate individual feelings and create a supportive network. This peer support is a lifeline that reinforces the idea that no one is alone in their emotional struggles. Implementing trigger awareness exercises can further improve this process. These exercises involve looking back on past incidents—possibly with the help of a professional—to identify common emotional triggers and develop personalized strategies to address them. Grounding techniques such as focusing on the five senses or engaging in physical activity can help maintain emotional equilibrium during stressful situations. Additionally, emotional regulation strategies like cognitive reframing empower individuals to reinterpret and manage their emotional responses effectively.

GROUNDING TECHNIQUES FOCUSING ON YOUR FIVE SENSES

Grounding techniques are strategies used to anchor you in the present moment, especially during times of anxiety and stress or when you feel particularly overwhelmed. One of the most effective methods involves focusing on your five senses to shift your attention away from distressing thoughts and toward concrete, immediate experiences. When you're caught up in anxious or dissociative thoughts, your mind can drift away from the here and now. By deliberately engaging your senses, you force your brain to process real-world stimuli. This sensory input helps disrupt negative thought patterns and reassures you that you are safe and present.

The 5-4-3-2-1 Grounding Technique makes use of all five senses (Gupta 2024):

- **Sight:** Take a moment to look around you. Identify five distinct objects in your environment. Notice their colors, shapes, and details. This helps you focus on tangible aspects of your surroundings rather than your internal worries.
- **Sound:** Listen carefully for four different sounds. These could be the hum of a fan, birds chirping outside, or even the distant sound of traffic—the key is to find four of them that are distinct from each other. Then, tune into the auditory world around you, which grounds you in the moment.
- **Touch:** Identify three textures or sensations. This might include the feeling of your clothing, the texture of the chair you're sitting on, or the sensation of a soft blanket. Focusing on how things feel under your fingertips can reconnect you with your physical presence.
- **Smell:** Recognize two distinct scents. Ideally, these should be pleasant or at least neutral—whether it's the aroma of freshly brewed coffee, a scented candle, or the natural smell of the outdoors. Engaging your sense of smell in this way can evoke memories and emotions that firmly root you in the present.
- **Taste:** Notice one taste. This could be a sip of water, a piece of candy, or simply a lingering flavor in your mouth. This helps complete the sensory cycle and brings your focus fully into your current experience.

There are also some practical tips for using this technique:

- **Practice regularly.** Like any skill, grounding improves with practice. Try incorporating the five senses exercise into your daily routine even when you're not feeling overwhelmed.
- **Adjust as needed.** If you find one sense particularly calming or grounding, you can emphasize that sense more to tailor the exercise to your personal preferences.
- **Combine with other techniques.** Grounding can be paired with deep breathing or mindfulness exercises for even greater benefit.

Regularly practicing grounding techniques helps you create a reliable tool to manage moments of high anxiety or dissociation. It's a simple yet powerful way to remind yourself of the here and now, nurturing a sense of safety and control.

EMOTIONAL REGULATION STRATEGIES AND COGNITIVE REFRAMING

Emotional regulation strategies are, in brief, techniques designed to help you understand, manage, and respond to your emotions in helpful, adaptive ways. One key strategy within this framework is cognitive reframing, which involves changing the way you interpret a situation in order to alter its emotional impact. It's basically a technique used to shift your perspective on a situation by changing how that situation is interpreted. It's widely applied in various settings, including stress management, conflict resolution, and resilience training (Morin 2024). The process typically involves several steps:

- **Identify distorted thoughts.** Recognize when you're engaging in cognitive distortions such as catastrophizing, overgeneralizing, or all-or-nothing thinking.
- **Challenge these thoughts.** Examine the evidence for and against your negative thoughts. Ask yourself if there's an alternative, more balanced perspective.
- **Reframe the situation.** Replace the negative thought with a more positive or neutral interpretation. Instead of thinking, "I always mess up," you might reframe it as, "Sometimes I make mistakes, but I learn and improve every time."

The benefits of cognitive reframing can be significant (Ezawa and Hollon 2023):

- **Reduced Stress:** By altering your perception, you can decrease the emotional intensity of stressful events.
- **Better Problem-Solving:** A more balanced view can lead to clearer thinking and better decision-making.
- **Improved Resilience:** Over time, reframing helps you build a more optimistic and adaptable mindset.
- **Greater Optimism:** Reframing encourages a problem-solving mindset rather than a defeatist attitude.
- **Burnout Prevention:** Reframing helps maintain motivation and a sense of purpose in high-pressure careers.

Instead of seeing change as a threat, cognitive reframing helps you recognize change as an opportunity for growth, learning, and adaptation. This mindset shift can significantly impact your mental well-being, reducing your stress and increasing your overall resilience. Let's look at some examples of how cognitive reframing could help various types of first responders:

1. **Firefighter**
   ◦ **Situation:** *A dangerous fire.*
   ◦ **Negative Thought:** *"This fire is overwhelming; we might not be able to contain it."*
   ◦ **Reframed Thought:** *"This is a challenging fire, but we have the skills, teamwork, and training to handle it safely and efficiently."*
2. **Paramedic or EMT**
   ◦ **Situation:** *A high-stress emergency call.*
   ◦ **Negative Thought:** *"I can't handle another traumatic call like this. It's too much, and it's not like people appreciate it anyway."*
   ◦ **Reframed Thought:** *"I am making a difference in someone's worst moment. My skills and composure help save lives."*
3. **Police Officer**
   ◦ **Situation:** *A potentially violent confrontation.*
   ◦ **Negative Thought:** *"This job is too dangerous. I never know what's going to happen next."*
   ◦ **Reframed Thought:** *"I am trained to handle unpredictable situations, and my preparation helps keep me and others safe."*
4. **Emergency Dispatcher**
   ◦ **Situation:** *A distressing 911 call.*

- **Negative Thought:** *"I feel helpless just sitting here giving instructions. I wish I could do more."*
- **Reframed Thought:** *"My calm voice and guidance do a lot to help people in crisis until responders arrive."*

5. **Search and Rescue Team**
   - **Situation:** *A difficult and seemingly impossible mission.*
   - **Negative Thought:** *"We've been searching for hours with no success; this is hopeless."*
   - **Reframed Thought:** *"Every second we search increases the chance of finding the missing person. Persistence saves lives."*

Practicing cognitive reframing allows first responders to shift their mindset to see obstacles as opportunities for growth, helping them maintain their mental and emotional well-being in the face of adversity. Along with routine practice, trauma-certified therapists and counselors can provide guidance and tools to work through complex emotional reactions and promote long-term mental wellness. Therapists, in particular, can provide personalized strategies and feedback, making it easier to implement cognitive reframing and other techniques effectively.

Developing a toolkit of emotional regulation strategies teaches you how to reframe negative thoughts while helping you create an environment for sustained emotional well-being. This two-pronged approach can help you respond more flexibly to life's challenges, leading to improved mental health and resilience. This, in turn, helps you remain equipped to tackle the challenges of your role.

THE WEIGHT OF THE BADGE: BALANCING DUTY AND VULNERABILITY

The duality of being a first responder involves a constant tug-of-war between duty and vulnerability. This contradiction demands composure during the most chaotic circumstances—a skill honed through rigorous training and relentless experience. Beneath the surface, though, the pressure to remain stoic can be overwhelming. Each call requires grit and resilience, qualities that act as both a shield and a burden. The challenge is finding the balance between being the protector and acknowledging the human beneath the uniform. In high-stakes environments where decisions must be made quickly, vulnerability often gets sidelined. The mask of stoicism becomes the default to hide the emotional turmoil within. But the price of this façade can be steep, with suppressed emotions simmering beneath the surface. The cultural expectation to remain stoic can take a toll on mental health and create a dissonance between the person you are and the role you play. Suppression of emotions might sometimes be necessary in the field, but it can also lead to long-term psychological impacts such as burnout and depression.

The transition from the chaos of the field to the sanctuary of home is fraught with all sorts of challenges. Personal sacrifices are made constantly. Birthdays are missed and precious moments lost, all in service of the greater good. The struggle to maintain a work-life balance is real. It's a delicate dance requiring strategies that prioritize both professional responsibilities and personal well-being. Setting boundaries, practicing self-care, and communicating openly with loved ones can all help you forge a path through this complex terrain.

Open communication is particularly important for nurturing a supportive environment, and emotional intelligence is a huge part of the process. Understanding and learning to manage your emotions—without simply burying them—can have a tremendous effect on your resilience and job performance. Developing emotional awareness allows you to recognize and process your feelings rather than pushing them down under layers of duty. Acknowledging these emotional responses creates space for healthier interactions and decision-making. Practical exercises in emotional regulation, such as pausing to breathe deeply before responding to stress, can make a significant difference.

The weight of the badge is a reality that touches every aspect of a first responder's life, and balancing the demands of duty with the need for vulnerability is a continuous process that requires courage and commitment. By embracing emotional intelligence and acknowledging the human side of the badge, you can thrive in your role with greater resilience and understanding.

Emotional Awareness Check

Take a few moments at the end of each shift to think about the emotions you've experienced throughout the day. Write them down while noting any patterns or triggers that jump off the page at you. Think about how what you were feeling affected your interactions and decisions. This exercise is a powerful tool that improves self-awareness while helping you develop strategies for managing your emotions in the future. The more you commit to this exercise, the more you'll see its benefits in your professional and personal life.

BUILDING BLOCKS OF PSYCHOLOGICAL STRENGTH

Let's talk about psychological strength. It's a subject a lot of first responders misunderstand, with many of us equating "strength" with stoicism. At its core, though, true psychological strength comprises self-efficacy and confidence. These elements empower you to face challenges while instilling a sense of control and capability. Confidence does not mean being sure you will succeed every time but believing in your capacity to handle whatever comes your way. Self-efficacy, meanwhile, is the internal acknowledgment of your competence. It propels you to take on tasks even when the outcome is uncertain. This belief in yourself is extremely important when you're faced with the unpredictable nature of emergency situations.

Emotional intelligence and adaptability are equally significant, as they allow you to deal with complex social environments with sensitivity and understanding. Emotional intelligence involves recognizing and managing your emotions while empathizing with others. This skill improves your communication and teamwork, which are both of extreme importance in high-pressure scenarios. Adaptability, meanwhile, is your secret weapon. It enables you to adjust your approach as situations change, keeping your performance effective even when circumstances change rapidly—as they so often do for first responders. Together, emotional intelligence and adaptability create a flexible yet sturdy psychological framework that supports your professional and personal endeavors.

Positive psychology, which focuses on the positive aspects of human experience, offers valuable tools for improving your resilience. Focusing on gratitude and optimism allows you to shift your perspective from solely managing stress to nurturing a mindset that thrives under pressure. Daily gratitude practices, such as jotting down three things you're thankful for, can surprisingly improve your mood and outlook. This sort of optimism can motivate you to persist in the face of adversity. Indeed, research has actually shown that a positive outlook can have beneficial effects on one's physical health (Park et al. 2014). Additionally, a strengths-based focus encourages you to identify and leverage your unique talents and abilities, which reinforces your self-confidence and self-efficacy.

Cultivating these components isn't something that happens by accident—it requires intentional effort. Goal-setting and achievement-tracking are practical ways to build your psychological strength. Set realistic, incremental goals that challenge you, then track your progress. Celebrate each milestone to boost your motivation and confidence, and know that you can achieve the inner changes necessary to thrive.

BODY SCAN MEDITATION

There are all sorts of mindfulness and meditation practices that can help you cultivate your emotional regulation, and we'll talk about a lot of them over the course of this book. Let's start with one of the simpler ones: body scan meditation.

A body scan is a mindfulness meditation practice that involves directing your attention sequentially through different parts of your body. The goal is to increase your awareness of your bodily sensations, reduce stress, and promote relaxation by grounding you in the present moment (Raypole 2022).

A body scan works by bringing focused attention to each area—starting from your toes or head and gradually moving through every part of your body—recognizing sensations such as tension, warmth, or relaxation. It helps you cultivate a mindful awareness of your physical self, allowing you to notice and release areas of stored stress.

Here's how to practice a body scan meditation:

1. **Preparation:**
   - **Find a quiet space.** Choose a calm and comfortable environment where you can lie down or sit without distractions.
   - **Set an intention.** Before you get started, set a gentle intention, such as cultivating awareness or simply relaxing.
2. **Starting the Scan:**
   - **Focus on your breath.** Begin with a few moments of mindful breathing. Allow your breath to become slow and natural to center your attention.
   - **Begin at a chosen point.** Typically, you might start at the toes or the crown of your head. Slowly move your attention through your body.
3. **Moving Through the Body:**
   - **Give your body parts sequential attention.** Concentrate on one part of your body at a time.

For instance, notice the sensations in your toes, then your feet, gradually moving up your legs, torso, arms, neck, and finally your head.

- **Observe without judgment.** Pay attention to how each area feels. If you encounter tension, warmth, or any unusual sensations, simply note them without trying to change or analyze them.
- **Acknowledge distractions.** If your mind wanders, gently redirect your focus back to the physical sensations in the area you're scanning.

4. **Concluding the Practice:**
   - **Be aware of your whole body.** Once you have scanned your entire body, take a few moments to feel the overall state of your being.
   - **Return to your breath.** Conclude by returning to your breath for a few moments before slowly opening your eyes and re-engaging with your surroundings.

Body scan meditations can have all sorts of benefits. They can help reduce stress by keeping you focused on the present moment while deepening your mind-body connection. They increase your awareness of your own body, helping you notice any sources of tension or discomfort. In turn, this can help you relax. They're highly customizable, as you can easily adjust the length and pace of your body scan to suit your needs. There's even some research that indicates body scan meditations can be beneficial for the management of chronic pain (Ussher 2014).

There are all sorts of tips to get the most out of the process. Consistency is the big thing; like so many of the practices we'll be talking about, engaging in body scan meditations regularly improves their efficacy. You can also use guided body scan recordings if you're new to the practice, as they can provide clear instructions and a supportive structure. One thing to always bear in mind: There's no "right" or "wrong" way to experience sensations during a body scan. The goal is simply to nurture awareness and acceptance.

Integrating resilience practices into your daily routine helps them become second nature. Establish routines that reinforce resilience, such as starting your day with a brief meditation or ending it with a look back on the day's accomplishments. Doing either of these things reinforces a positive mindset and prepares you to face challenges with a fortified mental state. When you regularly commit to them, it can have a huge effect on strengthening your psychological resilience, keeping you adaptable and emotionally intelligent in all aspects of your life.

As you continue to develop these building blocks of psychological strength, remember that resilience is a process rather than a destination. You can cultivate a strong psychological foundation by focusing on self-efficacy, emotional intelligence, and positive psychology. This foundation will support your ability to fulfill your role with confidence and adaptability. When you embrace these strategies as part of your daily life, you will be better equipped to handle the demands of your profession and the challenges that come your way.

2

TECHNIQUES FOR STRESS MANAGEMENT

O n a warm summer afternoon, a veteran police officer responded to a call about a domestic disturbance. His heart raced in a familiar yet disquieting rhythm as he approached the scene, and each step toward the unknown heightened the tension in his body. As he reached the door, however, a change occurred. He paused, took a deep breath, and employed a technique he had practiced countless times: tactical breathing. This simple act allowed him to regain focus and enter the situation with a calm, clear mind. These rapid stress-reduction techniques can turn chaos into calm, preparing you to face whatever the field might throw your way.

STRESS MANAGEMENT TOOLS AT A MOMENT'S NOTICE

Quick, calm methods of stress management are indispensable tools for first responders and healthcare workers. In the unpredictable world of emergency services, it's invaluable to have techniques at your disposal that can be employed at a moment's notice. Tactical breathing exercises are among the most effective. Inhaling deeply through your nose, holding your breath for a moment, and then exhaling slowly through your mouth activates your parasympathetic nervous system and helps reduce your heart rate and blood pressure. This physiological shift promotes a sense of calm and control, allowing you to tackle high-pressure situations with improved focus and calm (Solan 2023).

Adaptability is a powerful tool in your stress management arsenal. Techniques that you can adjust to different situations improve your ability to cope with stressors, giving you a sense of control over your emotional state. The "STOP" technique—Stop, Take a breath, Observe, Proceed—is a good example of one of these. It provides a structured way to interrupt your stress responses and recalibrate your focus (Magee 2020).

Emotion labeling is its own interesting technique. Naming your emotions—identifying whether you're feeling sad, anxious, angry, etc.—can help create distance between you and your feelings, making it easier to address them constructively. When you give something a name, it gives you some degree of power over it. You might be tricking your brain into establishing control, but it can work surprisingly well (Aldao 2014).

Techniques requiring minimal resources are particularly valuable here. A simple tactile object like a stress ball can serve as a focus point that anchors your attention and dissipates tension. Instant journaling prompts on mobile devices, on the other hand, can offer a quick way to process your emotions and experiences even during a hectic shift. These tools are both accessible and practical, as they require nothing more than your willingness to engage with them. They can help you feel prepared and resourceful even during the most challenging situations.

Finally, there's visualization. Visualization exercises can serve as mental escape routes that offer a respite from stress. It essentially involves picturing an outcome in order to make it more likely to occur. It's often used by professional athletes such as LeBron James (Baer 2020). While you're likely not trying to become the NBA's all-time scoring leader, visualization can still work for you in high-stress situations. You can use visualization in a stressful scenario by momentarily distancing yourself from a present challenge and imagining a peaceful scene or a successful outcome. It might sound silly, but it works.

Visualization for Success

Pause for a moment and gently close your eyes. Envision a scenario that you find particularly challenging—a high-pressure emergency call, a standoff in the line of duty, a demanding situation in a healthcare environment, etc. Picture yourself in the midst of this situation, handling it with unparalleled confidence and a serene composure. Focus on the sensations that surround that success. Immerse yourself in how victory feels within your body, the sounds accompanying this triumph, and the vivid imagery of a positive outcome. If you dedicate a few minutes each day to this visualization practice, it can yield surprising results. Visualization can be a powerful tool that equips you with the necessary skills to handle high-stress situations and improve your readiness to deal with the realities of a high-stress career.

ENCOURAGING COGNITIVE FLEXIBILITY

Cognitive distortions can wreak havoc on mental health, and they often go unnoticed in the blur of daily tasks. These distortions are patterns of thinking that skew reality and lead to undue stress and anxiety. Recognizing them is the first step to change, and doing so can help give you a sense of control. There are several types of cognitive distortions, each with its own unique flavor. Catastrophizing, for instance, is when you assume the worst will happen and magnify problems out of proportion. Overgeneralization, on the other hand, involves making broad assumptions based on a single event—like believing a single mistake defines your competence. There's also fortune-telling, where you predict how things are going to go wrong, and comparison, where you unduly compare yourself to others around you (Grinspoon 2022).

There are all sorts of strategies to counter these distortions and others like them. These include reality testing, where you assess the likelihood of your fears coming true and seek evidence that contradicts your negative thoughts. This process helps ground you in reality, reducing your anxiety and empowering you to take charge of your mental health. Thought record exercises are helpful, too. These involve writing down a distressing situation, identifying the thoughts and feelings it triggers, and then challenging these thoughts with evidence and rational alternatives.

Documenting your thoughts and emotions can help you gain clarity on the patterns that shape your reactions. Reframing negative experiences into positive learning moments is another effective tool. This is similar to the cognitive reframing we talked about in Chapter 1 but distinct in that it focuses on what you can learn from your experiences. This encourages a growth mindset that views challenges as opportunities for development (Silva 2021).

Cognitive flexibility is an important component of resilience, and it involves the ability to adapt your thinking in response to changing circumstances. This means being able to shift your perspective, change your approach, and consider new information when faced with a challenge. Embracing change and uncertainty becomes less daunting when you cultivate cognitive flexibility. The important thing is to be open to new approaches and adjust your perspective when you're faced with difficulties. This flexibility allows you to deal with the unpredictable nature of your work with greater ease and confidence.

Let's say you're facing a high-stakes incident. Your initial thoughts might spiral into worst-case scenarios, heightening your stress. But you can intercept and redirect these thoughts by employing the techniques we've talked about here. The more you practice these exercises, the more you'll strengthen your mental resilience, empowering you to meet challenges head-on and feel more confident and capable in your role as a first responder.

MINDFULNESS ON DUTY: STAYING PRESENT IN HIGH-STRESS SITUATIONS

Let's talk about mindfulness. Broadly speaking, mindfulness encompasses numerous practices that involve maintaining a heightened awareness of the present moment. The body scan meditation we talked about in the previous chapter is one type of mindfulness exercise, but it's not the only one. What they all have in common is that they play a key role in improving your focus and reducing your stress. Mindfulness can provide immediate stress relief, helping you stay present in the moment rather than getting lost in the whirlwind emotions of high-pressure situations. For first responders, the benefits of mindfulness extend beyond this immediate relief, too. Mindfulness practices can generally reduce emotional reactivity, allowing you to respond to emergencies with the level-headed clarity you need for effective decision-making. They can also improve your situational awareness. This helps you stay fully attuned to your environment, decreasing the likelihood of errors and improving your ability to assess rapidly changing situations. These are pretty important skills to have when lives depend on your actions.

Integrating mindfulness into your routine doesn't require extensive time or resources, making it particularly suitable for active duty. Mindful breathing, for example, can be practiced while waiting for dispatches. Focusing on each breath brings your attention back to the present, quieting your mind and encouraging a sense of calm. During team briefings, meanwhile, you can practice mindful listening to keep yourself fully present so you can absorb information without distraction. This attentiveness improves both your communication and collaboration, which has the added benefit of nurturing a more cohesive team dynamic. In routine checks, you can employ mindful observation of the environment to help you catch details you might otherwise miss (Ackerman 2017). This reduces the risk of oversight, potentially saving lives. It's important to keep in mind that mindfulness is not a separate activity from your job. Instead, it's a mindset that can permeate all aspects of your work, leading to greater efficiency and effectiveness.

The long-term benefits of consistent mindfulness practice can be significant. Over time, you might notice improved emotional regulation as mindfulness helps you respond to stress with greater equanimity. This improved regulation means emotions are less likely to overwhelm you, even in the most challenging situations. Mindfulness can also contribute to greater overall job satisfaction. You might find a deeper connection to your role and a renewed appreciation for your contributions by cultivating a sense of presence and purpose in your work. Studies have shown that a commitment to long-term mindfulness practices actually improves the parts of the brain responsible for attention and sensory processing (Keng, Smoski, and Robins 2011). Mindfulness can ultimately support both your professional success and your personal well-being, creating a foundation of resilience that will sustain you through the ups and downs of your career.

Mindfulness Journaling Prompts

In addition to practicing mindfulness on the job, it can also be helpful to engage in simple journaling prompts throughout the day. This doesn't have to be a long process; just take a few minutes to answer the following questions:

1. **Morning Check-In:**
   - "What am I grateful for this morning?"
   - "What is my intention for the day?"
2. **Midday Reflection:**
   - "What emotions am I experiencing right now?"
   - "How can I bring more presence to my current tasks?"
3. **Evening Reflection:**
   - "What was a moment of mindfulness I experienced today?"
   - "What did I learn about myself today?"

THE ROLE OF PHYSICAL FITNESS IN MENTAL HEALTH

Most people might think about physical fitness as just about staying in shape—but it can be so much more than that. Sure, a commitment to physical fitness keeps you in good shape, but it can also be a pillar that supports your mental well-being. The link between maintaining physical health and mental resilience is well-established. When you engage in physical activity, your body releases endorphins, natural mood elevators that create a sense of well-being. This biochemical reaction is a powerful antidote to stress and anxiety, as it offers a natural boost to your mood. Whether it's a firefighter battling a raging inferno, a paramedic rushing to save a life, or a police officer facing a high-stakes situation, exercise can be a powerful tool for reducing stress and anxiety levels. Physical exertion provides an outlet for the tension that builds up over long shifts. The sweat and effort expended during a workout can cleanse the mind, providing a sense of calm that carries over into your professional duties. This reduction in stress is also a cumulative benefit that builds resilience over time. Regular exercise also improves sleep quality—a necessity for recovery and mental sharpness. As a first responder, the quality of your sleep can influence your decision-making abilities and your emotional balance. Taken together, all of these benefits make exercise an urgent part of your mental health toolkit (Mahindru, Patil, and Agrawal 2023).

As a first responder, finding time for fitness amidst your demanding and often chaotic schedules may seem challenging, but it's both achievable and necessary for your well-being. Tailored routines such as high-intensity interval training (HIIT) can be particularly effective for those with limited time. These are short, intense bursts of exercise followed by rest periods. They can be completed in as little as twenty minutes, providing significant cardiovascular and strength benefits without taking up significant time (Reynolds 2021). Flexibility and mobility exercises are equally important, as they help prevent injuries that could sideline you from work. Simple stretching routines can be integrated into your daily schedule to maintain your body's readiness for the physical demands of your job. Creating a balanced fitness routine that suits your lifestyle is key to making exercise a sustainable habit.

Consistency in your workout routine is important—but so is variety. As a first responder, engaging in diverse exercises serves two purposes: maintaining interest and planning for comprehensive fitness. Combining cardio workouts with strength training helps build endurance and power, for example, which are extremely important traits for the physical demands of your role. Outdoor activities like hiking or cycling, on the other hand, can offer mental refreshment, providing a change of scenery and a break from the demands of your work environment. These activities contribute to both your physical health and your mental rejuvenation, offering a momentary escape that can refresh your perspective and reduce your stress.

You can also make physical exercise a social activity. Partner workouts can improve your motivation, turning exercise into a social activity that encourages consistency. Having a workout buddy (sometimes your literal partner) offers accountability and makes the experience more enjoyable. This sense of community can be a powerful source of support that reminds you that you're not alone on your fitness path.

OTHER BREATHING TECHNIQUES FOR INSTANT RELIEF

More than just an automatic function, breathing can be a powerful tool for stress reduction. Earlier in this chapter, we talked about the science behind tactical breathing and its effect on the parasympathetic nervous system. But there are a lot more breathing exercises out there than just tactical breathing.

One effective breathing exercise is box breathing, which is great for improving focus and calm. It involves inhaling for a count of four, holding for four, exhaling for four, and pausing again for four. This rhythmic pattern helps regulate your breath and encourages a sense of tranquility, making it an ideal practice for moments when you need to regain your composure quickly (Gotter 2025). Diaphragmatic breathing, meanwhile, involves deep inhalations that fill your lungs completely, followed by slow, deliberate exhalations. This promotes deep relaxation, helping you release tension and clear your mind (Jewell and Hoshaw 2023). The adaptability of these techniques allows you to use them in virtually any scenario, from the midst of a chaotic emergency to a moment of peace during a break.

Breath awareness plays an important role in emotional regulation. When emotions run high, focusing on your breath can anchor you, providing a stable point of reference amidst turmoil. Paying attention to the rhythm and depth of your breathing enables you to manage your emotional responses more effectively, preventing them from overwhelming your rational thoughts. Different breathing patterns can also influence mood states; slower, deeper breaths can instill a sense of calm, while quicker, more vigorous breaths can energize and invigorate you (Vogel 2022). This means breath awareness is a valuable skill in a wide variety of applications, depending on your needs at any specific moment.

Perhaps unsurprisingly, regular practice improves the effectiveness of breathing exercises. Integrating these techniques into your daily routine builds a toolkit you can access whenever the need arises. Set reminders throughout the day to practice mindful breathing in order to reinforce this habit. Over time, you'll likely notice changes in your mood and stress levels as these practices become ingrained in your behavior. On the whole, breathing techniques offer a simple yet effective solution to stress management. They require no equipment, take little time, and can be practiced anywhere, making them accessible to anyone in high-stress professions.

These techniques can be great tools to help manage stress effectively. From breathing exercises that calm the mind to cognitive strategies that reshape your very thought patterns, the methods you've learned here can help equip you to deal with the demands of your role with resilience and confidence.

3

OVERCOMING TRAUMA FROM CSI
AND PTSD

In the early hours of dawn, the air was thick with anticipation as I stepped into the station, the scent of smoke still clinging to my gear from the night before. Despite the camaraderie and shared purpose that often buoyed my spirits, something felt different that day. The memories of a particularly harrowing recent call replayed vividly in my mind in an unwelcome film reel that refused to stop. While my colleagues chatted over coffee, I found myself drifting away, lost in thought, as the images from that night unfolded repeatedly.

Moments like these highlight the importance of open discussion about mental health in our line of work. This relentless revisiting of traumatic events is a hallmark of Cumulative Stress Injury (CSI), a condition that can cast a long shadow over the lives of first responders. Combined with the better-known Post-Traumatic Stress Disorder (PTSD), they are issues we need to talk about if we want to serve our mental health.

DEFINING TRAUMA AND ITS IMPACT ON FIRST RESPONDERS

Trauma is an emotional and psychological response to extremely distressing or disturbing experiences. First responders frequently encounter traumatic events such as natural disasters, accidents, and violent crimes. This involves witnessing a lot of suffering, confronting life-threatening situations, and making split-second decisions that can mean the difference between life and death. These experiences can result in considerable emotional and physiological stress over time, which can wear down one's mental health.

It's important to remember, though, that trauma is not uniform. Its manifestation varies from individual to individual; every instance of trauma is unique. Understanding the distinction between CSI and PTSD is foundational to this discussion. They're not the same at all, and grasping this does a lot for early recognition, appropriate intervention, and, ultimately, long-term well-being. While both conditions arise from exposure to distressing experiences, they develop in different ways and have distinct implications for mental health and recovery.

Cumulative Stress Injury (CSI)

Unlike PTSD, which results from a single traumatic event, CSI develops over time due to repeated exposure to stress and trauma. It's sometimes referred to as "Cumulative PTSD." As that's somewhat confusing, though, we'll be referring to it as "CSI." Whatever you want to call it, it's often referred to as "the slow burn" because it builds gradually, accumulating over years of service. This condition is common among first responders who regularly face distressing and emotionally taxing situations—EMTs, in particular, deal with it a lot (Geronazzo-Alman et al. 2016).

Symptoms of Cumulative Stress Injury can include:

- **Persistent Fatigue and Emotional Exhaustion:** Feeling drained and disconnected from work and personal life
- **Cynicism and Irritability:** A tendency to develop a negative outlook, increased frustration, or difficulty connecting with others
- **Physical Symptoms:** Chronic headaches, digestive issues, muscle tension, and heightened susceptibility to illness
- **Reduced Performance and Engagement:** A loss of motivation, difficulties with concentration, and feelings of disengagement from work
- **Increased Risk-Taking and Isolation:** A tendency to engage in risky behaviors or to withdraw from loved ones

Cumulative Stress Injury may not seem as immediately debilitating as PTSD. If it's left unaddressed, however, it can lead to burnout, severe mental health struggles, and suicidal thoughts. Because it develops gradually, early intervention is extremely important for preventing long-term damage. Managing this condition requires a proactive, structured approach:

- **Acknowledge and identify the stress.** Recognize the symptoms of cumulative stress. Take a long, hard look at your emotional, physical, and behavioral changes. Accept that cumulative stress is an injury rather than a personal failure.
- **Seek support and communicate.** Talk to trusted colleagues, supervisors, or mental health professionals. Engage with peer support programs. Keep lines of communication open with family and friends.
- **Implement self-care strategies.** Prioritize sleep, healthy nutrition, and regular exercise for emotional support. For emotional support, meanwhile, practice mindfulness, meditation, and relaxation techniques. Lastly, social support involves maintaining meaningful relationships and social activities.
- **Set boundaries and manage your workload.** Take breaks and utilize your vacation time. Avoid excessive overtime or double shifts. Learn to say "no" when necessary.
- **Develop healthy coping mechanisms.** Engage in hobbies and activities that bring you joy. Practice stress management techniques such as deep breathing, journaling, and creative outlets. Avoid unhealthy coping mechanisms such as alcohol or substance use.
- **Utilize professional resources.** Access employee assistance programs (EAPs). Seek therapy or counseling for stress management. Attend workshops or training on resilience-building.
- **Monitor progress and adjust as needed.** Regularly assess your stress levels and mental health. Adjust

your self-care strategies based on their effectiveness. Remain open to seeking additional support when necessary.

Cumulative Stress Injury is a serious but manageable condition. Recognizing the signs early and taking proactive steps enables first responders to maintain resilience and continue to serve their communities effectively. Always keep in mind that seeking help is a sign of strength and that prioritizing your well-being helps your personal and professional longevity.

Post-Traumatic Stress Disorder (PTSD)

PTSD is a psychiatric disorder that can develop after experiencing or witnessing a single traumatic event. This could mean a mass casualty incident, a personal assault, a natural disaster, or potentially any other life-threatening situation. Regardless of the specific cause, PTSD involves intense, persistent psychological distress that interferes with one's daily life and work (Donohue 2022).

Symptoms of PTSD can include:

- **Intrusive Memories:** Flashbacks, nightmares, or distressing thoughts about the traumatic event
- **Avoidance Behaviors:** Steering clear of places, people, or situations that remind you of the trauma
- **Negative Mood and Cognition:** Feelings of guilt, shame, or emotional numbness
- **Hyperarousal:** Heightened alertness, irritability, difficulty sleeping, or being easily startled

PTSD typically requires structured treatment such as therapy, counseling, or medication to effectively manage your symptoms. There are several current forms of treatment (Schrader and Ross 2021), which can include:

- **Cognitive Processing Therapy (CPT):** Generally delivered through twelve sessions, CPT is designed to enable patients to confront and modify their unhelpful beliefs surrounding their trauma. In many ways, it's similar to the cognitive reframing we've been talking about.
- **Prolonged Exposure Therapy (PE):** It is a therapy focused on helping patients gradually approach the memories and feelings surrounding their trauma, facing their issues over time. It's designed to help patients understand that avoiding the idea of their trauma often has the effect of making it worse in the long run.
- **Eye Movement, Desensitization, and Restructuring (EMDR):** Somewhat unusual compared to the other two, EMDR involves patients focusing briefly on their traumatic memories while engaging in bilateral stimulation (most frequently in the form of eye movements). This bilateral stimulation has been shown to reduce the vividness and emotional weight associated with the memories in question. EMDR has shown remarkable efficacy in helping individuals process trauma without the need to verbalize every detail, making it a valuable option for those who find discussing their experiences challenging.

Why Recognizing the Difference Matters

First responders need to understand the distinction between CSI and PTSD to recognize their own mental health needs and seek appropriate care. PTSD often requires structured trauma-focused therapy, while CSI necessitates ongoing stress management strategies, lifestyle adjustments, and support systems to prevent escalation. Much as an EMT wouldn't treat a laceration with a splint, you need to utilize the right treatments for the right injury.

Recognizing that trauma is an inherent part of the first responder profession does not equate to accepting chronic suffering. With proper education, invaluable support from your peers, and access to mental health resources, both CSI and PTSD can be effectively managed. Whether you're experiencing acute symptoms after a traumatic event or feeling the cumulative toll of years of service, remember that help is available. Seeking support is not a sign of weakness; it is a proactive step toward maintaining resilience and another brave act in your long, fulfilling career of serving others.

TRAUMA-INFORMED CARE FOR SELF AND OTHERS

Trauma-informed care is a paradigm shift in how we approach mental health and well-being. This is particularly within the high-stress environments first responders regularly experience. It starts with a fundamental question shift: instead of asking, "What's wrong with you?" you ask, "What happened to you?" This change in perspective nurtures environments where safety and trustworthiness are paramount. In your daily inter-actions, both personal and professional, it's important to create spaces where people can feel secure and respected. This means setting clear boundaries and maintaining consistent, dependable behavior. Trust is the bedrock of any supportive environment, as it allows for open and honest communication—two crucial ingredients for healing and growth (Girolimon 2025).

Empowerment and collaboration are at the heart of any variety of trauma-informed care. Whether you're working with colleagues or trying to support those you rescue, encouraging others' participation in decision-making can significantly improve their recovery and support. This approach keeps everyone feeling valued and heard, which builds confidence in their treatment. Empathy and under-standing are extremely important components of this process, as they allow you to connect with the individual's experience. Non-judgmental communication practices, where you approach each interaction with an open mind and set aside preconceived notions as much as possible, nurture an environment where individuals feel safe to express their struggles without fear of judgment or reprisal.

A trauma-informed approach can dramatically reduce the stigma around trauma and mental health. Encouraging an environment that normalizes discussions about these issues helps diminish the shame that often keeps people from seeking help. And as stigma decreases, job satisfaction and team cohesion increase, with people feeling supported and understood rather than isolated. This supportive atmosphere encourages openness and vulnerability—extremely impor-tant components for building strong, resilient teams. Creating an environment like this requires practical strategies. Establishing clear communication channels for sharing concerns, such as regular feedback sessions or anonymous suggestion boxes, makes sure everyone has a voice. It's also a good idea to implement regular check-ins where team members can discuss their challenges and successes and mental health days where individuals can take a break from work to focus on their well-being. These provide a much-needed respite from the pressures of the job, which allows you to recharge and return refreshed.

Maintaining personal well-being is absolutely necessary for caregivers, and that's true whether they function in a professional or personal capacity. Setting boundaries is important for preventing compassion fatigue, which occurs when the emotional demands of supporting others become overwhelming. Engaging in peer support groups provides a space to share your experiences, vent your frustrations, and receive encouragement from others who understand your challenges. These groups can be lifelines for practical advice and emotional support.

Implementing trauma-informed practices into organizational culture requires commitment and action. Training sessions and workshops can educate teams on the principles of trauma-informed care, equipping them with the tools to apply these concepts in everyday interactions. Policy changes may be necessary to institutionalize these practices in order to make them an established part of the workplace fabric.

One good idea is to initiate a monthly workshop focused on trauma-informed care principles within your team or organization. These workshops can cover topics like the science of trauma, communication strategies, and self-care practices.

It's key to encourage participation from all levels of staff, as their involvement is a big part of the success of these workshops and the adoption of trauma-informed care principles. Additionally, it can help drive policy changes that support trauma-informed care, such as implementing mental health days or creating dedicated spaces for staff to decompress during shifts. These steps can lay the groundwork for a more supportive, empathetic, and resilient workplace culture.

SELF-HELP COPING MECHANISMS AND THERAPIES

In the world where you operate, the shadows of trauma can be long and persistent, making it important to have effective strategies for coping with CSI and PTSD. We talked about evidence-based therapies that provide structured approaches to alleviate symptoms and encourage recovery. There are also self-help strategies that empower you to actively participate in your recovery, though—and you can conduct these on your own in addition to seeking professional help.

Journaling is a simple yet surprisingly impactful practice that can allow you to process your thoughts and emotions on your own terms. Putting pen to paper creates a safe space to explore your feelings, unraveling the threads of trauma and paving the way for a better understanding of yourself. This practice can be cathartic, as it provides insight into patterns and triggers that might otherwise remain hidden from your conscious mind. Alongside journaling, mindfulness meditation—which we talked about a lot in Chapter 2—can be extremely helpful. These self-help strategies put you in the driver's seat of your recovery, giving you the tools to chart your course with confidence.

Social support networks also play a pivotal role in coping with CSI and PTSD, as they offer a sense of community and shared understanding. Building connections with others who face similar stressors creates a safety net where you can share your experiences without fear of being judged for them. Participating in group therapy or support groups brings the added benefit of collective wisdom, where you can draw strength from others' stories and offer your support in return. These networks reinforce the message that you are not alone. Don't underestimate the value of a sense of belonging and understanding in helping you feel less isolated and more connected in your process of recovery.

Despite the availability of effective therapies, accessing professional help can be fraught with challenges. Geographic limitations, financial constraints, and the stigma surrounding mental health can all act as barriers. However, solutions are emerging to bridge these gaps. Online therapy options offer a lifeline for those in remote areas or with demanding schedules, providing flexibility and convenience without sacrificing quality. Many platforms now connect individuals with licensed therapists via video calls, ensuring that help is accessible from the comfort of your home. Additionally, employer-provided mental health resources are becoming more prevalent, with many organizations recognizing the value of supporting their employees' well-being. These resources can range from on-site counselors to partnerships with mental health professionals—support that is just a conversation away.

As you deal with the ins and outs of trauma, CSI, and PTSD, always remember that seeking help is a sign of strength rather than weakness. I know I keep hammering this point, but there's a reason for it: It is extremely, extremely important to keep it at the front of your mind. Engaging with therapies and self-help strategies demonstrates a commitment to your well-being and resilience that better enables you to serve others. Far from being a selfish act, it's a selfless one. Building a support network and accessing available resources can completely alter your path to recovery for the better, offering hope and healing in the face of adversity.

CREATING A PERSONAL PTSD MANAGEMENT PLAN

Building a personal CSI and PTSD management plan is like putting together a customized toolkit to work through the challenges you face. It starts with identifying personal triggers and stressors that disrupt your mental peace. These can be specific sounds like sirens, places like crowded spaces, or situations like particular types of conflict. Acknowledging these triggers is the first step toward managing them, as once you have a clear understanding of your struggles, you can start setting realistic goals for recovery. These goals should be achievable and contain both short-term milestones and long-term aspirations. A short-term goal, for example, might be to reduce the frequency of intrusive thoughts, while a long-term goal could be achieving a balanced emotional state. Laying out the path in an achievable way empowers you to take deliberate steps toward healing.

Regular evaluation and adaptation of your plan are extremely important, as CSI and PTSD are not static. Instead, their manifestations can change over time and be influenced by various factors. It can be helpful to keep a symptom diary, which is a record of your symptoms, their severity, and any triggers or stressors that may have caused them. This lets you track your progress and offers valuable information about patterns and changes. This diary can also point to effective strategies and areas requiring adjustment. You might notice that a particular coping technique works well in one scenario but not in another. Flexibility is key here; as you gain knowledge from your observations, adjust your strategies to keep them effective and relevant. This iterative process equips you to confidently handle shifting circumstances.

A holistic approach to well-being is very important when it comes to managing CSI and PTSD. This involves integrating practices that nurture physical, mental, and emotional health. We talked about exercise a lot in Chapter 2, and that's a huge part of this. Likewise, we briefly mentioned nutrition and sleep, and we'll get into them in detail in Chapter 10. It can also be a good idea to incorporate creative outlets like art or music therapy into your routine. These activities offer a way to express emotions that might be difficult to articulate in words, providing relief and encouraging your creativity. They can be very therapeutic and rewarding, offering a sense of accomplishment and joy.

Involving trusted individuals in your management plan can greatly improve its effectiveness, too. Sharing your goals and progress with your family and peers creates a support network that encourages both accountability and motivation. They can offer perspectives you might overlook and provide support when you run into unexpected challenges. Establishing accountability partners makes sure you have someone to check in with, which in turn reinforces your commitment to the plan. This collaborative approach can actually strengthen your relationships—something we'll get into in Chapter 11—and remind you that you're not alone in this process. A shared process can really enrich your life in all sorts of unexpected ways.

As you develop and refine your CSI and PTSD management plan, remember that it's a living outline—one that's supposed to change as you do, based on new information and experiences. Its success lies in its flexibility and your willingness to engage with it. Taking an active role in your healing helps create a future where CSI and PTSD no longer define you but merely become a part of your story. Managing CSI and PTSD is an ongoing process that requires dedication and support. As you carry this knowledge forward, know that each step brings you closer to a balanced, fulfilling life.

4

MENTAL HEALTH AWARENESS
AND STIGMA REDUCTION

During a quiet shift change a few years ago, I sat across from a fellow first responder. As the fluorescent lights hummed softly above and the weight of the night's calls settled in, she began to share. Her voice, barely above a whisper, told of the sleepless nights and overwhelming anxiety that trailed her like a shadow. The relief that washed over her face as she shared her burden was palpable, a testament to the emotional release that can come from breaking the silence.

At that moment, it became clear how powerful speaking up could be—not just for her but for our entire team. Her courage to break the silence was a catalyst that sparked conversations that had long been buried under the guise of toughness and resilience. All of this highlighted a simple truth: To fix problems, you first have to talk about them.

COMMUNICATING YOUR MENTAL HEALTH CONCERNS

Discussing mental health openly is not just beneficial; it is absolutely necessary. The veil of silence surrounding mental health can be suffocating for first responders, perpetuating a cycle of stigma and isolation. Open discussions are the first step in dismantling these barriers, as they allow for healing and understanding. Sharing stories, as my colleague did, does a lot to help break down the misconception that mental health struggles are a sign of weakness. Statistics from the National Alliance on Mental Illness (NAMI) highlight that when first responders engage in open mental health discussions, they experience significantly improved outcomes—both personally and professionally (Weaver 2021). Through these conversations, we find solidarity in realizing we are not alone in our struggles. It's a reminder that we're part of a community—united by our shared experiences.

Initiating conversations about mental health can feel overwhelming, particularly in environments where stoicism is generally valued—but there are practical strategies to ease into these discussions. In team meetings, introduce conversation starters that make discussing mental health less intimidating. Questions like "How can we support each other better?" or "What's one thing we can do to reduce stress?" can open the door to meaningful dialogue without making anyone feel pressured to share more than they're ready to. Encouraging leaders to share their own experiences with mental health can also set a powerful precedent. When those in leadership roles speak openly, it helps normalize these discussions, making it easier for others to follow suit.

Leadership plays an important role in nurturing an environment of openness and acceptance. A study by Corporate Wellness Magazine (n.d.) found that empathetic leadership significantly improves workplace mental health dynamics. This highlights the importance of making everyone feel valued and understood.

Despite the benefits, discussing mental health openly does come with its own set of challenges. Fears of judgment, career repercussions, or being perceived as unfit for duty can often silence those who need support the most. Misunderstandings about mental health conditions can further exacerbate this issue. Many still view mental health struggles through a lens of stigma rather than recognizing them as legitimate health issues that deserve attention and care. Addressing these misconceptions is an important part of creating a culture where mental health is treated with the same seriousness as physical health. There are numerous ways to do this: providing education and resources about mental health, sharing personal stories of overcoming mental health challenges, and promoting a culture of empathy and understanding—to name just a few.

Allies within the workplace play a pivotal role in facilitating these conversations. It's important for people to act as advocates and offer support and encouragement to those hesitant to speak up. Training sessions for allies can provide them with the tools to support colleagues effectively. These sessions cover active listening, empathy development, and strategies to approach mental health topics with the appropriate level of sensitivity. Creating a buddy system for peer support is a good idea, too. Pairing individuals together helps develop a network of support that encourages both trust and accountability. This system guarantees everyone has someone to turn to, which reduces feelings of isolation and promotes a sense of community.

Breaking the silence around mental health isn't a one-time event, though. Instead, it's an ongoing commitment to creating spaces where everyone feels safe to share their experiences. It requires courage, empathy, and a willingness to challenge the status quo. As you continue to engage in these discussions, remember that this commitment is a continuous effort that we all must uphold in order for it to be successful.

STIGMA BUSTING: CHANGING PERCEPTIONS IN THE WORKPLACE

Stigma is a heavy and often invisible burden. It hovers over mental health discussions within the workplace, casting long shadows over those who need support. Strength and bravery are important among first responders, sure, but addressing mental health issues might take even more courage. Stigma, in this case, generally manifests as negative stereotypes that portray mental health struggles as a sign of weakness or incompetence. Such misconceptions can erode self-esteem and make people hesitate to seek the help they need. This stigma doesn't just affect the person in question, though; it ripples through the workplace, impacting morale and team cohesion. When first responders feel they must hide their struggles, it creates an environment of mistrust and isolation where team members may work side by side yet still feel worlds apart.

Many departments have initiated programs to reduce stigma and create a culture of acceptance in order to change these perceptions. These initiatives are ultimately about creating a more positive and supportive workplace environment. Mental health awareness campaigns often involve educational materials, workshops, and seminars led by mental health professionals who provide factual information and dispel those persistent myths. In addition, departments have implemented workshops focusing on resilience and stress management to equip first responders with the tools they need to maintain their mental health. By providing these resources, organizations take a proactive stance and show that mental health is a priority rather than an afterthought.

Leadership plays a pivotal role in setting the tone for mental health acceptance. When leaders are open about their own mental health struggles, it sends a powerful message that seeking help is both accepted and encouraged. This transparency from the top can inspire similar openness throughout the ranks. Leaders have a unique capacity to influence workplace culture, and by implementing supportive mental health policies, they can encourage an environment of trust and safety. Such policies might include flexible work arrangements, access to mental health resources, and confidentiality assurances that protect those who seek help. Measures like these are important for creating an environment where employees feel valued and supported. This is a responsibility that all leaders should embrace, and it's a power that can truly make a difference.

The benefits of a stigma-free workplace can be tremendous. Reducing the stigma makes employees more willing to seek help, safe in the knowledge that they will not face judgment or repercussions (Henderson, Evans-Lacko, and Thornicroft 2013). This willingness to address mental health issues early on can lead to quicker recovery and a stronger workforce. As a result, organizations often see decreased absenteeism and turnover rates, as employees are better equipped to manage their mental health and thus remain engaged in their work (de Oliveira et al. 2022). The workplace becomes a more supportive and productive environment where people feel empowered to bring their whole selves to work without fear of discrimination or exclusion.

Creating a stigma-free workplace is an ongoing process that requires commitment and effort from all levels of an organization. It involves continuous education, open dialogue, and a willingness to challenge and change outdated perceptions. It's a lot of work, no doubt—but it's worth it.

ENCOURAGEMENT OF OPEN DIALOGUE: COMMUNAL SUPPORT

In the high-pressure world of first responders, encouraging an open dialogue about mental health can be a lifeline. This approach strengthens trust among team members while creating a cohesive unit that can stand firm against even the most challenging circumstances. Open discussions about mental health can dismantle the walls that often isolate individuals in their struggles. These conversations improve collective problem-solving, allowing teams to tackle mental health challenges with the same determination and cooperation they bring to their day-to-day duties. Sharing experiences and knowledge enables team members to develop innovative solutions and strategies that benefit everyone. Ultimately, this creates a more supportive and effective workplace.

Practical tools and techniques are invaluable for encouraging this kind of dialogue. One method is using anonymous suggestion boxes specifically for mental health topics. These can provide a safe avenue for individuals to voice concerns or suggest improvements without having to deal with a fear of reprisal. They can be placed in common areas where team members gather in order to make for easy access. Regular town hall meetings focused on mental wellness can also serve as platforms for open dialogue, which creates opportunities for team members to share their experiences, ask questions, and learn from each other in an inclusive environment. The key is to create a space where everyone's voice is heard and valued.

Creating safe spaces for mental health discussions is an important part of encouraging honest and open communication. Likewise, it's key that these spaces should be neutral areas separate from the usual work environment, where individuals can feel comfortable expressing themselves. Establishing non-punitive reporting mechanisms for mental health concerns is also extremely important. When team members know they can speak up without fear of negative consequences, they're more likely to seek help and support. These mechanisms include confidential reporting systems or trained mental health officers who can provide guidance and resources. Making sure that these spaces are free from judgment and stigma creates an environment where individuals feel safe to share their thoughts and feelings. In turn, this helps create a culture of openness and acceptance.

Mental health champions have a huge role when it comes to facilitating dialogue. These individuals act as advocates and leaders in mental health initiatives who inspire others to engage in open discussions and seek support when needed. Training select people as mental health ambassadors equips them with the knowledge and skills to effectively guide and support their peers. They can then lead workshops, facilitate support groups, and serve as a resource for team members seeking guidance. Recognition for contributions to mental health advocacy is also important. Acknowledging the efforts of those who champion mental health causes helps reinforce the value of these initiatives, encouraging others to get involved. It's ultimately a way of showing appreciation and value for the efforts of those who advocate for mental health.

BUILDING A CULTURE OF MENTAL HEALTH ADVOCACY

Creating a culture of mental health advocacy within your organization may seem like an ethical goal—and it is. But it's also a strategic move that can significantly improve your workplace environment. It starts with integrating mental health education into training programs to make sure every team member understands the importance of mental wellness and has the tools to maintain it. This education should not be a one-time event but a continuous process that works in tandem with the team's needs. Regular assessments of organizational mental health initiatives, meanwhile, are necessary to gauge their effectiveness and make necessary adjustments. These assessments can take various forms: surveys, feedback sessions, performance metrics, etc. The important thing is that they evaluate the overall mental health climate of the workplace. A culture of mental health advocacy is characterized by openness, support, and a commitment to ongoing improvement, so that's what their results should reflect.

Actionable steps must be taken to encourage and sustain a culture of mental health advocacy. Establishing mental health committees within organizations is a good start. These committees can consist of volunteers from various roles who are passionate about mental health. Their mission should be to oversee mental health initiatives and make sure they align with the organization's goals and the team's needs. Set annual goals for mental health improvement to give the committee and the entire team tangible targets to work toward. These goals could include increasing participation in mental health programs, reducing overall stigma, and improving access to resources. Organizations can create a roadmap for progress by linking metrics to these objectives to encourage a culture where mental health is prioritized.

Continuous education and training are also important components of mental health advocacy. Hosting annual mental health workshops and retreats allows team members to deepen their understanding and expand their skills. There are a lot of topics to go over here, from stress management techniques to resilience-building strategies. Incorporating mental health topics into professional development makes sure these discussions remain integral to career growth and workplace dynamics. This approach reinforces the message that mental health is not separate from professional responsibilities but is a key component of overall well-being and effectiveness.

As you think about these elements of mental health advocacy, dare to envision a workplace where every individual feels empowered to prioritize their mental well-being. Mental health should be actively supported and celebrated rather than just a topic of discussion. Integrating these practices into your organization contributes to a culture that values and supports each team member, improving their ability to perform their duties with resilience and confidence. This commitment to mental health advocacy lays the foundation for a supportive and thriving workplace where people can deal with the demands of their roles with both strength and compassion.

5

CREATING A SUPPORT NETWORK

I t was a late August day at the station. The radio crackled to life, and a call came in—a complex situation that demanded immediate attention. As I gathered my gear, the familiar face of my fire chief, Samantha, offered a reassuring nod. It was the nod of someone who had stood in my shoes, faced the same chaos I had, and understood the unspoken words that often lingered in the silence. It may have been a small gesture, but Samantha's support meant the world to me.

This exchange is the essence of peer support, an incredibly important lifeline in the world of first responders. Peer support is an anchor in the storm that can save you when things get rough. These bonds create the kind of trust that can't be bought, building a network of reliability you can rely on when the pressures of the job start to feel overwhelming.

PEER NETWORKS: A WAY FORWARD

Establishing peer support groups has become an increasingly recognized tool within first responder departments (Donovan 2022). These groups offer a structured environment where individuals can share experiences, voice concerns, and offer support without fear of judgment. They're a safe space to process the emotional aftermath of particularly traumatic incidents while nurturing a deep sense of community and solidarity. Mentorship programs that pair seasoned responders with newcomers can also strengthen these bonds and help with employee retention. Experienced individuals can offer guidance, share wisdom, and help newer members acclimate to the demands of the role. Additionally, such mentorships help with the transfer of valuable knowledge and skills, improving the team's overall effectiveness.

Building reliable peer networks requires a deliberate effort to encourage trust and open communication. Regular team-building activities can play an important role in strengthening these connections. These might involve more organized activities such as collaborative problem-solving exercises or something as simple as shared meals. Both types allow team members to bond outside of high-pressure situations. However, both pale in comparison to the regular check-ins, which truly help maintain a sense of support. Regular formal or informal check-ins keep everyone feeling connected, providing a platform for individuals to voice concerns and offer mutual encouragement.

Peer-led initiatives and programs have proven to be particularly effective. Introducing peer-led debriefing sessions after significant incidents allows for emotions to be processed in a supportive environment. These sessions allow first responders to discuss their experiences with others and eventually find closure. The "buddy system," another peer-led initiative, pairs individuals for mutual emotional support. This system helps make sure everyone has someone they can turn to when they need it.

While the benefits of peer support are clear, potential challenges also have to be acknowledged and addressed. Confidentiality is a big concern, as some first responders may fear that sharing personal information could lead to unintended professional or personal consequences. Establishing clear guidelines to make sure all participants understand the importance of maintaining confidentiality within the group is thus extremely important. Interpersonal dynamics can also pose challenges, as differing personalities and communication styles may lead to misunderstandings. Facilitators play an important role in working through these dynamics, helping to mediate conflicts and promote inclusivity in a way that makes everyone feel supported and understood. Encouraging consistent participation and engagement is another challenge; it's important to realize busy schedules and competing priorities can sometimes hinder attendance. Offering flexible meeting times and incorporating engaging activities can help maintain both interest and commitment, though.

Creating a strong peer support network is an ongoing process that requires unwavering commitment, deep empathy, and seamless collaboration. And it's worth it; through these connections, we find strength, resilience, and the ability to thrive even in the most challenging circumstances.

ENGAGING WITH MENTAL HEALTH PROFESSIONALS

The role of mental health professionals in the lives of first responders is invaluable. These professionals bring expertise and guidance that can help work through the complex emotions associated with high-stress careers. This makes sense when you think about it, as even among first responders, different jobs have different purposes. You wouldn't ask a dispatcher to put out a burning building or a police officer to deliver critical emergency medical care, would you? In both fire response and mental health situations, it's best to trust those who have trained to deal with the problem.

Therapy can offer a space to process experiences in a structured and supportive environment to anyone who faces trauma and pressure regularly. Individual therapy sessions can be tailored specifically to your unique challenges, providing personalized coping and resilience strategies. The one-on-one focus in these sessions enables the therapist to guide you through the intricacies of stress, trauma, and any accompanying mental health concerns you might have. Group therapy, meanwhile, offers shared healing experiences and a sense of community. In these settings, you can connect with others who understand your struggles, sharing stories and solutions in a collective process of attaining wellness. This communal aspect can greatly boost the therapeutic process through the power of support and perspective.

Recognizing the need for professional help is a big step in building a support network. It's not always easy to know when to reach out, but there are usually signs that therapy may be beneficial. Persistent symptoms that linger despite self-help efforts—anxiety, depression, intrusive memories, etc.—can indicate that additional support is needed. When these symptoms begin to impact your personal or professional life, affecting your relationships or your job performance, it's definitely time to set aside your qualms and seek guidance. This is not a situation to be taken lightly; remember those statistics about suicidal ideations from the very beginning of this book. Therapy can provide tools to address these issues and help restore balance and functionality. Identifying these signs within yourself is an act of strength and self-awareness. After all, you're recognizing that seeking help is a proactive and positive step, and what could be more self-aware than that?

Finding the right mental health professional is also important. It's important to choose someone who understands the unique demands of your role. Check the credentials and experience of potential therapists; many mental health professionals specialize in working with first responders and have training in dealing with trauma and occupational stress. Seeking recommendations from trusted peers or organizations can also guide you toward reliable practitioners. Colleagues who have had positive experiences with therapists can offer valuable knowledge about the process, helping you find someone who fits your needs. Also, don't be discouraged if the first therapist you try doesn't work out; not every therapist will click with every client—and that's okay. Keep at it, and you'll eventually find a therapist who works for you.

You can't just sit back and fail to engage, either; maximizing the effectiveness of professional help involves active participation. Prepare for your therapy sessions by setting goals, considering the issues you'd like to discuss and the outcomes you hope to achieve. This preparation guarantees that the time spent in therapy is focused and productive. During sessions, actively participate and provide feedback. Open communication with your therapist can help tailor the approach to your changing needs. Don't just assume there's no reason to speak out; if something isn't working, expressing your concerns can lead to adjustments that improve the therapeutic process.

Ongoing professional support is a huge part of long-term well-being. Sporadic visits may provide temporary relief, but it's regular engagement that nurtures truly durable healing and growth. Scheduling consistent appointments—and making sure you actually attend them—helps track progress and maintain momentum. Through this continuity, you can build a strong therapeutic relationship that supports your path toward resilience. Incorporating what you've learned in therapy into your daily life, meanwhile, helps extend benefits beyond the therapy room. Applying what you've learned in real-world situations reinforces new habits and coping mechanisms, embedding them into your routine. This integration is where the fundamental change occurs as you harness the power of professional guidance to improve every aspect of your life.

STRENGTHENING FAMILY TIES FOR EMOTIONAL SUPPORT

At the heart of your resilience lies a network that literally sits close to home: your family. For many people, family is the one who stands by you and helps you emotionally weather any number of catastrophes. Strong family relationships are extremely impactful for maintaining mental health. Open communication within your family can be a lifeline that connects your experiences with their understanding. Sharing the highs and lows of your work invites your loved ones into your world and allows them to offer the support you need. Involving family members in mental health awareness and education empowers them to recognize signs of stress or trauma, creating a nurturing environment where you can express your feelings openly.

It's likewise important to note that not everyone has access to a supportive family environment—or indeed could even create one easily. Sometimes, family members will be toxic and unsupportive. It's, therefore, extremely important to clarify that even if you don't have a great relationship with your family or a supportive network more broadly, it isn't hopeless at all. You can still build support networks with coworkers, friends, or any number of others.

For others, though, it is possible to increase the amount of help you get from your family in everyday life. Improving your level of family support requires deliberate actions that fortify the bonds you share. Establishing regular family meetings provides a platform for discussing challenges and celebrating your achievements. These meetings need not be formal; they can be as simple as a weekly dinner where everyone has a chance to speak. During these conversations, focus on listening as much as you share. Be sure to validate each other's experiences and emotions even if you don't always agree with them. Creating family rituals or traditions, such as a monthly outing or a shared hobby, can also be a way to reinforce unity and provide touchpoints that everyone can look forward to. These traditions can become part of the family identity and turn moments of joy and togetherness into your everyday routine.

While a lot of the above is good advice regardless of profession, first-responder families face unique challenges that can strain relationships if not addressed proactively. The nature of your job means that stress and anxiety related to shift work can bleed into home life and affect how you interact with your loved ones. Balancing work commitments with family responsibilities is a delicate process that often requires compromises and adjustments. One way to manage these demands is by setting clear boundaries and expectations to make sure everyone is on the same page. Communicate openly about your schedule and any anticipated changes, as this allows your family to plan and adapt accordingly. Encourage them to express their needs and concerns, take a collaborative approach to problem-solving, and let them know you care about their feelings.

Family involvement in mental health initiatives can significantly improve your support system. Much like with your coworkers, getting your family involved in organized workshops on mental health topics can educate everyone about the challenges associated with your role and equip them with the tools they need to offer informed support. These workshops can be facilitated by mental health professionals or community organizations well-versed in the unique pressures first responders face. Another option is encouraging family participation in stress-relief activities like yoga and meditation or outdoor activities like hiking or cycling. This both benefits individual wellness and strengthens family cohesion. All of these activities promote shared relaxation, allowing everyone to unwind and build resilience as a unit.

Your family can often be a source of color, strength, and stability in your life. Nurturing these relationships and involving your loved ones in your mental health struggles can help you create a strong support network that sustains you through your inevitable ups and downs. Your family's love and understanding, coupled with empathy for the unique challenges you face, can be a powerful buffer against the stresses of your profession. It can provide solace and strength when you need it most—provided you're willing to do the work required to let them in.

COMMUNITY RESOURCES AND HOW TO ACCESS THEM

Every community possesses a wealth of resources designed to support those who serve it—as long as you're willing to seek them out. For first responders like you, these resources can be valuable allies in dealing with the challenges of your demanding role. Employee Assistance Programs (EAPs) are among the most accessible, providing immediate support for various personal and professional challenges such as stress, trauma, financial difficulties, and legal issues (Paychex 2024). These programs often offer confidential counseling tailored to your needs. They can be a lifeline for those moments when the weight of your duties feels particularly heavy, offering a safe space to explore solutions and find support.

Additionally, local mental health organizations often have specialized programs for first responders. These programs are likely to recognize your unique pressures and offer targeted support, including stress management and resilience-building workshops. Community centers, too, can be a hub of wellness activities such as yoga classes, meditation sessions, and art therapy workshops. These centers provide an opportunity to connect with others in a relaxed, low-pressure environment.

Accessing these community resources does require a proactive approach, though. Research the programs available in your area; many organizations have online portals where you can learn about their services and how to register. Contacting these organizations directly can also yield valuable information and guidance. Networking with fellow first responders helps, too. This can involve joining professional associations, attending local meetings, or participating in online forums. Attend local meetings or events where resource information is shared to create opportunities to learn and connect with others who understand your experiences. This doesn't just benefit you; sharing information about the resources you've found helpful creates a ripple effect that spreads awareness and encourages others to seek the support they need. Establishing a resource-sharing network makes sure valuable information is accessible to everyone, which improves the collective support within your community.

Engaging with community resources extends beyond accessing services and involves active participation that enriches your mental health. Local events can encourage a sense of belonging, which grounds you within your community. These might include health fairs, workshops, or social gatherings. All of these provide a platform to interact with others, share experiences, and build meaningful connections. Volunteering opportunities also offer a unique way to connect and find purpose. Giving your time and skills to community projects or initiatives can cultivate a sense of fulfillment and contribute to the well-being of others. This involvement benefits the community while improving your sense of purpose and satisfaction, creating a symbiotic relationship that nurtures both.

Despite the numerous benefits, accessing community resources can present challenges. Much like with all other ways to help your mental health, stigma remains a significant barrier that often deters individuals from seeking help due to fear of judgment or misunderstanding. Overcoming this stigma involves shifting perceptions within yourself and the broader community. Recognize that seeking help is a sign of strength and a proactive step toward maintaining your well-being. Scheduling flexibility can also be a hurdle, particularly for those with unpredictable work hours (which includes most first responders). Look for programs that offer evening or weekend sessions. Transportation can be another obstacle, so explore options like carpooling with colleagues or using public transportation to make sure logistical challenges don't prevent you from accessing the support you need. Addressing these barriers head-on will help you maximize the community resources available to you.

Remember that community resources are part of a broader network of support that extends beyond your immediate circle—along with family support, mental health professionals, and peer networks. All these can empower you, providing tools and connections that improve your ability to thrive in your role. Engaging with these resources strengthens your resilience and contributes to a culture of support and well-being that benefits everyone.

6

IMPROVING YOUR COMMUNICATION SKILLS

On a blistering summer afternoon, the sun beating down and the air shimmering with heat, my fire chief Rick stood before our team of firefighters and paramedics. A wildfire had broken out on the outskirts of town, its flames threatening the community's edge. Rick's voice was steady and deliberate, cutting through the thick tension with purpose. Every word carried weight as Rick guided us with precision and clarity. The blend of urgency and command Rick displayed in this moment highlights the power of effective communication under pressure. Chaos often prevails in the world of first responders, and the ability to communicate clearly can make the difference between order and disarray.

COMMUNICATION DURING EMERGENCIES

Maintaining clear communication during high-stress situations is important, as it impacts both the safety and the efficiency of teamwork among first responders. When directives are clear, teams can function like a well-oiled machine, with each member knowing their role and the expectations. In emergency response scenarios, concise communication both makes sure that vital information isn't lost in translation and prevents misunderstandings that could lead to costly errors.

Specific techniques can be invaluable for remaining calm and articulate during emergencies. Breathing exercises, which we've talked about a few times now, can be a simple yet powerful tool to help calm your nerves before speaking. Visualization is another subject we've touched on, and it can be particularly helpful here. Before stepping into a tense situation, picture the successful resolution of the task at hand. This mental rehearsal prepares you to deal with the scenario with poise and assurance, keeping your communication steady and effective.

The use of concise and direct language is extremely important, especially when every second counts. In urgent situations, clarity and precision are your allies. Using standardized codes and phrases can significantly improve your ability to communicate clearly and effectively. These codes are a universal language between different teams and agencies, and they do a lot to empower effective communication. Let's take the example of a 911 dispatcher relaying information to field units. The use of clear, direct language makes sure responders receive the information they need without delay.

Developing these communication skills requires practice, and there are a few ways to achieve it. Simulated emergency response exercises can allow you to hone these abilities in a controlled environment. During these drills, you can practice issuing and receiving directives with precision, guaranteeing that all participants understand the communication flow. Role-playing different high-pressure scenarios both improves your skills and encourages empathy and understanding (Lanzoni 2021). Stepping into various roles also enables you to gain insight into the communication challenges others might face, making your own communication better in turn. These exercises allow you to experiment with different strategies, refining your approach until it becomes second nature.

Effective communication is a necessity in the high-stakes realm where you operate daily. It's the lifeline that allows teams to work together seamlessly, even under the most trying conditions. By practicing these techniques and engaging in regular drills, you can improve your ability to communicate clearly and effectively, allowing you to remain a steady and reliable presence in the face of chaos.

WORKING THROUGH DIFFICULT CONVERSATIONS WITH EMPATHY

We've touched on the subject of empathy before, and now it's time to take a look at what makes it a powerful tool in the high-stakes world of first responders. Empathy has the potential to change even the most confrontational relationships into ones built on mutual respect and cooperation. Empathy mapping, a technique used to understand others' perspectives, can make a huge difference. By considering what the other person sees, hears, thinks, and feels, you can better understand their mindset and motivations. This approach helps break down barriers and paves the way for constructive dialogue.

Preparing for challenging dialogues, however, requires a thoughtful approach, so you have to know where to start. It's a good idea to prepare talking points that consider the other person's feelings and perspectives. Anticipate their concerns and acknowledge them in your discussion. This preparation shows that you value their input and are committed to finding common ground. But don't let it veer into preemptively anticipating their arguments; make sure your focus is on how you can validate their feelings. Setting a positive intention before the conversation is equally important. Approach it with a mindset focused on resolution and understanding rather than confrontation; this positive framing can help defuse tension and create an atmosphere conducive to open communication.

Non-verbal communication cues play a significant role in empathetic communication, too, and can often convey even more than words (Carmichael and Mizrahi 2023). Your body language and tone can radically change how the interaction goes. Maintain an open and inviting posture to signal that you are approachable and receptive. Keep your arms uncrossed, make eye contact, and nod occasionally to show engagement. Modulate your tone to convey understanding and respect if you need to help calm a tense situation. A soft, steady voice can reassure the other person that you are listening and present. These non-verbal cues amplify the empathy conveyed in your words.

Practicing empathetic communication involves exercises that help build these skills. Active listening exercises with peer feedback can be particularly beneficial. Pair up with a colleague and take turns sharing a challenging experience, such as a difficult call or a high-stress situation. As the listener, focus on fully engaging with the speaker and providing feedback on what you've heard and understood. Don't focus on what you're going to say next, but really listen. This exercise improves your ability to listen empathetically and respond appropriately. Empathy-building role reversal scenarios offer another avenue for development. This involves switching roles with a partner and each taking on the other's perspective. This practice nurtures a deeper understanding of different viewpoints and strengthens your ability to communicate with empathy.

Integrating these strategies and exercises into your routine can greatly improve your ability to deal with difficult conversations with empathy. This will, in turn, improve interactions on the job and strengthen relationships with your colleagues, patients, and the public. All of this makes for a more compassionate and effective workplace.

LISTENING SKILLS: THE FOUNDATION OF STRONG RELATIONSHIPS

"Listening" is a term a lot of people misunderstand. For many of us, listening is something we do halfheartedly while waiting for our turn to talk. Unfortunately, this isn't the best way to communicate—but active listening is. Active listening relies on truly doing your best to understand the message you're receiving. Perhaps unsurprisingly, paying full attention is foundational; this requires that you focus entirely on the speaker without distractions. Genuine interest in what the speaker is saying encourages openness and honesty across the board, which helps encourage an environment where ideas and concerns can be freely exchanged.

Reflective listening can help, too. This involves paraphrasing or summarizing what you've heard to make sure you understand the message you've received. This has the added benefit of making sure the other person knows you've understood, too. If a colleague says, "I'm feeling overwhelmed by this project," you might respond with, "It sounds like the project is causing you a lot of stress." This technique confirms that you've accurately understood the message and shows the speaker that you value their input. Be careful with its usage, however. If you just start continuously parroting back what another person is saying, they're likely to be more than a little annoyed. For this reason, it's a good idea to limit your usage of reflective listening to key moments.

The impact of active listening on relationship building can be significant. The sort of trust it can help build forms the basis of human connection, which is clearly important in both professional and personal interactions. In team settings, specifically, listening attentively can lead to improved dynamics and collaboration. When a team member feels heard and understood, they're more likely to contribute openly and work cohesively toward your shared goals. I recall an instance where a simple act of listening changed a tense meeting into a productive discussion. Terry, a firefighter in my unit, felt overwhelmed by a project, but he was scared to voice his concerns. The air felt weirdly tense as it was clear something was on his mind. Our station chief Samantha, though, addressed it directly by asking Terry what was wrong—then, just as importantly, she actively listened to him and acknowledged his challenges. By following Samantha's example, the team was able to address the issues collectively, reaching a resolution with a renewed sense of unity and purpose.

Improving your listening abilities requires deliberate practice. Mindfulness exercises—yes, we're back to those again, although these are new ones—can improve your focus and presence, allowing you to engage fully with the speaker. We've talked about taking a moment to center yourself, but it's just as important to figure out techniques for reducing internal distractions that work for you. Silencing your electronic devices is a good choice here, as when you're not distracted by your phone's constant buzzing, it's a lot easier to pay attention to what's in front of you. You can also choose to mentally set aside pressing tasks before engaging in a conversation, placing them in a box you can get to later. Minimizing these distractions can help create a space where active listening can flourish, allowing for deeper and more meaningful exchanges.

Common listening barriers can hinder effective communication, but recognizing these obstacles is the first step toward overcoming them. Preconceived notions and biases cloud everyone's perception at times, leading to misunderstandings and misinterpretations. One good way of addressing this involves approaching each conversation with an open mind and suspending judgment. This means refraining from forming opinions or conclusions about the speaker or their message until you've fully understood their perspective. This requires a conscious effort, but it gets easier over time. Additionally, managing environmental distractions is very important. A noisy background or frequent interruptions can make communication difficult, if not impossible. Circumventing this can involve solutions like finding a quiet space or setting ground rules for discussions. Creating an environment conducive to active listening facilitates more effective and impactful communication, making it a good idea for a whole host of reasons.

Listening is the foundation upon which strong relationships are built, and getting good at it requires patience, empathy, and a commitment to understanding. As you hone your listening skills, you'll find that your interactions become more genuine and fulfilling, laying the groundwork for trust and collaboration. These skills improve your professional relationships and enrich your connections, helping you remain an attentive and supportive presence in the lives of those around you.

COMMUNICATING YOUR NEEDS CLEARLY

In the demanding world of first responders, the ability to clearly communicate your needs and boundaries is absolutely crucial. Clear communication serves to both help prevent misunderstandings and conflicts and empower you, allowing you to maintain professional and personal harmony. My friend Marie was once nearly on the point of collapse from the relentless demands of the job. She didn't want to rock the boat—but when I begged her to clearly articulate her need for a break to a supervisor, she finally gave in. She might have expected this to be met with hostility, but that wasn't the case at all; her boss was actually just shocked she hadn't asked for one sooner.

Expressing needs like this directly and without ambiguity enables the paramedic to both alleviate their immediate stress and take control of the situation. It also sets a precedent for open communication within the team. You can't expect your teammates or bosses to read your mind; the only way to achieve effective communication is to do just that: communicate.

Effectively articulating your needs requires assertiveness. This is the skill that enables you to confidently express yourself while respecting others. Using "I" statements is a powerful technique here. Opting for "I need to focus on this task without interruptions" instead of "You're always interrupting me" emphasizes your needs without casting blame on anyone else. Coupled with effective body language and tone, this approach encourages and improves cooperation, reducing the likelihood of defensiveness and conflict. Setting clear and achievable expectations is also extremely important. You want to clearly outline what you need and why in order to make sure your message is understood. Doing so is the fastest and most effective path to resolution.

Assertiveness plays a pivotal role in communicating your needs, as it guarantees that other people are able to understand (and hopefully respect) them. Maintaining composure when asserting what you need is key, as calm situations are far more likely to lead to good outcomes than arguments. Even in the face of resistance or misunderstanding, you should try to stay as calm and collected as possible. Balancing assertiveness with empathy and flexibility is equally important, though. While it's crucial to stand firm, it's also beneficial to listen to others' perspectives and be willing to negotiate when appropriate. This balance demonstrates respect for your needs while encouraging a sense of connection and understanding with others. As a side benefit, this can work wonders to reduce any feelings of isolation.

Engaging in role-playing and reflection activities can be immensely beneficial to practice communicating these needs. Role-playing scenarios allow you to rehearse important conversations in a safe and controlled environment, and by simulating real-life situations, you can experiment with different approaches and receive feedback on your communication style. As far as reflection exercises go, we're back to our old friend journaling. Writing about what you need to be happy and how to communicate that can help you see areas for improvement as well as better understand your inner world. You could also journal about a time when you successfully stood up for yourself and how it positively impacted your work, reinforcing productive habits. These exercises can help you gain clarity on what is important to you and assess the effectiveness of your communication strategies.

In the context of your demanding role, mastering the communication of your needs—not to mention all other types of good communication practices—is a continuous process. Good communication, in general, requires self-awareness, practice, and a willingness to adjust as circumstances change. As you refine your communication skills, you improve your interactions with others and strengthen your resilience and capacity to thrive in both your personal and professional life.

7

BALANCING YOUR WORK AND PERSONAL LIVES

I f you want to get the most out of your life and improve your well-being as a first responder, it's not enough to simply do meditation exercises and cultivate family relationships. Instead, you have to figure out your work-life balance —and how to set boundaries around it. For first responders, building a proper work-life balance is absolutely necessary to preserve your mental health and guarantee you have the time you need to recharge. The unique demands of your profession mean that without these boundaries, work can seep into every corner of your life, leaving little room for personal fulfillment or rest.

ESTABLISHING A ROUTINE

Routines are more important than you might realize. Setting specific work hours and adhering to them, for example, is a foundational step in establishing work-life balance. Defining when your workday begins and ends carves out protected time for yourself and your loved ones. This is a valuable practice for everything regardless of profession, but it's especially important in fields such as first response, where the lines between personal and professional life often blur.

It may feel like an uncomfortable conversation to have, but you need to be sure to communicate these boundaries to your colleagues and supervisors. Letting them know that your off-hours are dedicated to your personal time reduces the likelihood of work encroaching on your downtime. It may feel challenging at first, especially if your work culture doesn't typically encourage boundaries like these. You might even feel guilty, like you're doing something wrong or selfish. In fact, it's just the opposite; you're making sure you have what you need in order to be at your best when it's time to serve others. Moreover, the empowerment that comes from setting these boundaries is immense, and the long-term benefits to your mental health and relationships are significant.

Identifying and communicating your boundaries involves practical strategies that enable you to protect your personal time without guilt. It's especially important to learn to say "no" confidently. Whether you're declining an extra shift or turning down a non-essential task, saying "no" can be a powerful tool for maintaining balance. Part of your brain might initially view it as being uncooperative, but that's not it at all. Instead, what you're doing is prioritizing your well-being to avoid all of the negative consequences we've talked about so far. Delegating tasks is another effective method of managing your workload. Sharing responsibilities can lighten your burden and allow others to contribute when you need them. The sense of teamwork this instills can even be a powerful motivator in maintaining your work-life balance.

Technology can have both positive and negative impacts on boundary management. On the one hand, apps designed for scheduling personal time and setting reminders can be instrumental in keeping work at bay during your off-hours. These tools help you plan leisure activities and help you allocate time for relaxation and self-care. On the other hand, technology can also encroach on your personal time if you don't manage it carefully. Constant email notifications and work-related messages can erode the boundaries you've set. You can manage these by setting specific times to check your emails or using features that silence alerts during your personal hours. This can significantly reduce work's intrusion into your personal life.

Regular re-reassessment of your boundaries is extremely important for keeping them practical and relevant as your work and personal demands change over time. This process involves exercises that help you evaluate how well your current boundaries serve you. This can involve answering questions like "Do I feel rested and recharged during my personal time?" or "Are there areas where work is still encroaching on my life?" Based on your answers, you can adjust your boundaries to better meet your needs. This proactive approach allows you to adapt to changing circumstances and make sure your work-life balance always aligns with your priorities.

TECHNIQUES FOR DETACHING FROM WORK STRESS AT HOME

Leaving work stress at the station or hospital door is key if you want to maintain a healthy balance between your professional responsibilities and your personal life. For those in the thick of emergency services, mental separation from the work environment is nothing less than how you maintain your sanity. Consciously detaching from the day's stresses helps prevent burnout and enables you to relax in a way that is absolutely necessary for your well-being. Allowing your mind to rest from the day's demands also helps your body kickstart its natural recovery processes. Stress reduction at home can lead to numerous physiological benefits, including lower blood pressure and improved immune function (Moore 2022). Unsurprisingly, these are pretty important for maintaining your long-term health and job performance. Detaching from work stress provides a significant amount of control over your mental well-being, making it a powerful tool in your professional arsenal.

Achieving this mental detachment is easier if you establish transition rituals—simple actions that signal the end of your workday and the beginning of your personal time. In addition to getting you in the right mindset, these rituals can also serve to reassure you that you're on the right path to a healthy work-life balance. Changing out of your work clothes when you get home can be a powerful symbol of this transition, helping you physically and mentally separate your work stress from home life. Taking a shower can serve a similar purpose, as it can wash away the tension and create a fresh start. Setting up a calming home environment helps, too; play relaxing music or use scented candles to create a soothing atmosphere right after you get home. The gentle notes of a favorite song or the familiar aroma of lavender can cue your mind to relax and unwind, helping your home achieve its potential as a sanctuary from the rigors of your job.

Physical and mental activities can also be practical tools for further detaching from work stress. Physical exercises such as yoga or jogging promote relaxation and boost your endorphin levels; this naturally improves your mood and reduces your stress (Woodyard 2011). These activities can also provide the sort of mental clarity that's often elusive amidst the chaos of emergency response. Practicing mindfulness or meditation before and after shifts can also help, as these practices encourage presence in the moment, allowing you to process stress and restore balance. Even a few minutes of deep breathing or guided meditation can provide a mental reset, which helps you transition more smoothly from work to home life.

Establishing evening routines is another important part of encouraging relaxation and detachment. A consistent bedtime ritual can signal to your body and mind that it's time to wind down and prepare for rest. This might include activities such as reading or engaging in a low-stakes hobby that brings joy and satisfaction. Leisure activities before sleep help create a buffer between the demands of the day and the tranquility of night, helping your mind be ready to rest when your head hits the pillow. Consistency in these routines reinforces their effectiveness, providing a reliable framework for unwinding after a demanding shift.

SCHEDULING SELF-CARE INTO BUSY SHIFTS

The idea of self-care might seem like a luxury rather than a necessity when you're caught up in the whirlwind of a particularly demanding shift. But integrating self-care into your workday is incredibly important for maintaining your health and overall performance. Moreover, it actually empowers you to take control of your well-being. Brief moments of respite, like short breaks for stretching or deep breathing, can make a world of difference. These quick pauses allow your body to reset and your mind to regain focus, reducing both tension and fatigue. Hydration and nutrition also play pivotal roles in self-care, as a well-nourished body is better equipped to handle your job's physical and mental demands. You want to stay alert and ready to respond to emergencies, and taking care of yourself is exactly how you achieve it.

Incorporating self-care into your workday requires some deliberate planning. Setting reminders for regular short breaks throughout your shift can make sure you don't overlook these important moments of rest. This might mean a quick walk around the building, a moment of deep breathing in a quiet corner, or anything that gives you at least momentary peace. Whatever you pick, these breaks are extremely important for refreshing your mind and body. Packing healthy snacks and meals is another good idea, as having nutritious options readily available helps maintain your energy levels and prevents blood sugar crashes that can sap your strength and focus. Simple choices like fruit, nuts, or yogurt can provide the nutrients needed to power through a busy day without the crash that often follows sugary or processed snacks.

Micro self-care practices are small yet powerful tools that can be seamlessly integrated into even the busiest days. Desk exercises can relieve tension without requiring much time or space, reducing the muscle stiffness that often accompanies long hours of sitting or standing. Quick mindfulness exercises like a minute of focused breathing or a brief mental check-in—or any of the others we've talked about—can be performed between tasks, helping to clear your mind and center your thoughts. These moments of mindfulness enable you to approach each task with renewed vigor and focus—without disrupting your workflow.

The benefits of consistent self-care extend far beyond the immediate relief they provide. Over time, these practices contribute to a more resilient and balanced state of mind, improving your mood and overall well-being. Regular self-care improves your focus and productivity during shifts, allowing you to perform at your best, even when the pressure ratchets up. Investing in these small acts of care builds a foundation of resilience that supports you through all of the myriad challenges of your role. This commitment, in turn, encourages a sense of balance and satisfaction, which reinforces your ability to thrive personally and professionally. It's hard not to have a more positive outlook for the future in these circumstances.

CULTIVATING HOBBIES AND INTERESTS OUTSIDE OF WORK

Finding time for hobbies might seem like frivolity amidst the demanding life of a first responder. This isn't the case, though; engaging in hobbies is a powerful way to achieve work-life balance. They can work wonders in offering relaxation and promoting personal growth. When you immerse yourself in a creative outlet, you allow your mind to wander away from the day's stressors, helping you achieve a sense of calm and tranquility. These activities serve as a form of temporary escapism, which provides a much-needed break from the routine, helping to significantly reduce your stress levels. Creative outlets engage different parts of your brain, but they might be most powerful for the sense of accomplishment and satisfaction they give you. That sort of feeling can be elusive in the high-pressure environments you deal with daily.

Individual fulfillment is valuable enough on its own, but hobbies often provide opportunities for social interaction, too. Remember when we talked about support networks back in Chapter 4? These can be particularly beneficial there. Joining a book club, a cooking class, or a community gardening group both enriches your interests and connects you with others who share similar passions. This social aspect is a huge part of mental health, as it combats feelings of isolation and creates a sense of belonging. Engaging with others in a relaxed setting allows you to forge new friendships while strengthening existing ones. The end result can be a community that supports you both personally and professionally. This sense of connection and support can be a powerful tool in maintaining your mental and emotional well-being.

Finding and developing hobbies might require exploration and effort, but it's ultimately an extremely rewarding endeavor. Try new activities that grab your interest. Painting, for instance, can provide a creative outlet for self-expression, while gardening offers the satisfaction of nurturing and growth. Cooking, on the other hand, can be both practical and enjoyable, offering a sensory experience that engages your creativity (also, you get to eat tasty food out of it). If you're unsure of where to start, joining clubs or groups that line up with these interests can be a good way to kick things off. Many communities offer classes or workshops—a great low-pressure way to explore new activities and meet like-minded individuals.

Scheduling regular leisure time for hobbies is extremely important. It's easy to let personal interests fall by the wayside, especially if you feel like your professional responsibilities are all that matter. However, prioritizing these activities is absolutely necessary if you want to maintain balance. Allocating specific time slots each week for leisure activities helps keep hobbies a part of your routine rather than an occasional indulgence. You could dedicate an hour each evening to writing, playing guitar, or painting. Alternatively, you could reserve a weekend afternoon for a round of golf. This time can be even more rewarding when you share it with family or friends. Family game nights or weekend hikes can combine your hobbies with your loved ones to add an extra mental and emotional boost.

The mental health benefits of engaging in fulfilling activities go far beyond immediate pleasure. Hobbies provide a sense of accomplishment and satisfaction that greatly improves your overall well-being. Completing a project instills a sense of achievement and pride that can be difficult to find anywhere else. This boost in self-esteem can carry over into other areas of your life, improving your mood and reducing your anxiety. The immersive nature of hobbies also offers a respite from the constant demands of work, giving you ample time to recharge and reset. This stress reduction naturally improves your mental health and boosts your ability to perform effectively in your professional role. In the long run, those "frivolous" hobbies can work wonders to make you better at the things you might have already decided are all that matter.

Pursuing interests outside of work is about more than filling time. The goal is to enrich your life and nurture your overall mental and emotional well-being. By cultivating hobbies, you create a well-rounded existence that supports your personal satisfaction and professional resilience. As you explore the diverse array of activities available, remember that you want to find what brings you joy and fulfillment. These pursuits can do a lot to provide stability and joy amidst the challenges of your demanding profession. Your path toward balance and well-being is unique, and the interests you cultivate will guide you along the way.

MAKE A DIFFERENCE WITH YOUR REVIEW

THE POWER OF GENEROSITY

The best way to find yourself is to lose yourself in the service of others.

— MAHATMA GANDHI

As first responders, healthcare providers, and public servants, we know what it means to give our best for others —day after day, call after call. We do it without expecting anything in return. That's just who we are. Now, I'm asking you to help in one more small but powerful way.

Would you help someone just like you—someone working in a high-stress, high-stakes job—who is looking for tools to care for their mind, body, and relationships? Someone who wants to thrive rather than just survive? My mission is to make mental resilience and emotional well-being something every first responder can build—easily, practically, and without shame. But I can't reach them alone.

Most people choose books based on what others say about them. Your review of *First Responder Self-Help Solutions* could be the guiding light for another responder just like you, leading them toward hope and healing. Your voice matters in our community.

It's quick, it's easy, and it's free. Your review could make a world of difference in just a minute. It could help:

- one more firefighter hold on through tough times
- one more paramedic find strength after a hard call
- one more officer strengthen their marriage
- one more nurse or doctor find peace in their heart
- one more responder know they are not alone

To make a difference, scan the QR code below and leave a review:

If you believe in helping others, you're my kind of person. Thank you for all you do, on and off the job.

8

LEADERSHIP AND MENTORSHIP IN HIGH-STRESS CAREERS

The echo of a radio call and the rush of adrenaline as you race to the scene is an inextricable part of the life of a first responder. In high-stakes situations and tense moments, effective leadership means everything—but it matters a lot in the quiet moments between emergencies, too. Leadership in both action-packed scenarios and everyday interactions helps shape team dynamics and influences mental health awareness. As someone who has stood in your boots, I understand your unique pressures. Leadership in our context means setting the tone for mental health advocacy. It's a grave responsibility that rests on the shoulders of those who guide and support our teams, and it's integral to our collective well-being.

LEADING BY EXAMPLE: PROMOTING MENTAL HEALTH AWARENESS

Leaders have a unique opportunity to champion mental health awareness in the high-stress emergency response environment. By sharing their personal experiences with mental health struggles, leaders can help dismantle the barriers that allow these issues to do untold damage from the shadows. Their openness both normalizes these conversations and helps others feel connected and understood. Publicly supporting mental health initiatives through event participation or vocal advocacy sends a clear message: Mental health is a priority rather than an afterthought.

Leaders play a big role in modeling healthy behaviors. By prioritizing self-care and wellness in their own lives, they demonstrate the importance of these practices to the first responders under their charge. Whether it's taking regular breaks, engaging in physical exercise, or practicing mindfulness, all of these actions speak volumes. Encouraging regular mental health check-ins within teams nurtures an environment where everyone feels seen and supported. It also can't be something conducted without being personally involved; it's extremely important to participate in mental health training sessions alongside team members. This visibly solidifies a leader's commitment to the process and shows that mental health education is for everyone, regardless of rank or experience.

Transparent communication, meanwhile, is a foundational element for leaders in nurturing a culture of trust and support. Regular updates on organizational mental health policies keep everyone informed and engaged, while open discussions about available mental health resources make sure team members know where to turn when they need help. Maintaining transparency enables leaders to build a foundation of trust that encourages open dialogue and collaboration. This approach supports individual well-being while improving team cohesion and effectiveness.

Leaders play a pivotal role in reducing the stigma associated with mental health conversations. By integrating mental health topics into regular meetings, leaders make these discussions a routine part of workplace culture—just another part of taking care of one's well-being. Recognizing and rewarding mental health advocacy efforts within the team further reinforces the importance of these initiatives. It's important to acknowledge those who contribute to mental health awareness. Doing so cultivates an environment where everyone feels valued and empowered to make a difference in reducing the mental health stigma.

Bettering Your Leadership Practices

Think about your current leadership practices and consider how you can incorporate mental health advocacy into your daily interactions. Are there personal experiences you can share to normalize mental health discussions? It's important to model self-care and wellness for your team, as it sets a positive example and promotes a healthy work-life balance. Set goals to improve your leadership in mental health awareness and revisit them regularly to track your progress and growth.

LEADING WITH EMPATHY AND UNDERSTANDING

Empathy in leadership is a world-altering force in high-stress environments. Leaders who lead with empathy nurture trust and loyalty within their teams while also inspiring and motivating them. I once worked with a seasoned paramedic named Kelly who transitioned into a leadership role after years in the field. Instead of enforcing authority through rigid protocols, she embraced empathy as her guiding principle. Kelly listened to her team's concerns, really making an effort to understand their struggles and aspirations. This empathetic approach completely changed the team's dynamics for the better, creating a cohesive unit where morale soared and unity was the new normal. Empathy does more than soothe wounds; it builds bridges, improving team morale and encouraging a spirit of collaboration that thrives even under pressure.

Developing empathetic leadership skills requires intentional effort, and active listening sessions play an important role here. Dedicating time to truly hearing team members enables leaders to gain deep insight into the challenges and triumphs of their colleagues. You don't simply want to hear the words people say but understand the emotions and motivations behind them. This understanding, in turn, nurtures a deeper connection, which makes leaders more effective in guiding their teams. Role-playing exercises also offer a practical avenue to cultivate empathy, as they allow leaders to step into their team members' shoes and experience first-hand the pressures and expectations they face. Through these activities, leaders can hone their ability to respond with empathy, building responses that acknowledge and validate the feelings of others while guiding them toward effective long-term solutions.

Balance is key in leadership, especially when it comes to empathy and authority—a delicate act that requires setting clear expectations while remaining approachable and open. Leaders can even maintain authority by using empathetic language to enforce rules and standards. This approach makes sure that guidelines are respected and understood as part of a supportive framework rather than a top-down directive. As a leader, you want to strike the right balance between guiding with firmness and nurturing with compassion. Leaders who master this balance create an environment where mutual respect and authority are upheld without fear or resentment. When executed successfully, this instills confidence in the team, making them feel competent and capable.

The impact of empathetic leadership on team performance can be significant. Studies have shown that teams led by compassionate leaders often experience increased productivity and satisfaction (Ramachandran 2023). This isn't altogether surprising when you think about it; when team members feel understood and valued, their commitment to their work and colleagues deepens. In turn, this leads to lower turnover and absenteeism. This chain reaction creates a stable, motivated workforce ready to tackle challenges with resilience and dedication. Empathy-driven leadership doesn't just improve outcomes; it completely changes the fabric of team culture for the better. Nurturing an environment where everyone feels empowered to contribute and grow creates a culture of collaboration, innovation, and continuous improvement.

CREATING SUPPORTIVE ENVIRONMENTS: POLICIES AND PRACTICES

In the demanding world you inhabit, a supportive workplace is even more important than you might realize. There are all sorts of ways to create this environment, and implementing flexible work arrangements can make a significant difference. Whether this means allowing for shift swaps or offering remote work options whenever feasible, flexibility helps first responders manage the demands of both their personal and professional lives. This approach acknowledges the unique challenges of your role and provides the adaptability necessary to maintain mental health and job satisfaction. Alongside flexibility, providing access to mental health resources is extremely important. There do exist on-site counseling services or partnerships with mental health professionals who understand the specific pressures you face, and it would be a good idea to look into these. These resources should also be easily accessible so that support is just a conversation away.

Training and development programs play a pivotal role in encouraging a supportive culture. Offering mental health first aid training equips you and your colleagues with the skills to recognize and respond to mental health issues, which can potentially save lives and reduce absenteeism. You wouldn't send an EMT into the field without knowledge of CPR, so why should knowing how to deal with mental health issues be any different? This training demystifies mental health and empowers first responders to support each other effectively. Regular workshops on stress management and resilience further strengthen this culture by providing practical tools and techniques people can apply at work and in their personal lives. This, in turn, helps improve first responders' ability to cope with the stresses inherent in the profession. Organizations that prioritize continuous education signal their commitment to your well-being and growth.

A comprehensive Employee Assistance Program (EAP) can be a huge part of providing support. These programs offer confidential counseling services, providing a safe space to discuss personal or professional challenges. Access to mental health professionals through an EAP guarantees you have the support to work through difficult times. These programs often include various services, from financial counseling to legal advice. Altogether, these issues address multiple aspects of a first responder's life that may impact their mental health. By providing such comprehensive support, EAPs contribute significantly to a healthier, more resilient workforce (Paychex 2024).

There are plenty of good options if you want to engage in successful, supportive practices for mental health. Peer support networks within organizations can create a sense of community, facilitating support and reducing feelings of isolation. Recognition programs for mental health champions, meanwhile, improve workplace culture by acknowledging and rewarding those individuals who advocate for mental health awareness, making them feel valued and appreciated. These programs highlight the importance of mental health and inspire others to get involved in advocacy efforts. Initiatives like these demonstrate the power of collective action and the impact of a workplace committed to supporting its members at every level.

ENCOURAGING OPEN DIALOGUE: FACILITATING IMPORTANT CONVERSATIONS

You've probably heard this before: Communication is important. When it comes to first responders and mental health, open dialogue is what connects individuals, breaking down barriers and encouraging inclusivity. A powerful sense of community emerges when spaces are created where people can share their experiences without any fear of judgment. The benefits of these sorts of environments are numerous, including improved mental well-being, increased job satisfaction, and stronger team cohesion. Encouraging feedback and suggestions on mental health initiatives can further strengthen this environment. When team members feel their voices are heard and valued, they're far more likely to engage actively, contributing ideas and solutions that might otherwise be lost in the silence of apprehension.

Facilitating difficult conversations requires a delicate balance of sensitivity and assertiveness. It starts with active listening, a skill that we've talked about and which enables each participant to feel genuinely heard. Empathy is even more important, as it connects diverse perspectives and encourages people to understand each other better. Setting clear goals and boundaries for discussions is equally important. This provides structure and focus while making sure conversations remain productive and respectful. This approach helps defuse potential tension while cultivating a culture of respect and collaboration where each voice contributes to the collective wisdom of the group.

Regular team meetings and forums serve as important platforms for open dialogue. By incorporating mental health check-ins into routine meetings, leaders signal that mental well-being is an ongoing priority rather than an occasional concern. These check-ins, whether they're carefully structured or just as simple as a quick "How are you really doing?" can be a tangible demonstration of care and support. Hosting forums specifically dedicated to discussing mental health challenges and solutions, meanwhile, allows for a deeper exploration of issues that impact the team. These gatherings encourage transparency and offer a space for collective problem-solving. This has the ultimate effect of turning challenges into opportunities for growth and innovation.

Inclusive leadership is the linchpin that holds these efforts together. Leaders who champion diversity of thought and encourage varied perspectives—along with seeking out and hiring those with diverse experiences—create an environment where all voices can be heard. This inclusivity enriches discussions and encourages a culture where collaborative problem-solving can thrive. More importantly, leaders play a key role in promoting mental health initiatives and creating a safe space for open dialogue. When leaders provide opportunities for team members to contribute their knowledge and ideas, they empower those working under them to take ownership of their mental health—not to mention that of their colleagues. This leads to a more resilient, cohesive team that stands ready to face the challenges of their demanding roles with confidence and solidarity.

MENTORSHIP IN MENTAL HEALTH: GUIDING THE NEXT GENERATION

Mentorship is a key part of professional development, as it offers a bridge between seasoned experience and fresh energy. When offered productively, mentorship can offer growth and facilitate the transfer of knowledge—a process that allows both mentors and mentees to flourish. For mentors, guiding the next generation can be a rewarding experience in and of itself. Many find it enriches their professional lives while keeping them engaged with new ideas and perspectives. For mentees, having a mentor means having access to invaluable knowledge and guidance, which can significantly accelerate their career advancement and personal development. This relationship nurtures both parties, creating a cycle of continuous learning and support.

Effective mentorship is not a random process but one which requires careful planning and intention. Setting clear objectives and expectations is the bedrock of this process; both mentor and mentee should have a shared understanding of their goals. This might mean improving specific skills, figuring out career paths, or working on personal growth. Regular check-ins are important for tracking progress and addressing challenges as they arise. These meetings provide an opportunity for course correction and reaffirmation of your shared goals, helping the mentorship stay productive and aligned with the needs of both mentor and mentee.

The qualities of a successful mentor go way beyond just having expertise in a subject area. Patience is extremely important, as guidance often involves listening and understanding at a deep level. A mentor must be able to provide constructive feedback, offering truthful and supportive answers without veering into the unproductive type of judgment. This balance helps mentees grow without feeling overwhelmed or discouraged. Additionally, a mentor's willingness to share their experiences openly is important. A mentor who can look back on their own story and share both their failures and successes provides their mentee with a fuller picture of their learning. As an added bonus, this openness further nurtures trust and encourages a closer connection between the two.

Mentorship doesn't have to be spontaneous and scattershot; institutionalizing the practice within organizations can amplify its benefits. It can make a huge difference to have structured mentorship pairing programs that match mentors and mentees based on shared goals and interests. Pairing people up this way does a lot to make sure the relationship is mutually beneficial and relevant. Recognizing and incentivizing mentors who actively contribute to such programs can further encourage participation. Celebrating successes and highlighting the impact of mentorship also motivates current mentors and inspires others who might have been hesitant. On the whole, embedding mentorship into the organizational culture creates an environment that values growth, collaboration, and the development of future leaders. This culture of growth and collaboration isn't just a byproduct of the process—it's a direct result of effective mentorship.

BUILDING A RESILIENT TEAM CULTURE

Part of being a first responder is the keen awareness that each day is going to bring with it unforeseen challenges. In this sort of environment, building a resilient team culture is incredibly important. A resilient team thrives on adaptability and flexibility, which in turn enables its members to effectively pivot and respond to unexpected situations. This adaptability defines the ability to change course when needed, maintaining composure and focus in the face of adversity. It requires strong communication and collaboration skills—the glue that holds a team together. In a resilient culture, team members share information freely, support one another, and work collaboratively to solve problems. The resulting environment is one where everyone feels empowered, confident, and capable of contributing, safe in the knowledge their input is both valued and respected.

Nurturing resilience within a team involves deliberate and consistent efforts. Regular resilience training sessions and workshops are an important part of equipping team members with the skills they need to productively handle stress and adversity. Resilience is ultimately the ability to rebound from setbacks, to keep focused and productive under pressure, and to adapt to changing circumstances. Resilience training sessions can cover various topics, from stress management techniques to strategies for maintaining emotional balance under pressure. Leaders will also want to encourage their teams to look back on their own experiences —both the good and the bad. Reviewing and learning from setbacks enables teams to identify areas for improvement and develop strategies to prevent similar issues in the future.

This improves individual growth and strengthens the team, creating a culture that values learning and continuous improvement.

Leaders play a pivotal role in cultivating resilience. They can inspire others by sharing personal resilience stories, demonstrating that challenges are not insurmountable but opportunities for growth. These stories provide real-life examples of overcoming adversity, which can offer hope and motivation to team members mired in their own struggles. Recognizing and rewarding resilient behaviors within the team is a big part of this. By highlighting team member achievements, leaders show their appreciation for the team's efforts. In turn, this encourages team members to persevere and to continue striving for excellence.

The long-term benefits of a resilient team culture are significant. A team that can thrive amidst changing circumstances is better equipped to handle the demands of their roles. Improved team cohesion and mutual support also lead to a more harmonious work environment where individuals feel connected and committed to the team's goals. This sense of unity does a lot to improve feelings of loyalty, reducing turnover and improving job satisfaction. In a resilient team, challenges become growth opportunities, and each success contributes to the strength and resilience of the team as a whole. These benefits highlight the importance of resilience and should motivate leaders and team members to invest in its development.

9

PERSONAL GROWTH AND PROFESSIONAL DEVELOPMENT

We've talked a lot about self-help involving techniques like mindfulness and general stress relief for your mental well-being. While all of that is important, and your mental health is certainly important for its own sake, that's not the only benefit you get out of the process. Growing as a person and as a professional matters just as much—but how do you manage that? There are a whole bunch of aspects to this process, it turns out: being adaptable, building your self-confidence, committing to continuous learning, etc. But it all starts with knowing how to set goals for yourself.

GOAL-SETTING FOR FIRST RESPONDERS

An important part of everything we've talked about involves setting goals. After all, if you don't know where you're headed, how can you expect to get there? For first responders like you, goal setting is less a tool for growth than it is a compass that guides you through your demanding role.

When executed properly, set goals should give you a sense of control and confidence. Each goal illuminates the way forward and motivates you to overcome any obstacles in your way.

Setting goals is an exercise in clarity and intention. The SMART framework—Specific, Measurable, Achievable, Relevant, and Time-bound—serves as a powerful guide here. Defining "Specific" goals enables you to pinpoint areas for development, addressing skill gaps that might otherwise hinder your progress. "Measurable" goals allow you to track achievements, which helps build a sense of accomplishment that improves your confidence. It's likewise important to make your goals "Achievable" so that your ambitions remain within reach, preventing the burnout that often accompanies shooting for the moon and missing entirely. "Relevance," meanwhile, helps keep your efforts in alignment with your career objectives, maintaining focus on your long-term growth. Finally, "Time-bound" goals create a sense of urgency and accountability, which drives consistent progress (Ponciano 2025).

It's also important to set goals that promote self-care and balance; you want to look after your well-being even as you strive for growth. For a first responder, a short-term goal could be mastering a new life-saving technique, while a long-term goal might be to become a team leader. Balancing these two types of goals allows for a harmonious pursuit of growth, making each step meaningful and strategic.

Reflection and reassessment are integral to the goal-setting process. Regularly checking your progress allows you to evaluate your successes and identify your biggest obstacles.

This process is not static but requires flexibility and an openness to change. As circumstances shift, so too might your goals and priorities—and that's okay. Embracing this change and adjusting your goals in response to these shifts helps keep them relevant and achievable.

Achieving goals should bring you tremendous motivation and satisfaction in a way that positively impacts your personal fulfillment and career success. I once knew a paramedic named Alex who set a goal to complete a specialized certification. It wasn't easy, but he ultimately achieved that milestone through dedication and service, gaining improved skills that enriched his work and contributed to his career advancement. At least one study has shown that reaching significant milestones can have a hugely beneficial effect on a person's mental health, as well as improving their feelings of agency (Wang et al. 2017).

Goal setting can ultimately be a source of significant empowerment. It serves as a foundation in the pursuit of personal growth and professional development, providing direction, motivation, and a sense of purpose. It empowers you to deal with the challenges of your role with confidence and clarity. As you continue to set and achieve goals, remember that each step forward brings you closer to the life and career you ultimately envision for yourself.

EMBRACING CHANGE AND ADAPTABILITY

The nature of emergency services is such that no two days are the same. One moment, you might be responding to a routine call, and the next, you get thrust into a scenario that tests every skill you possess. This unpredictability demands a mindset open to change and resilience against the unexpected. Adaptability improves your performance by allowing you to pivot as circumstances change. It strengthens your resilience, helping you remain steady and focused when chaos reigns. Preparing mentally for sudden shifts in your environment is an absolute necessity. Your ability to adapt means you can respond effectively—a must for the safety and well-being of those you serve.

Developing adaptability skills is a process of intention and practice that can lead to a sense of pride and accomplishment. One effective strategy is scenario planning, which involves envisioning potential situations and thinking about various potential responses. This mental rehearsal prepares you for a range of possibilities, which helps reduce your anxiety when you are actually faced with these situations in real life. Contingency thinking further improves this preparedness by encouraging you to develop backup plans. This proactive approach makes sure you're not caught off guard even when the unexpected occurs. Engaging in activities that require creative problem-solving also sharpens your adaptability. Team exercises that simulate high-pressure scenarios, or individual challenges that push you out of your comfort zone, can build the mental flexibility needed to work through complex situations.

The role of your mindset in embracing change is extremely important. A positive, growth-oriented mindset turns challenges into opportunities for learning and development. Remember when we talked about cognitive reframing way back in Chapter 1? That comes back into play here. The mindfulness practices we've discussed also complement this by helping you remain present and open-minded. Together, this approach encourages a calm, clear mind that stands ready to adapt and respond to whatever challenges get tossed its way.

Another thing to consider is that adaptability leads to personal and professional growth by opening doors to new opportunities. One time, a friend of mine, a firefighter named Connor, transitioned to a leadership role within his department. Initially, the shift demanded significant adjustment, challenging him to adopt new skills and perspectives. However, by embracing adaptability, he succeeded and innovated, eventually introducing new strategies that improved his team's overall performance. In this case, as in so many others, adaptability is a catalyst for career advancement—one that enables you to step into new roles with confidence. In leadership, adaptability is invaluable, as it allows you to guide others through change with vision and assurance.

The benefits of adaptability are not just professional; they also extend to personal growth and fulfillment. Adaptability cultivates a mindset of lifelong learning and growth, which in turn encourages you to continuously seek improvement. This openness to change further boosts your resilience, equipping you to face future challenges with strength and optimism. As you embrace adaptability, you improve your capacity to handle the demands of your role and enrich your personal and professional life. This ability to adapt and thrive amidst uncertainty is helpful for everyone, but it especially defines the most successful and fulfilled first responders. With each change you embrace, you lay another brick in the foundation for yourself and those you serve.

CONTINUOUS LEARNING: STAYING INFORMED AND SKILLED

In the ever-shifting world of emergency response, what you know today might not be enough for tomorrow. The techniques and protocols that define your work are constantly in flux, driven by advancements in technology, changes in regulations, and new knowledge about human behavior. This environment demands a commitment to lifelong learning, a practice that keeps your skills sharp and relevant. Ongoing education doesn't simply mean keeping up but staying ahead and equipping yourself with the knowledge and tools you need to excel in your role. Every new piece of information you acquire improves your ability to serve effectively and confidently, which ultimately empowers you in your mission.

You really can't overemphasize the importance of staying informed for first responders. Continuous learning opens doors to career advancement, providing opportunities that might otherwise remain out of reach. Your superiors are likely to notice, too, as engaging in professional development signals a readiness to take on new challenges and responsibilities. This proactive attitude benefits your career and improves the quality of service you provide. Whether you're mastering the latest life-saving technique or understanding new communication protocols, each learning experience adds to your expertise and fortifies your role within your team and your community.

Numerous resources and strategies are available to support your educational process. Online courses and certifications tailored to first responders offer flexibility and allow you to learn at your own pace and schedule. These programs might cover various topics, from advanced medical procedures to leadership skills, providing a comprehensive foundation for your growth. Attending workshops, seminars, and conferences further enriches your knowledge base, in addition to offering opportunities to network with peers and industry leaders. These events can serve a useful role as platforms for sharing ideas and best practices.

Embracing self-directed learning is equally important. Much like the goal-setting we talked about earlier, taking personal responsibility for your education means setting learning goals and actively seeking information. Open-source materials and industry publications are invaluable resources offering great information about the latest developments and trends. Dedicating time to reading and exploring these materials cultivates a deeper understanding of your field. This commitment to learning shows a desire to excel, both for your benefit and the greater good of those you serve. It's also important to learn from your mistakes and failures, as they can provide valuable lessons and help you develop resilience and adaptability. Unsurprisingly, these are key qualities in the fast-paced and unpredictable world of emergency response.

The benefits of continuous learning go a lot further than personal satisfaction, too. They can even significantly impact your career progression. Staying informed improves your job performance, enabling you to respond more effectively to the diverse challenges you face on a daily basis. Specialized skills acquired through education can totally alter your team dynamics and position you as a leader and innovator within your organization. A paramedic who pursues advanced training in critical care might see their confidence and competence rapidly improve. In turn, this would boost the team's overall capabilities, inspiring others to pursue their educational goals and leading to a more fulfilling and satisfying career.

Continuous learning is an absolute necessity and the foundation upon which you can build a successful, fulfilling career. Remaining open to new information and actively seeking growth opportunities guarantees that you're always prepared to meet the shifting demands of your profession. This commitment to education shows a dedication to your craft and a deep sense of responsibility to those you serve. As you continue to learn and grow, you contribute to a legacy of excellence that inspires and empowers those around you.

BUILDING CONFIDENCE AND SELF-EFFICACY

In a nutshell, self-efficacy is your belief in your ability to accomplish tasks and achieve goals. As a first responder, it's a huge part of your personal and professional success. This belief can massively influence how you approach challenges. When you trust your capabilities, you're more likely to take decisive action and tackle your problems head-on. Self-efficacy is also intricately linked to resilience, as it provides the confidence to work through setbacks and obstacles. This mindset is very important for decision-making and problem-solving, where confidence can be the difference between hesitation and action. On the scene of an emergency, every second counts. In these moments, self-belief fuels your ability to make quick, informed decisions, empowering you to take control of the situation and guaranteeing the best possible outcomes for those in your care.

Positive affirmations and self-talk can be very effective for building this skill. You reshape your internal narrative by consistently reinforcing positive beliefs and replacing doubt with certainty. Repeating affirmations like "I am capable" or "I can handle challenges with grace" can shift your mindset and nurture a positive self-image. It can also help build a reservoir of confidence that you can draw upon in important moments, improving your overall sense of empowerment.

Experience and skill mastery also play pivotal roles in confidence-building. Seeking out challenging opportunities is a huge part of developing improved competence. Each new experience should add to your repertoire, expanding your skill set and reinforcing your abilities. Looking back on your past successes is also extremely important. Take the time to acknowledge your achievements, as this will remind you of your capabilities and strengthen your confidence. Compiling a mental or physical list of accomplishments will remind you of your growth and potential. Over the long run, this boosts your self-efficacy and cultivates a mindset of continuous improvement, which encourages you to seek out new challenges and opportunities to master.

Confidence also significantly impacts your personal and professional interactions for the better. In crisis situations, confident leadership can inspire calm in your fellow first responders. When team members see you acting with assurance, they're more likely to follow suit in maintaining composure and focus. The self-assured demeanor of a confident paramedic leading a team through a critical incident can guide the team's actions while inspiring and reassuring those in their care. Leaders with high self-efficacy naturally encourage environments where collaboration and innovation thrive, which empowers others to contribute their best efforts. This creates a positive feedback loop where confidence begets success, and success begets further confidence. This is the sort of situation that forges influential and inspiring leaders.

Self-efficacy and confidence form the backbone of personal and professional development. They are the forces that drive you forward, enabling you to meet the demands of your role with courage and assurance. Building these qualities is not a one-time effort but an ongoing process that requires careful consideration, practice, and a willingness to grow. As you continue cultivating self-efficacy, you improve your capabilities while inspiring those around you to reach their fullest potential.

10

SELF-CARE ROUTINES FOR FIRST RESPONDERS

At the end of another challenging shift, I drove home, the city slowly waking as the sun peeked over the horizon. The adrenaline that kept me sharp and focused was ebbing away, now replaced by a heavy fatigue. As the road stretched ahead, I realized how important it was for me to recharge before the next call. Moments like these are where self-care steps in. The best self-care sustains your mental and physical well-being in a career that demands so much of you. But how do you make sure the self-care you're practicing is healthy and productive? It starts with a self-care plan.

YOUR PERSONALIZED SELF-CARE PLAN

Creating a personalized self-care plan is absolutely essential if you want to get the most out of the process. Tailoring self-care strategies to your needs helps them fit seamlessly into your lifestyle, greatly improving their effectiveness. Think about your personal stressors and relaxation preferences; maybe certain sounds or situations trigger stress, while a particular hobby or activity brings you peace. Understanding these elements helps you build a self-care plan that addresses your unique challenges and supports your well-being. Matching your self-care activities to your values and interests also increases their sustainability. If you value connection, for instance, incorporating social activities into your routine can provide relaxation and fulfillment. This process of tailoring your plan empowers you, as it puts you in control of your well-being.

Crafting a personalized self-care plan starts with assessing your current habits and identifying any gaps in what you need. Think about your daily routine and note where your self-care is lacking. Are there moments when you feel overwhelmed or stretched thin? Recognizing these patterns can highlight areas that could use some improvement. Next, set specific and achievable self-care goals. These could involve dedicating ten minutes each morning to meditation or committing to a weekly exercise class. Again, much like the goal-setting we've previously talked about, make sure these goals are realistic to avoid adding pressure to your already demanding schedule. Breaking down self-care into manageable steps creates a structure that supports gradual change and long-term adherence.

Flexibility and adaptability are key components of an effective self-care plan, just as they are with so many other things we've talked about. As a first responder, your days can be unpredictable, with demands shifting rapidly. Developing contingency plans for busy or unforeseen circumstances ensures self-care remains a priority. This might mean having a list of quick relaxation techniques ready for a hectic day or keeping a stress ball in your pocket for immediate relief.

Incorporating small, manageable activities into your routine —a five-minute breathing exercise or a short walk around the block, for instance—allows you to maintain self-care even when time is tight. These brief activities can provide a refreshing mental reset, which helps you stay grounded amidst the chaos. Walking a set of stairs at work during breaks is a great way to get away, do breathing exercises, work on your mindset, and stimulate the release of endorphins that can improve your mood and well-being, reduce your stress and anxiety, and boost your energy levels.

Regular evaluation and modification of your self-care plan are extremely important for its long-term success. Life doesn't stand still, and your needs will change along with it— a truth that will require adjustments to your routine. Keeping a self-care journal to track progress and challenges can provide valuable information. Documenting your experiences allows you to see what works and what doesn't, which makes it a lot easier to refine your strategy. Schedule periodic reviews to assess your plan's relevance and effectiveness. Are there activities you no longer find beneficial? Are there new stressors that need to be addressed? Regular check-ins keep your self-care plan right in line with your current life circumstances, supporting your path toward resilience and well-being. This proactive approach puts you in charge of your well-being and empowers you to make the necessary adjustments.

Self-Care Plan Template

1. **Identify stressors and relaxation preferences.**
   - List common stressors in your day-to-day life.
   - Note activities or environments that help you relax.
2. **Set specific self-care goals.**
   - Choose one short-term and one long-term goal for self-care.
   - Make sure your goals are attainable and tailored to your needs.
3. **Develop contingency plans.**
   - Identify quick self-care practices for busy days.
   - Think about portable activities that can be done anywhere.
4. **Evaluate and modify your plan regularly.**
   - Use a journal to track your progress, noting successes and challenges.
   - Schedule monthly reviews to adjust your self-care plan as needed.

This self-care plan is designed to help first responders proactively manage stress and maintain their well-being in high-pressure environments. Identifying stressors, setting goals, developing contingency plans, and evaluating your progress greatly helps with sustainability and adaptability.

Stressors and How to Deal with Them

Before developing an effective self-care plan, it's also extremely important to identify your potential sources of stress as well as your personal relaxation strategies. There are all sorts of potential common stressors for first responders. First up, the stressors:

Work-Related Stressors

- Exposure to trauma, violence, or critical incidents
- High workloads, long shifts, or unpredictable schedules
- Pressure to make split-second, life-altering decisions
- Lack of control in certain emergency situations
- Workplace conflicts or team dynamics

Personal Stressors

- Family and relationship strain due to work demands
- Financial concerns
- Health issues (e.g., chronic pain, fatigue, sleep disturbances)
- Emotional exhaustion or burnout

There are all sorts of relaxation options to deal with these stressors. Here are a few good ideas involving a mix of environments and activities:

- **Relaxing Environments:** Nature, quiet spaces, your home, a gym, or the beach
- **Physical Activities:** Exercise, stretching, or deep breathing
- **Mental Activities:** Reading, listening to music, or guided meditation
- **Emotional Activities:** Journaling, talking to a friend, or watching a movie

- **Social Activities:** Spending time with loved ones or attending peer support meetings

Self-Care Goals Template

Setting intentional self-care goals helps guarantee your commitment and accountability. It's important to lay out both your short- and long-term goals in order to have a clear handle on both.

- **Short-Term Goal (1-3 Months):** "I will engage in physical activity at least three times a week for stress relief."
- **Long-Term Goal (6+ Months):** "I will establish a healthier sleep routine by going to bed before midnight on work nights."

SMART Goals Approach

Remember the SMART framework we talked about in Chapter 9? That comes back into play here. Laying out a SMART approach for deep breathing and exercise might look like this:

- **Specific:** Define clear objectives ("I will practice deep breathing for five minutes daily").
- **Measurable:** Track your progress over time ("I will exercise three days per week").
- **Attainable:** Make sure your goals are realistic given your schedule and demands ("I will not stress if I can't practice deep breathing for more than five

minutes per day, or if I miss a day of exercise on occasion").

- **Relevant:** Match your goals to your overall well-being ("Exercise and deep breathing will both help me feel better").
- **Time-bound:** Set a time frame for achievement ("I will pursue these goals for no less than three months").

Because first responders face unpredictable schedules, it's also important to have backup self-care strategies for busy or high-stress days. These contingency plans aren't something you'll need to make use of all the time, but when you need them, you'll be glad to have them in your back pocket. What route you go with these plans is up to you, but you can potentially rely on some strategies we've already discussed.

Quick Self-Care Practices for Busy Days

It's likewise important to establish some potential self-care practices for when you need them—or simply for when you have a bit of free time. These can be broken down into two categories: five-minute strategies and fifteen-minute strategies:

Five-Minute Strategies

- **Deep Breathing Exercises:** These include box breathing and tactical breathing (Chapter 2).
- **Mindfulness Check-ins:** These include things like body scan meditations and grounding techniques such as the 5-4-3-2-1 method (Chapter 1).

- **Hydration and Healthy Snacks:** Hydration is self-explanatory (drink water!), but we'll get more to healthy snacks in a moment.
- **Stretching or Brief Physical Movement:** A quick walk around the block or a few jumping jacks can work wonders. Don't strain yourself, but at least get your body in gear.

Fifteen-Minute Strategies

- **Audio Relaxation:** This includes things like listening to calming music or a motivational podcast.
- **More Involved Physical Movement:** This can include things like taking a brisk walk or stepping outside for fresh air. Basically, it's the same as the brief physical movement strategy under five-minute strategies but slightly longer.
- **Short Power Nap:** This doesn't work for everyone, but a lot of people swear by brief power naps. This might be helpful if you're the sort of person who can fall asleep quickly and easily.

Meanwhile, it's also a good idea to know which activities are good to practice where. If you're at the station or in a vehicle, guided meditation apps, breathing exercises, or listening to an audiobook or motivational speech are all good options. If you're at home, you can take a hot shower or bath to decompress, schedule a family game night or movie time, or unplug from social media for a mental detox.

Incorporating structured self-care habits enables first responders to build resilience, prevent burnout, and sustain their long-term mental and physical well-being. This framework ultimately enables you to create a self-care plan that fits your lifestyle and evolves with you, allowing you to remain resilient and ready for whatever the day might bring.

Monthly Review Checklist

You'll also want to check in each month and ask yourself some important questions in order to track your progress. Having these questions ready to go—not to mention using them consistently over time—can make a huge difference in your efforts to better yourself. Here are some good examples:

- "Did I achieve my short-term goal? Why or why not?"
- "Are my self-care activities effective?"
- "What challenges did I face in implementing my plan?"
- "What adjustments can I make to improve my well-being?"

Final Commitment Statement

Use the following as a template to make a pledge to yourself that you'll not just establish a self-care plan but stick with it. Really give yourself a chance to let the process work.

"I, [Your Name], commit to prioritizing my well-being by implementing this self-care plan. I will regularly assess my progress and make adjustments as needed to maintain resilience in my role as a first responder."

Signature: _____

Date: _____

NUTRITION: THE FIRST PILLAR OF WELLBEING

As we've stressed over and over, first responders have a difficult job. But while that's pretty common knowledge, what you might not realize is the importance of nutrition to everything we've been talking about. In brief, nutrition is a pillar that upholds your physical and mental resilience. Understanding the direct impact of what you consume on your energy levels and mood empowers you to make informed choices. A balanced diet rich in nutrients can provide sustained energy, stabilize your mood, and sharpen your focus (Cena and Calder 2020). Foods high in omega-3 fatty acids, proteins, and vitamins (we'll cover each of these in a moment) have been shown to support brain health, which improves your ability to manage stress and maintain your emotional balance (Gómez-Pinilla 2008). The goal here is not simply to avoid the crash but to fuel your body with what it needs to function optimally. This is especially important when the stakes are high.

Supporting your overall health through nutrition means making an intentional effort to consume nutrient-dense foods that provide the things you need: omega-3 fatty acids, proteins, and vitamins. Let's start with omega-3s, which are extremely important for brain function, heart health, and reducing inflammation (Hjalmarsdottir 2025). Here are a few good sources of omega-3s:

- **Fatty Fish:** Salmon, mackerel, sardines, tuna (especially albacore), herring, trout
- **Plant-Based Sources:** Flaxseeds, chia seeds, walnuts, hemp seeds, seaweed, and algae (e.g., nori, spirulina)
- **Oils:** Flaxseed oil, chia seed oil, walnut oil

Protein, meanwhile, is extremely important for muscle repair, immune function, and energy levels (Gunnars 2025). Most people think of protein as being the province of meat, and while there are certainly plenty in that category, there are a whole host of good options for vegetarians, too:

- **Animal-Based Proteins:** Chicken breast, turkey, lean beef, eggs, Greek yogurt, cottage cheese, fish (again)
- **Plant-Based Proteins:** Lentils, chickpeas, black beans, quinoa, tofu, tempeh, edamame, almonds, peanuts
- **High-Protein Dairy Products:** Milk, cheese, whey protein

Vitamins, meanwhile, accomplish a wide variety of beneficial effects. They support your immune health, skin, vision, and energy production, to name just a few (Srakokic 2023). Here's a list of various vitamins and how they help you:

- **Vitamin A—Vision and Immune Response:** Carrots, sweet potatoes, spinach, kale, liver

- **Vitamin B Complex—Energy and Brain Function:** Whole grains (brown rice, oats), eggs, lean meats, legumes, nuts and seeds
- **Vitamin C—Immune Response and Skin Health:** Oranges, strawberries, bell peppers, kiwi, broccoli
- **Vitamin D—Bone Health and Immune Response:** Fatty fish (salmon, mackerel), fortified dairy products, egg yolks, mushrooms
- **Vitamin E—Skin Health and Heart Health:** Almonds, sunflower seeds, avocados, spinach
- **Vitamin K—Blood Clotting and Bone Health:** Kale, spinach, Brussels sprouts, broccoli

You might have noticed there are a few foods that appear on multiple lists. These are known as superfoods—specifically because they cover multiple of these categories (Hill 2023). Here are a few good examples of superfoods:

- **Salmon:** Omega-3s, Protein, Vitamin D
- **Eggs:** Protein, B Vitamins, Vitamin D
- **Chia Seeds:** Omega-3s, Protein, Fiber, Antioxidants
- **Spinach and Kale:** Vitamins A, C, K, Iron, Plant Protein
- **Quinoa:** Protein, Fiber, B Vitamins

Taken together, all of these foods show the importance of good nutrition. But how can you keep track of all this on a day-to-day basis? Luckily, you have a few options at your disposal. Preparing meal plans that include quick and healthy options is a good one, while batch cooking on your days off can make sure nutritious meals are always within reach. If you're not a fan of cooking, just look for simple recipes that incorporate lean proteins, whole grains, and a variety of colorful vegetables. These meals can be stored and reheated, which offers you convenience without compromising your health. Choose snacks like nuts, fruit, or yogurt over processed items when you're on the go; these choices provide the energy needed to stay alert and focused without the pitfalls of sugar crashes.

On the whole, getting your diet right is one of the best things you can do to help both your physical and mental well-being. Nutrition isn't the only way to help, however—there's also sleep.

SLEEP: THE SECOND PILLAR OF WELLBEING

Sleep is an absolutely fundamental part of securing your well-being. Much like how you'll eventually starve to death, if you don't sleep at all, you will eventually die. While you're unlikely to run into that exact circumstance, lack of quality sleep is common—and it can be devastating.

We've talked at length about how cognitive function and emotional regulation are extremely important for first responders. Sleep deprivation can impair these faculties, leading to slower reaction times and heightened irritability. Quality sleep, on the other hand, improves your memory retention, decision-making, and mood stability. It also allows your body to repair and your mind to reset, equipping you to face the challenges of each new day. The link between restorative sleep and mental health is well-established, with research indicating that adequate rest can mitigate symptoms of depression and anxiety—common issues in high-stress professions such as first response (Watson and Cherney 2024).

Much like nutrition, getting quality sleep amidst unpredictable schedules can be harrowing. Establishing good sleep hygiene is a huge part of it. Knowing how to create a conducive sleep environment and manage sleep disturbances can provide a sense of relief. Keeping your room cool, dark, and quiet are all good ways to create this sort of environment. You can also invest in blackout curtains or a white noise machine if necessary. Limit your screen time before bed, as the blue light emitted by devices can disrupt your natural sleep cycle (Hersh 2024).

For those working irregular shifts, managing sleep disturbances can be particularly challenging. It's a good idea to maintain a consistent sleep schedule even on your days off, as this helps regulate your internal clock. Taking short naps can also be effective if you really need daytime sleep, but aim to nap for no more than half an hour to avoid grogginess.

The benefits of consistent sleep habits extend far beyond daily energy and focus. Over time, it greatly improves your stress management and resilience, which, as we've talked about, are extremely important traits for those in emergency services. When your body is well-rested, you can cope better with your role's physical and mental demands. This improved resilience translates into improved performance and a reduced risk of burnout. Additionally, maintaining these habits supports your long-term health, reducing the risk of chronic illnesses that could impact your ability to serve.

Prioritizing both sleep and nutrition is not simply a matter of immediate gains but an investment in your future well-being. As you continue to dedicate yourself to your demanding role, remember that taking care of your body and mind is a huge part of your commitment to your work. Paying attention to these foundational aspects of health helps you achieve a career marked by service, personal well-being, and longevity. The long-term benefits of these habits should motivate you to continue prioritizing your health.

11

FAMILY DYNAMICS AND IMPACT

W ork can be hectic and chaotic for first responders—it certainly has been for me in the past. This doesn't even necessarily mean on calls themselves; the time my Halligan bar mysteriously went missing right before an important call wasn't exactly a moment filled with serenity. Unfortunately, that chaos is all too often reflected by similar emotional turmoil found at home. When the demands of duty meet the sanctuary of family life, you and your loved ones can often run straight into complex challenges. The unpredictability of your work schedule, with its ever-changing shifts and unexpected calls, can ripple through your household, disrupting all of the carefully laid routines and plans you and your family wanted to accomplish. Your courage and sacrifice in serving others can be a source of pride and appreciation for your family—but if you're not careful, it can also cause all sorts of issues.

HOW FAMILY MEMBERS CAN HELP YOU

There's no getting around it: Being a family member of a first responder means shouldering the emotional weight of their commitment to others. The constant worry about the inherent dangers of their job can be overwhelming; the knowledge that every call they respond to carries risks can lead to chronic stress. Some family members may even experience secondary trauma, a psychological strain that arises from their empathy and concern for the first responder's safety (White-Gibson 2022). This emotional burden can result in feelings of isolation as the irregular hours and long shifts leave family members feeling disconnected from each other.

Open communication is extremely important for working through these challenges. Regular family meetings can provide a platform for discussing concerns and sharing feelings, which allows everyone to express themselves freely. Active listening during these meetings, meanwhile, makes sure everyone feels heard and validated. Prioritizing this open dialogue creates a supportive environment where everyone can address their worries and work together to find solutions. This communication is ultimately nothing less than the glue that holds the family together, even when external pressures threaten to pull it apart. Never underestimate the importance of this type of communication in helping your family to feel heard, understood, and valued.

Establishing routines and rituals that nurture a sense of stability is a huge part of strengthening family resilience. Family meals, even if shared only a few times a week, are a regular opportunity for connection and grounding. Less frequent joint activities like a weekend hike or a game night are equally important, as they promote bonding and strengthen the familial ties that support you through the challenges of your work. These shared experiences work together to build a reservoir of positive memories and reinforce a sense of belonging, which counteracts the isolating effects of your demanding schedule.

Family Resilience Journal

Start a family resilience journal and use it to document shared experiences such as family vacations, celebrations, or even challenging times you've overcome together. Record the outcomes of family meetings and jot down joyous moments that brought the family together. Look back on the ways these interactions have supported and strengthened your family. Encourage family members to contribute their thoughts to further deepen these connections. The goal here is ultimately to remind you of your family's strength and unity.

INVOLVING LOVED ONES IN YOUR HEALING PROCESS

Involving your family in your healing process can greatly improve your resilience and recovery. When loved ones gain a greater understanding of your mental health struggles, it creates a foundation of empathy and support that is absolutely necessary for healing. This shared understanding allows for a collaborative approach where family members become active participants along your path toward well-being. They're not just observers, nor do you want them to be. Instead, it's important that your family acts as partners who can provide emotional support and practical assistance, reinforcing the bond that holds you together.

I mentioned much earlier that there's often a culture of silence around first response. You might think that sharing your experiences will hurt them or that they won't understand. This isn't the case at all, and it's important you shake off that misconception. Not only are they not going to dismiss your experiences, but their ability to offer meaningful support will only increase as they learn more about what you face daily. This can be incredibly beneficial for your healing, as this collaboration nurtures an environment where recovery is not a solitary endeavor but a shared mission.

Educating your family about the challenges you encounter as a first responder is a big step in this process, as it's important to empower them with the knowledge they need to support you effectively. Educational workshops and seminars can be invaluable resources that provide a look into your profession's unique stressors and psychological impacts. These sessions offer a structured way for family members to learn about the ins and outs of your role, in turn equipping them with the knowledge they need to provide you with support. Sharing articles or books on related topics can also help, as these offer a glimpse into the world you walk through daily. Encouraging your family to engage with these resources empowers them to become informed allies in your healing story.

Supportive family activities can also work wonders. The focus of these is ultimately on strengthening the bond that holds your family together. Family therapy sessions are a good example; they offer a safe space for open dialogue where everyone can express their thoughts and feelings in a guided setting. These sessions are capable of addressing individual concerns and strengthening the family unit as a whole. Joint participation in resilience-building exercises such as yoga or mindfulness practices can further reinforce this connection. As we've already talked about, these activities promote physical and emotional well-being, but in a group setting, they also create opportunities for shared growth. Making an intentional effort can allow your family to become a cohesive support system united by the common goal of nurturing a healing atmosphere.

Establishing clear boundaries and expectations is likewise important. Setting rules is less important here than instilling a culture of open and respectful communication. Communicating your needs and limits helps prevent misunderstandings and sets the stage for healthy interactions. You might worry about pushing them away, but it's important to express when you need space to process your thoughts or when you require additional support. Ultimately, what matters is how you communicate this—ideally, you want to be as calm and collected as possible. Developing a family support plan can facilitate this communication by outlining roles and responsibilities for each member ahead of time, guiding your family through the challenges you face together. Setting these boundaries and expectations creates an environment where everyone feels respected and understood, which can do a lot to encourage a sense of security and stability.

MAKING A FAMILY SUPPORT PLAN

First-responder families face unique challenges, including unpredictable work schedules, high-stress environments, and emotional tolls. A family support plan can help make sure everyone understands their roles and responsibilities as well as the support systems available to deal with these challenges together. Before creating a structured plan, it's important to assess the specific challenges your family encounters. Here are a few possibilities:

- **Unpredictable Work Schedules:** Late shifts, overtime, or emergency call-ins can disrupt family time.
- **Emotional and Mental Health Strain:** Exposure to traumatic events can lead to stress, anxiety, or PTSD.
- **Limited Quality Time:** Rotating shifts and long hours make it hard to connect with loved ones.
- **Parental Responsibilities:** Balancing child-rearing can be difficult when one parent is frequently away.
- **Communication Barriers:** Struggles in discussing work-related stress while protecting the family from emotional burdens can cause miscommunications.

There are a couple of ways you can potentially deal with this issue. One good idea is to hold a family discussion to identify specific challenges unique to your household. Another—possibly in conjunction with this—is to have everyone write down the top three stressors they feel affect family life. It's important to discuss the results if you want to help resolve the situation.

As we've previously talked about, establishing personal boundaries can help reduce misunderstandings and stress while maintaining a respectful and supportive home environment. Here are a few good ideas for boundaries to set:

- **Work-Life Balance:** You should set boundaries on how much work-related stress is shared at home. ("I will limit the amount of my work stress I allow to enter the house.")
- **Respecting Decompression Time:** Allow time to unwind after a shift before jumping into family activities. ("After a long shift, I need thirty minutes alone to decompress before engaging in conversations.")
- **Scheduled Family Time:** Prioritize quality moments despite a busy schedule. ("We will schedule a family night once a week, regardless of shift changes.")
- **Emotional Boundaries:** Family members should express when they need space to process emotions. ("I can't talk about this right now; I need some time to work through how I feel first.")

Clear and consistent communication is the backbone of any support plan. It's a good idea to always keep the avenues open for discussions about individual needs. Equally important is to create mutual agreements on personal space, work-life balance, and support. Here are a few ways to manage this:

- **Check-In Conversations:** It's a good idea to regularly ask, "How are you feeling today?"
- **Shared Calendar Apps:** These help everyone stay informed about work schedules and family plans.
- **Journaling or Message Notes:** If verbal conversations are tough, leave written notes for encouragement.
- **Code Words for Support:** Establish a phrase or word that signals when someone needs extra emotional support (e.g., "I need a reset").

First-responder families often also need additional support to manage stress, trauma, and emotional exhaustion. There's nothing wrong with seeking help when needed. Here are a few good ways you can seek out help:

- **Professional Counseling:** Individual or family therapy sessions for mental well-being
- **First Responder Peer Groups:** Support groups for sharing experiences with others who understand
- **Spousal Support Networks:** Partner groups that offer guidance on coping strategies
- **Stress-Relief Activities:** Meditation, family walks, or designated "tech-free" evenings

Lastly, a family support plan needs to be flexible. It should be able to shift in tune with changing work schedules, emotional needs, and life events. You always want to ask questions like, "What's one thing we did well as a family this month? What can we improve?" There are a few good ways to make sure your plan stays on track:

- **Quarterly Family Check-Ins:** Reassess and update roles and boundaries during a scheduled check-in.
- **Reflection Journals:** Encourage family members to track their emotional well-being.
- **Adjusting as Needed:** Modify rules as children grow, careers shift, or needs change.

Developing a family support plan helps first-responder families create a structured, balanced, and emotionally supportive environment. Setting boundaries, improving communication, and planning for emergencies enable families to work through the challenges of this demanding profession as a single unit.

Final Commitment Statement

Use the following as a template to make a pledge to yourself that you'll involve your family in your healing journey. The language can certainly be changed based on your unique circumstances, and it's important everyone involved has input on the process.

> "As a first-responder family, we commit to nurturing open communication, respecting personal boundaries, and supporting each other through the challenges of our unique lifestyle. We will work together to maintain emotional well-being, balance responsibilities, and strengthen our bond."

Signatures: _____

Date: _____

MAINTAINING STRONG FAMILY CONNECTIONS

Amid the chaos from sirens and shifts, prioritizing family relationships often serves as the glue that keeps everything together. For many first responders, strong family bonds are a huge part of overall well-being and provide refuge from the demands of the profession. It's likewise important to note that investing in family time can also improve your work performance by reducing your stress and increasing your motivation. Despite the whirlwind of your schedule, carving out regular family time is non-negotiable. It might seem challenging, but scheduling a few hours each week for dedicated family interactions can work wonders. These moments of connection are a huge part of nurturing relationships and guaranteeing that your family remains a priority despite the demands of your job.

Luckily, there are all sorts of ways to nurture these connections further. Family game nights or outings can nurture togetherness and offer a break from the routine. Don't underestimate the value of a chance to create lasting memories. These activities don't have to be elaborate; a board game or a walk in the park can suffice. The key is to be present with each other without the distraction of work. Regular check-ins with your family are equally important. There's no hard and fast rule on what these need to look like; they can be casual conversations over dinner or more structured discussions where everyone shares their thoughts. Ultimately, it's whatever works for you. The important thing is to establish an ongoing dialogue to help maintain an emotional connection with each other. Keep in mind that it's the simple things that often make the biggest difference.

Technology can also play a pivotal role in bridging the gaps created by long shifts and unpredictable schedules. Video calls and messaging apps can keep you connected with loved ones in real time, no matter where you are. You might think you don't have the time to spare to enable these things to matter, but you're wrong. A two-minute video call during a break or a heartfelt text message can make all the difference in reminding your family that you're thinking of them. Sharing digital calendars can also be great for helping coordinate family events and activities. Syncing schedules makes sure that important dates and times are not missed, facilitating better planning and participation in your family life.

Creating family traditions and memories is another powerful way to build lasting bonds. Annual family vacations—or even just staycations—offer a much-needed escape from the daily grind and provide opportunities to relax and reconnect. These traditions can become cherished memories that your family looks forward to each year. Documenting family stories and histories together, meanwhile, encourages a sense of belonging and continuity. Whether through photo albums, journals, or digital scrapbooks, capturing these moments preserves your family's legacy and creates a web of shared experiences.

SUPPORTING CHILDREN IN FIRST-RESPONDER FAMILIES

The unique challenges children face in first-responder families can often be overlooked—but they're too significant to ignore without consequence. Needless to say, your role as a parent is incredibly important in your child's life. The absence of a parent during holidays and significant events—often very busy times of the year for first responders—can create understandable feelings of disappointment and confusion. The unpredictability of your schedule means that your child might not always understand why you miss their soccer game or a family gathering. Over time, these absences can lead to feelings of neglect, sadness, and resentment as your child grapples with the void left by your commitments.

Understanding the risks and responsibilities associated with your role is another layer of complexity for your children. Your kids might overhear snippets about the dangers you face or see news reports that paint a stark picture of your work. Without the proper context, this awareness can fuel anxiety as they worry about your safety each time you leave the house. It's thus extremely important to explain your role in an age-appropriate and reassuring way. Storybooks and resources designed for children can help demystify emergency services, presenting your work as meaningful and important while still addressing their fears. Open discussions about your job can further alleviate their concerns. It's all in how you communicate; speaking candidly yet gently helps your children understand that while your job can be dangerous, you are trained and equipped to handle it.

Supporting your children's emotional well-being requires sensitivity and attentiveness. One effective method is encouraging your child to express their feelings through art or play. These creative outlets allow them to convey emotions they might struggle to articulate with words. Setting aside one-on-one time with them is equally important. These moments allow your child to share individual concerns and feel heard. Moreover, making time for just the two of you does a lot to tacitly reinforce their importance in your life. Dedicating uninterrupted attention to them strengthens your emotional bond and provides reassurance that they're a priority.

Involving your children in family resilience efforts can further strengthen your family unit. Engage in problem-solving sessions where everyone contributes ideas to encourage a sense of belonging and teamwork. Many of the methods we've talked about for dealing with stress can be valuable for them, too. Teaching children coping strategies such as deep breathing or positive visualization ultimately empowers them to manage their emotions effectively. These techniques equip them with the tools to deal with the uncertainties of being part of a first responder family. This both prepares them to handle challenges and instills a sense of agency and confidence that will serve them well throughout their lives.

CONFLICT RESOLUTION IN HIGH-STRESS MARRIAGES

For first responders, marriage often involves unique stressors. Unpredictable schedules can wreak havoc on your personal plans, straining the relationship in myriad ways. You might plan a weekend getaway only to have it upended by an unexpected shift. This constant flux can lead to resentment and frustration, creating a rift between you and a partner who yearns for stability. Emotional withdrawal after challenging shifts is another common source of conflict.

After a taxing day, you might find yourself retreating into silence, needing space to process the day's events. Sometimes, this is a necessary part of the healing process— but if you leave your partner in the dark, they're likely to feel shut out or unimportant. If you don't communicate, you're likely to spark feelings of neglect or misunderstanding. These scenarios are not uncommon, but they require intentional strategies to deal with effectively.

Luckily, there are some structured approaches that can be effective in addressing these conflicts. These include the "win-win" negotiation model, which prioritizes solutions that meet both partners' needs and encourages a sense of partnership rather than opposition. It encourages you to view challenges as shared problems to be solved together, which can instill a sense of hope and empowerment (Shonk 2025). Mediation techniques for couples also provide a framework for resolving disputes. These techniques might involve a neutral party or feature guided exercises. While they can be varied, what they share in common is that they aim to promote healthy dialogue. The goal is to create a safe space for both partners to express their perspectives without fear of judgment.

Timing and environment are pivotal when it comes to addressing conflicts. Choosing a neutral ground can help both partners feel comfortable and heard. This might mean stepping away from your home environment and finding a quiet café or park instead. Equally important is timing; addressing conflicts during high-stress periods often only exacerbates tensions. Instead, wait for moments of calm when both partners are more receptive and open to discussion. Selecting the right time and place creates an atmosphere conducive to resolution where emotions can be expressed freely and constructively.

Rebuilding trust and intimacy after conflicts is extremely important for maintaining a strong marital bond. A good way to strengthen this bond is to engage in activities that build trust, like setting aside dedicated time for each other or engaging in shared hobbies. These activities remind you both of the joy and companionship that brought you together in the first place. Intimacy-improving communication practices, like sharing daily highs and lows or making a commitment to expressing gratitude, further strengthen the relationship. These practices nurture a deeper understanding and appreciation for each other, which can help to mend wounds created by conflict. Dedicating time and effort to these exercises nurtures the relationship, keeping it resilient and supportive even amidst the challenges of your first responder life.

WORKING THROUGH RELATIONSHIP CHALLENGES WITH PARTNERS

Maintaining a relationship often comes with unique challenges for first responders. Communication breakdowns are common, which isn't surprising; the fatigue and stress from demanding jobs can make it difficult to connect meaningfully at the end of a long day. The exhaustion that follows a shift can leave you or your partner (or both) feeling drained, leading to misunderstandings. Balancing the demands of your shift work with your relationship needs can become a delicate dance. Dealing with this requires intention and effort to make sure both of you feel valued and heard.

Prioritizing quality time together is a huge part of nurturing and sustaining a healthy partnership. Date nights might seem like a simple and even clichéd solution, but they can really help with keeping your connection alive. A quiet dinner at home or a stroll in the park can allow you to focus on each other away from the pressures of work. But while date nights are important, regular communication truly makes you feel heard and understood. Making it a point to address concerns and express your appreciation helps maintain a strong emotional bond. Acknowledging even just the small things reinforces the relationship's foundation.

Empathy and patience are indispensable in understanding each other's perspectives. Empathy-building exercises such as role reversals, where each partner expresses their feelings from the other's perspective, can help you see things from their point of view. Managing emotional responses is another important part of working through issues. It's important to develop strategies to remain calm and composed during discussions to prevent escalation and facilitate constructive dialogue.

Mutual support and understanding are a huge part of overcoming relationship challenges. Attending couples' workshops or therapy sessions can offer shared growth opportunities, providing the tools to strengthen your partnership in the process. Practicing gratitude and regularly recognizing each other's efforts also play a significant role. These practices create a nurturing environment where each of you feels appreciated and valued.

Setting joint goals and dreams can further solidify your relationship. It can be a great idea to plan future projects or set goals together to encourage a sense of teamwork and shared purpose. These could include home improvement projects, travel plans, or any pursuit that brings you both joy. These shared goals encourage a sense of unity, making you feel more connected in your relationship.

12

LONG-TERM CAREER
SUSTAINABILITY

As the sirens faded, I stepped into the quiet of the station, the adrenaline slowly ebbing away from my body after yet another demanding shift. What replaced it was something a lot more insidious: the feeling that I couldn't handle another shift. In these moments, it's extremely important to recognize the early signs of burnout. When you're away from the immediacy of crisis, the long shadows of fatigue can begin to creep in. Burnout isn't just an abstract concept; it's a tangible weight many first responders carry. Keeping an eye on your personal burnout meter is a big deal for your well-being and for maintaining the quality of service you provide to the community. Chronic fatigue—a relentless exhaustion that no amount of sleep seems to shake —can often serve as the first red flag. You might find your-self growing detached, a protective cynicism creeping in as a barrier against the emotional toll your work takes on you. Your performance at work might wane next, leading to decreased satisfaction and a sense of futility. But how do you get ahead of these issues?

PREVENTING BURNOUT WITH A SUPPORTIVE WORK ENVIRONMENT

The root causes of burnout are as varied as they are insidious, but one of the more common ones is an excessive workload that stretches your resources thin. This can be exacerbated by a lack of control over your job roles, as rigid structures leave little room for autonomy. Emotional exhaustion might become a constant companion, fueled by the relentless pressure of life-and-death situations.

Understanding these factors is a huge part of creating strategies to combat burnout. Regular breaks and rest periods are incredibly important, even if they're often difficult to prioritize. You need to make time for them whenever possible, as these moments of respite allow you to recharge and return with renewed vigor. Stress-relief activities, whether that means a hobby like painting or simple physical exercise, can help release pent-up tension. When the burden becomes too heavy, it's time to seek professional support. Seeking this help provides a space to process these experiences and develop coping mechanisms, and it's a big step in preventing and recovering from burnout.

A supportive workplace culture, meanwhile, can often be the deciding factor in how burnout develops. Environments that encourage appreciation and recognition validate your efforts, which does a lot to reinforce your sense of purpose. Encouraging open communication about workload and stress allows for adjustments that alleviate the pressure you might feel. Work cultures like these see burnout not as a personal failing but as an occupational hazard that can be managed and mitigated.

Recovery from burnout—once it has already hit—requires deliberate steps. Establishing firm boundaries to protect your personal time is a huge part of reducing work-related stress. As we've talked about, it's important to prioritize self-care by attending to your physical, mental, and emotional needs. You might feel like you're somehow betraying your community or your fellow first responders by taking time to rest and recover, but you're not. No one can continue down a path toward burnout indefinitely. Taking the rest you need serves your community by making sure you're able to help them over the long term.

Awareness of Burnout

Take a moment at the end of your week to assess your current state. Identify signs of burnout, such as fatigue or detachment. Now, think about which activities have provided you with relief or joy. How can you incorporate more of these into your routine in order to help maintain a healthier work-life balance? Recognize the importance of seeking support through peer discussions or professional counseling to deal with these challenges effectively. Embracing these practices helps you to continue serving with dedication while preserving your health and well-being.

FINANCIAL PLANNING FOR LONG-TERM STABILITY

The world of first responders is notoriously fast-paced, and every second counts. Under these circumstances, it's easy to let long-term financial planning fall by the wayside. What's important to remember, though, is that financial security is a pillar of career sustainability that can offer peace of mind and satisfaction in your professional life. The financial demands of your role, coupled with your personal responsibilities, can create a perfect storm of stress if you don't manage them proactively. Reducing your financial stress through careful planning enables you to focus more on what truly matters: your work and your personal life.

An emergency fund is your safety net, providing a sense of security and preparedness. It cushions against unforeseen expenses like sudden car repairs or unexpected medical bills. Having something in reserve helps guarantee that these surprises don't derail your financial stability. Planning for future goals—buying a home, funding a child's education, enjoying a comfortable retirement, etc.— requires foresight and discipline.

Effective financial management is ultimately about making your money work for you. Creating a realistic budget is the first step. This budget should reflect your income, fixed expenses, and discretionary spending, giving you a clear overall picture of where your money goes each month. You can then redirect funds toward savings and investments by identifying areas where you can cut back. Speaking of investments, exploring options for long-term growth can significantly improve your financial stability. Think about diversifying your portfolio with a mix of stocks, bonds, and real estate to balance risk and reward. The stock market can seem overwhelming, the exclusive province of rich people, but that doesn't have to be the case. Investing can help build your wealth over time in order to provide a more secure financial future.

Retirement may seem distant, especially in the early years of your career, but preparing for it is extremely important. Regular contributions to retirement savings accounts such as a 401(k) or IRA can allow your money to grow through compound interest (Friedberg 2025). Understanding your pension plan and benefits is equally important, as they form a significant part of your retirement income. Early and consistent planning empowers you to retire with dignity, free from financial constraints. Consulting with a financial advisor can also provide personalized guidance tailored to your unique needs as a first responder, making you feel supported and guided in your financial decisions. It's a good idea to seek out advisors experienced in public service careers, as they're more likely to understand your specific challenges and can help you work through complex financial decisions.

Professional financial advice is invaluable when you're planning for the future. Attending financial planning workshops or seminars can improve your knowledge base and equip you with the tools you need to manage your finances more effectively. These resources offer information about saving strategies, investment opportunities, and retirement planning. They can do a lot to empower you to take control of your financial destiny and feel confident about your future.

PLANNING FOR CAREER TRANSITIONS AND RETIREMENT

The rhythm of a first responder's career is often punctuated by transitions, with each bringing its own set of challenges and opportunities. Moving from fieldwork to an administrative role, for instance, can feel like stepping into a new world with its own language and customs. The direct adrenaline rush of responding to emergencies changes into the strategic demands of managing teams and resources. Similarly, transitioning into specialized units or departments might require the acquisition of entirely new skills, a process that demands adaptability and a willingness to embrace change.

These transitions can certainly be enriching, but they also require thoughtful preparation. Identifying transferable skills is a big part of this. The leadership skills developed in managing a team during an emergency can be applied to project management in a corporate setting. The critical thinking skills used to assess a crisis situation, meanwhile, can be useful for problem-solving in any professional setting, while the communication abilities honed on the job can be assets in any role that requires clear and effective communication. Networking is invaluable here, as it offers a way to explore diverse career paths and connect with mentors who can provide guidance.

As retirement looms on the horizon, preparation becomes an extremely important part of the process. The transition from a fast-paced career to the slower rhythms of retirement is both a practical and emotional shift. Gradually reducing your work hours can ease this change and help you adjust to a new pace. Engaging in hobbies or volunteer work can fill the void left by work, providing you with fulfillment and purpose. Continuous learning plays an important role in career transitions, as education keeps your mind sharp and skills relevant. Setting clear retirement goals is a big part of steering this new chapter of life. Defining personal and financial aspirations can create a roadmap that guides you toward a fulfilling retirement and instills a sense of focus and determination.

The emotional aspect of retirement is as significant as the practical one. Shifting from a structured work environment to the freedom of retirement can be disorienting at first. Exploring hobbies can do a lot to provide structure in this changing environment (not to mention joy). Volunteering, meanwhile, offers a chance to give back and stay engaged. When approached with intention and flexibility, this transition can become a rewarding phase full of new experiences and opportunities for growth. The path of a first responder is marked by constant evolution, adapting to new roles, and embracing the future with resilience and an open heart. Whether you're climbing the career ladder or walking into retirement, each step holds the promise of new beginnings and the continuation of a life dedicated to service.

CELEBRATING ACHIEVEMENTS AND REFLECTING ON YOUR GROWTH

In the midst of the chaos that defines the life of a first responder, it's important to take the time to recognize and celebrate your achievements. These moments of acknowledgment can breathe life into your career, offering a much-needed boost to both your morale and motivation. Keeping a journal of milestones and successes can likewise be a tangible reminder of your accomplishments. Whether you saved a life, learned a new skill, or simply made it through another demanding shift, each achievement deserves recognition. Celebrating with family, friends, and colleagues solidifies these moments and strengthens the bonds that support you through your most challenging times.

Reflection, meanwhile, can be a powerful tool for personal and professional growth. Regular self-assessments help identify your strengths and highlight areas where improvement can be made. Set aside time to thoughtfully look back on your past experiences. Consider what went well and what you could have done differently. This introspection can do a lot to provide clarity and direction, guiding your future actions and decisions. Practice gratitude by writing thank-you notes to mentors and colleagues acknowledging their support, as this does a lot to encourage a culture of appreciation. Take a moment each day to think about what you're grateful for, whether that's a career opportunity or a small moment of growth. This shifts your focus from challenges to possibilities.

As you celebrate your past achievements, think about how they can inform your future goals. Your successes should be a foundation for setting new objectives that inspire you to reach even greater heights. You can also create a vision board to encourage your continued growth, as a visual representation of your goals can help fuel your motivation and commitment. You want to be sure to set objectives that align with your core beliefs to keep your career fulfilling. This is extremely important for dealing with the complications inherent to your role, maintaining enthusiasm, and cultivating a sustainable career.

Recognizing and celebrating your achievements is both a personal affair and a collective one. Sharing these moments within your community encourages a sense of camaraderie and shared purpose, reminding you that you're part of a more extensive network of professionals dedicated to service and excellence. These celebrations reinforce the connections that sustain you, offering a pause, a chance to breathe, and a time to acknowledge the path you've traveled. In doing so, you honor your story and pave the way for future triumphs.

MANAGING REPUTATION: BUILDING A LEGACY OF INTEGRITY

In public safety, your reputation is a currency that can either open doors or erect impenetrable barriers. Your reputation is a reflection of your actions and character, and a strong reputation encourages trust and respect from peers and the community, amplifying your credibility and authority. For a seasoned paramedic known for their calm demeanor and expertise during crises, for example, their reputation precedes them. They carry the weight of respect and confidence from those around them when they walk into a situation. This sort of trust isn't built overnight but through consistent, ethical behavior that lines up with the profession's values. Once this trust is earned, it can serve as a solid foundation for your future in public safety, providing reassurance about the long-term benefits of your efforts.

Maintaining your professional integrity requires an unwavering commitment to ethical standards and transparency. Adhering to guidelines and codes of conduct makes sure your actions reflect the principles of your role. Following rules is a byproduct rather than the point; what actually matters is demonstrating accountability in every decision you make and interaction you have. A police officer might face a situation where they have to choose between upholding the law and showing compassion. In scenarios like these, transparency in your actions reassures others of your integrity. In moments of doubt, your steadfast adherence to these principles will strengthen your standing and reinforce the foundation of your reputation.

On and off duty, your personal behavior significantly impacts your professional reputation. The choices you make in your personal life can echo into your career. A single social media post, for example, can have far-reaching implications. Dealing with personal spaces with caution and mindfulness is thus extremely important. Professional interactions should always reflect the values you uphold, whether they occur in the field or online. This consistency in behavior solidifies your reputation and reinforces the trust others place in you. Always be mindful of your actions, as they can shape your reputation as a public safety professional.

Nevertheless, mistakes are inevitable. When they do happen, repairing and rebuilding your reputation is extremely important. The first step is acknowledging your error and taking responsibility. This act of ownership is powerful, as it sets the stage for genuine change. Learning from your mistakes involves implementing positive changes, demonstrating growth, and committing to improvement. You always want to try to turn setbacks into opportunities for personal and professional development if you possibly can. These actions restore trust and reaffirm your dedication to integrity. The power of accountability is in your hands and can be a potent tool in maintaining a strong reputation, empowering you to take control of your professional narrative.

The path to building a legacy of integrity is ongoing—every interaction and decision contributes to the mosaic of your reputation. It's important to hold yourself to the highest standards and know that your actions ripple beyond the immediate moment. In the world of public safety, where lives and trust are on the line, this legacy is your most enduring contribution.

PROFESSIONAL NETWORKS: BUILDING COMMUNITY SUPPORT

For first responders and healthcare workers, building professional networks is a hugely important part of your professional life. Networking opens doors to career advancement and offers a platform for exchanging knowledge about best practices. Building a community of like-minded professionals, a place where you belong and can provide the guidance and support needed to thrive in high-stress careers, can be enormously fulfilling, both emotionally and professionally.

Developing practical networking skills involves active participation in industry conferences and events. These gatherings are fertile grounds for meeting peers and leaders in your field, and they offer opportunities to build relationships that can lead to future collaborations. Online professional groups and forums provide another avenue for connection, allowing you to engage with colleagues globally to stay informed about the latest trends and developments. These activities demonstrate your dedication to service and can introduce you to like-minded individuals who share your passion for making a difference.

Mentorship–a key topic in Chapter 8–is a key component in strengthening professional networks. It's important to seek out mentors both within and outside your organization to discover new perspectives and guidance. There are some things, after all, that only experience can teach. A mentor can help you work through any career difficulties, empowering you to face challenges with greater confidence. Providing mentorship to others can be equally rewarding, as it allows you to give back by sharing your own experiences and knowledge. This reciprocal relationship nurtures a culture of learning and growth, improving the overall strength of your network.

Don't underestimate the importance of diversity in networking, either. Building connections across different roles and industries—as well as with people from different backgrounds—broadens your perspective and enriches your professional life. Collaborating with professionals from various fields encourages innovative thinking and problem-solving while engaging with community leaders and stakeholders offers a good look into broader societal needs and challenges. These diverse connections both further your career and contribute to your personal growth, helping you become a more well-rounded and effective professional. Embracing the power of networking can totally change your career for the better by providing the support and opportunities needed to thrive in even the most challenging environments.

CONCLUSION

We've finally reached the end of our time together. As you think about what you've learned from this book, consider how the tools and knowledge you've gained can be applied to your unique experiences. Remember that resilience doesn't mean being invincible but about having the ability to adapt and grow in the face of adversity. You can strengthen your mental and emotional well-being by incorporating practices like mindfulness, cognitive restructuring, and self-care into your daily routine. Engaging in open and honest conversations about mental health with your colleagues, family, and friends can create a supportive environment that nurtures understanding and encourages others to seek help, too.

The path toward improved mental health and personal fulfillment is an ongoing process, and I want you to know that you are not alone. As a first responder or healthcare worker, your dedication and service to your community are invaluable, and your resilience in the face of challenges is truly inspiring. Remember to prioritize your well-being, as taking care of yourself is key to effectively caring for others. Society cannot function without you, and we appreciate and recognize your efforts.

So, get out there and take action to implement the techniques and practices discussed in this book. Start by setting small, achievable goals such as practicing mindfulness or prayer for ten minutes a day or having a weekly check-in with a trusted colleague about your mental health. Gradually build upon them by seeking opportunities for personal and professional development, and never hesitate to reach out for support when needed. Actively engaging in improving your mental health enables you to cultivate a greater sense of purpose, fulfillment, and resilience in your personal and professional life.

As you step out on this path, know you have the strength and capacity to overcome your challenges. You are part of a community of dedicated professionals who understand your work's unique struggles and triumphs. Embrace the support of your colleagues, family, and friends, and always keep in mind that seeking help is a sign of strength, not weakness. Together, we can break down the stigma surrounding mental health and create a culture of understanding and support within our professions. Your actions and your support for others can make a significant difference in this collective effort.

I encourage you to approach the future with hope and optimism. What you've learned throughout this book will serve as a solid foundation as you deal with the ups and downs of your career and personal life. Embrace the opportunities for growth and self-discovery that lie ahead, and know that you have the resilience and strength to overcome any obstacle. In the end, you are not defined by your struggles but by your ability to rise above them and thrive.

REFERENCES

Ackerman, Courtney E. 2017. "21 Mindfulness Exercises & Activities for Adults." *Positive Psychology*, January 18. https://positivepsychology.com/mindfulness-exercises-techniques-activities/.

Aldao, Amelia. 2014. "Why Labeling Emotions Matters." *Psychology Today*, August 4. Accessed on March 24, 2025. https://www.psychologytoday.com/us/blog/sweet-emotion/201408/why-labeling-emotions-matters.

Baer, Drake. 2020. "Use LeBron James' Simple Visualization Ritual to Get What You Want Out of the New Year." *Business Insider*, January 6. Accessed on March 19, 2025. https://www.businessinsider.com/forget-resolutions-use-lebron-james-visualization-ritual-for-success.

Ballenger, James F., Suzanne R. Best, Thomas J. Metzler, David A. Wasserman, David C. Mohr, Akiva Liberman, Kevin Delucchi, Daniel S. Weiss, Jeffrey A. Fagan, Angela E. Waldrop, and Charles R. Marmar. 2010. "Patterns and Predictors of Alcohol Use in Male and Female Urban Police Officers." *The American Journal on Addictions* 20 (1): 21–29. Accessed on March 24, 2025. https://doi.org/10.1111/j.1521-0391.2010.00092.x.

Carmichael, Cheryl L. and Moran Mizrahi. 2023. "Connecting Cues: The Role of Nonverbal Cues in Perceived Responsiveness." *Current Opinions in Psychology* 53: 101663. Accessed on March 27, 2025. https://doi.org/10.1016/j.copsyc.2023.101663.

Carson, Leslie M., Suzanne M. Marsh, Margaret M. Brown, Katherine L. Elkins, and Hope M. Tiesman. 2023. "An Analysis of Suicides Among First Responders — Findings From the National Violent Death Reporting System, 2015–2017." *Journal of Safety Research* 85: 361-370. https://doi.org/10.1016/j.jsr.2023.04.003.

Cena, Hellas and Philip C. Calder. 2020. "Defining a Healthy Diet: Evidence for the Role of Contemporary Dietary Patterns in Health and Disease." *Nutrients* 12 (2): 334. Accessed on March 30, 2025. https://doi.org/10.3390/nu12020334.

Cherry, Kendra. 2024. "What Is the Fight-or-Flight Response?" *Verywell Mind*, June 17. Accessed on March 24, 2025. https://www.verywellmind.com/what-is-the-fight-or-flight-response-2795194.

Columbia Lighthouse Project. n.d. "Asking About Suicide is Vital for First Responders and the Public They Serve." Accessed on March 24, 2025. https://cssrs.columbia.edu/the-columbia-scale-c-ssrs/first-responders/.

Corporate Wellness Magazine. n.d. "The Importance of Empathy in Leadership and Employee Well-being." Accessed on March 26, 2025. https://www.corporatewellnessmagazine.com/article/the-importance-of-empathy-in-leadership-and-employee-well-being.

de Oliveira, Claire, Makeila Saka, Lauren Bone, and Rowena Jacobs. 2022. "The Role of Mental Health on Workplace Productivity: A Critical Review of the Literature." *Applied Health Economics and Health Policy* 21 (2): 167–193. https://doi.org/10.1007/s40258-022-00761-w

Donohue, Maureen. 2022. "Post-Traumatic Stress Disorder (PTSD)." *Healthline*, February 18. Accessed on March 25, 2025. https://www.healthline.com/health/post-traumatic-stress-disorder%23symptoms.

Donovan, Nicole. 2022. "Peer Support Facilitates Post-Traumatic Growth in First Responders: A Literature Review." *Trauma* 24 (4): 277-285. Accessed on March 27, 2025. https://doi.org/10.1177/14604086221079441.

Ezawa, Iony D. and Steven D. Hollon. 2023. "Cognitive Restructuring and Psychotherapy Outcome: A Meta-Analytic Review." *Psychotherapy (Chic)* 60 (3): 396–406. https://doi.org/10.1037/pst0000474

Fincham, Guy William, Clara Strauss, Jesus Montero-Marin, and Kate Cavanagh. 2023. "Effect of Breathwork on Stress and Mental Health: A Meta-Analysis of Randomised-Controlled Trials." *Scientific Reports* 13: 432. Accessed on March 24, 2025. https://doi.org/10.1038/s41598-022-27247-y.

Friedberg, Barbara A. 2025. "Traditional and Roth IRAs: Benefits and Drawbacks." *Investopedia*, January 5. Accessed on March 31, 2025. https://www.investopedia.com/articles/financial-advisors/120815/iras-advantages-disadvantages-and-which-one-right-you.asp.

Geronazzo-Alman, Lupo, Ruth Eisenberg, Sa Shen, Christina S. Duarte, George J. Musa, Judith Wicks, Bin Fan, Thao Doan, Guia Guffanti, Michaeline Bresnahan, and Christina W. Hoven. 2016. "Cumulative Exposure to Work-related Traumatic Events and Current Post-traumatic Stress Disorder in New York City's First Responders." *Comprehensive Psychiatry* 74: 134–143. Accessed on March 26, 2025. https://doi.org/10.1016/j.comppsych.2016.12.003.

Girolimon, Mars. 2025. "What is Trauma-Informed Care?" *Southern New Hampshire University*, February 28. Accessed on March 26, 2025. https://

www.snhu.edu/about-us/newsroom/health/what-is-trauma-informed-care.

Godos, Justyna, Giuseppe Grosso, Sabrina Castellano, Fabio Galvano, Filippo Caraci, and Raffaele Ferri. 2021. "Association Between Diet and Sleep Quality: A Systematic Review." *Sleep Medicine Reviews* 57: 101430. Accessed on March 24, 2025. https://doi.org/10.1016/j.smrv.2021.101430.

Gómez-Pinilla, Fernando. 2008. "Brain Foods: The Effects of Nutrients on Brain Function." *Nature Reviews Neuroscience* 9 (7): 568–78. Accessed on March 30, 2025. https://doi.org/10.1038/nrn2421.

Gotter, Ana. 2025. "Box Breathing." *Healthline*, February 4. Accessed on March 25, 2025. https://www.healthline.com/health/copd/box-breathing.

Grinspoon, Peter. 2022. "How to Recognize and Tame Your Cognitive Distortions." *Harvard Health Publishing*, May 4. Accessed on March 25, 2025. https://www.health.harvard.edu/blog/how-to-recognize-and-tame-your-cognitive-distortions-202205042738.

Gunnars, Kris. 2025. "10 Science-Backed Reasons to Eat More Protein." *Healthline*, February 18. Accessed on March 30, 2025. https://www.healthline.com/nutrition/10-reasons-to-eat-more-protein.

Gupta, Sanjana. 2024. "Feeling Anxious? Try the 5-4-3-2-1 Grounding Technique." *Verywell Mind*, April 29. Accessed on March 25, 2025. https://www.verywellmind.com/5-4-3-2-1-grounding-technique-8639390.

Henderson, Claire, Sara Evans-Lacko, and Graham Thornicroft. 2013. "Mental Illness Stigma, Help Seeking, and Public Health Programs." *American Journal of Public Health* 103 (5): 777–780. Accessed on April 8, 2025. https://doi.org/10.2105/AJPH.2012.301056

Hersh, Erica. 2024. "12 Healthy Sleep Hygiene Tips." *Healthline*, March 27. Accessed on March 30, 2025. https://www.healthline.com/health/sleep-hygiene.

Hill, Ansley. 2023. "16 Superfoods That Are Worthy of the Title." *Healthline*, October 30. Accessed on March 30, 2025. https://www.healthline.com/nutrition/true-superfoods.

Hjalmarsdottir, Freydis. 2025. "17 Science-Based Benefits of Omega-3 Fatty Acids." *Healthline*, February 19. Accessed on March 30, 2025. https://www.healthline.com/nutrition/17-health-benefits-of-omega-3.

Huang, Garry, Hsin Chu, Ruey Chen, Doresses Liu, Kondwani Joseph Banda, Anthony Paul O'Brien, Hsiu Ju-Jen, Kai-Jo Chang, Jeng-Fong

Chiou, Kuei-Ru Chou. 2022. "Prevalence of Depression, Anxiety, and Stress Among First Responders for Medical Emergencies During COVID-19 Pandemic: A Meta-Analysis." *Journal of Global Health* 12: 05028. Accessed on March 24, 2025. https://doi.org/10.7189/jogh.12. 05028.

Jewell, Tim and Crystal Hoshaw. 2023. "What Is Diaphragmatic Breathing?" *Healthline*, May 19. Accessed on March 25, 2025. https://www.healthline. com/health/diaphragmatic-breathing.

Keng, Shian-Ling, Moria J. Smoski, and Clive J. Robins. 2011. "Effects of Mindfulness on Psychological Health: A Review of Empirical Studies." *Clinical Psychology Review* 31 (6): 1041–56. Accessed on March 25, 2025. https://doi.org/10.1016/j.cpr.2011.04.006.

Koskie, Brandi, and Crystal Raypole. 2023. "Depression Facts and Statistics." *Healthline*, October 31. Accessed on March 24, 2025. https://www.health line.com/health/depression/facts-statistics-infographic.

Lanzoni, Susan. 2021. "How Role-Playing Can Enhance Empathy." *Psychology Today*, April 8. Accessed on April 8, 2025. https://www. psychologytoday.com/us/blog/empathy-emotion-and-experience/ 202104/how-role-playing-can-enhance-empathy

Magee, Rhonda. 2020. "The S.T.O.P. Practice: Creating Space Around Automatic Reactions." *Mindful*, March 23. Accessed on March 25, 2025. https://www.mindful.org/the-s-t-o-p-practice-creating-space-around-automatic-reactions/.

Mahindru, Aditya, Pradeep Patil, and Varun Agrawal. 2023. "Role of Physical Activity on Mental Health and Well-Being: A Review." *Cureus* 15 (1): e33475. Accessed on March 25, 2025. https://doi.org/10.7759/ cureus.33475.

Mariotti, Agnes. 2015. "The Effects of Chronic Stress on Health: New Insights Into the Molecular Mechanisms of Brain–Body Communication." *Future Science OA* 1 (3): FSO23. Accessed on March 24, 2025. https://doi.org/10.4155/fso.15.21.

Moore, Marissa. 2022. "6 Benefits of Managing Your Stress Better." *PsychCentral*, July 25. Accessed on March 28, 2025. https://psychcentral. com/stress/the-benefits-of-stress-management.

Morin, Amy. 2024. "How Cognitive Reframing Works." *Verywell Mind*, December 5. Accessed on March 24, 2025. https://www.verywellmind. com/reframing-defined-2610419.

Obuobi-Donkor, Gloria, Folajinmi Oluwasina, Nnamdi Nkire, and Vincent I.O. Agyapong. 2022. "A Scoping Review on the Prevalence and

Determinants of Post-Traumatic Stress Disorder among Military Personnel and Firefighters: Implications for Public Policy and Practice." *International Journal of Environmental Research and Public Health* 19 (3): 1565. Accessed on March 24, 2025. https://doi.org/10.3390/ijer ph19031565.

Oginska-Bulik, Nina and Zygfryd Juczynski. 2021. "Burnout and Posttraumatic Stress Symptoms in Police Officers Exposed to Traumatic Events: The Mediating Role of Ruminations." *International Archives of Environmental and Occupational Health* 94 (6): 1201–9. Accessed on March 24, 2025. https://doi.org/10.1007/s00420-021-01689-9.

Park, Nansook, Christopher Peterson, Daniel Szvarca, Randy J. Vander Molen, Eric S. Kim, Kevin Collon. 2014. "Positive Psychology and Physical Health." *American Journal of Lifestyle Medicine* 10 (3): 200–6. Accessed on March 25, 2025. https://doi.org/10.1177/ 1559827614550277.

Paychex. 2024. "What Is an Employee Assistance Program (EAP) & What Are the Benefits?" June 14. Accessed on March 27, 2024. https://www. paychex.com/articles/employee-benefits/employees-stressed-an-eap-can-help.

Ponciano, Jonathan. 2025. "How to Set Financial Goals for Your Future." *Investopedia*, April 2. Accessed on March 29, 2025. https://www.investo pedia.com/articles/personal-finance/100516/setting-financial-goals/.

Ramachandran, Sunder, Sreejith Balasubramanian, Wayne Fabian James, and Turki Al Masaeid. 2023. "Whither Compassionate Leadership? A Systematic Review." *Management Review Quarterly* 74 (3): 1473–1557. Accessed on March 29, 2025. https://doi.org/10.1007/s11301-023-00340-w.

Raypole, Crystal. 2022. "How to Do a Body Scan Meditation (and Why You Should)." *Healthline*, December 5. Accessed on March 25, 2025. https:// www.healthline.com/health/body-scan-meditation.

Reynolds, Gretchen. 2021. "Does High-Intensity Exercise Affect Our Hearts? Minds? Life Spans? Waistlines?" *New York Times*, December 20. Accessed on March 25, 2025. https://www.nytimes.com/2021/11/10/ well/move/hiit-high-intensity-interval-training.html.

Roberts, Nicole F. 2023. "Sounding The Alarm: Firefighters Remain More Likely to Die by Suicide than on Duty." *Forbes*, March 19. Accessed on March 24, 2025. https://www.forbes.com/sites/nicoleroberts/2023/03/ 19/sounding-the-alarm-firefighters-remain-more-likely-to-die-by-suicide-than-on-duty/.

Ryals, Athena. 2024. "Burnout, Mental Health and the First Responder Compassion Crisis." *Journal of Emergency Medical Services*, November 13. Accessed on March 24, 2025. https://www.jems.com/mental-health-wellness/burnout-mental-health-and-the-first-responder-compassion-crisis/.

Sareen, Jitender, Brian J. Cox, Murray B. Stein, Tracie O. Afifi, Claire Fleet, and Gordon J. Asmundson. 2007. "Physical and Mental Comorbidity, Disability, and Suicidal Behavior Associated With Posttraumatic Stress Disorder in a Large Community Sample." *Psychosomatic Medicine* 69 (3): 242-48. Accessed on March 24, 2025. https://doi.org/10.1097/PSY.0b013e31803146d8.

Saunders, T., J.E. Driskell, J.H. Johnston, and E. Salas. 1996. "The Effect of Stress Inoculation Training on Anxiety and Performance." *Journal of Occupational Health Psychology* 1 (2): 170-86. Accessed on March 24, 2025. https://doi.org/10.1037//1076-8998.1.2.170.

Schein, Jeffrey, Christy Houle, Annette Urganus, Martin Cloutier, Oscar Patterson-Lomba, Yao Wang, Sarah King, Will Levinson, Annie Guérin, Patrick Lefebvre, and Lori L. Davis. 2021. "Prevalence of Post-Traumatic Stress Disorder in the United States: a Systematic Literature Review." *Current Medical Research and Opinion* 37 (12): 2151-61. Accessed on March 24, 2025. https://doi.org/10.1080/03007995.2021.1978417.

Schrader, Christian and Abigail Ross. 2021. "A Review of PTSD and Current Treatment Strategies." *Missouri Medicine* 118 (6): 546–551. Accessed on March 26, 2025. https://pmc.ncbi.nlm.nih.gov/articles/PMC8672952/.

Sharp, Marie-Louise, Noa Solomon, Virginia Harrison, Rachael Gribble, Heidi Cramm, Graham Pike, and Nicola T. Fear. 2022. "The Mental Health and Wellbeing of Spouses, Partners and Children of Emergency Responders: A Systematic Review." *PLoS One* 17 (6): e0269659. Accessed on March 24, 2025. https://doi.org/10.1371/journal.pone.0269659.

Shonk, Katie. 2025. "What is a Win-Win Negotiation?" *Harvard Law School*, February 26. Accessed on March 30, 2025. https://www.pon.harvard.edu/daily/win-win-daily/what-is-a-win-win-negotiation/.

Silva, Sandra. 2021. "9 Tips to Change Negative Thinking." *PsychCentral*, July 29. Accessed on March 25, 2025. https://psychcentral.com/lib/fixing-cognitive-distortions.

Solan, Matthew. 2023. "Try This: Take a Tactical Breather." *Harvard Health Publishing*, October 1. Accessed on March 25, 2025. https://www.health.harvard.edu/mind-and-mood/try-this-take-a-tactical-breather.

Srakokic, S. 2023. "What Are Vitamins and Can They Help Your Health?"

Healthline, November 29. Accessed on March 30, 2025. https://www.healthline.com/health/nutrition/what-are-vitamins.

Ussher, Michael, Amy Spatz, Claire Copland, Andrew Nicolaou, Abbey Cargill, Nina Amini-Tabrizi, and Lance M. McCracken. 2014. "Immediate Effects of a Brief Mindfulness-Based Body Scan on Patients with Chronic Pain." *Journal of Behavioral Medicine* 37 (1): 127-34. Accessed on March 25, 2025. https://doi.org/10.1007/s10865-012-9466-5.

Vogel, Kaitlin. 2022. "Breathing Rhythms Can Affect Your Emotions: Here's How." *PsychCentral*, March 3. Accessed on March 25, 2025. https://psychcentral.com/lib/change-how-you-feel-change-how-you-breathe.

von Bernhardi, Rommy, Laura Eugenín-von Bernhardi, and Jaime Eugenín. 2017. "What Is Neural Plasticity?" *Advances in Experimental Medicine and Biology* 1015: 1-15. Accessed on March 24, 2025. https://doi.org/10.1007/978-3-319-62817-2_1.

Wang, Wangshuai, Jie Li, Gong Sun, Zhiming Cheng, and Xin-an Zhang. 2017. "Achievement Goals and Life Satisfaction: The Mediating Role of Perception of Successful Agency and the Moderating Role of Emotion Reappraisal." *Psicologia: Reflexão e Crítica* 30 (1): 25. Accessed on March 29, 2025. https://doi.org/10.1186/s41155-017-0078-4.

Watson, Stephanie and Kristeen Cherney. 2024. "The Effects of Sleep Deprivation on Your Body." *Healthline*, August 23. Accessed on March 30, 2025. https://www.healthline.com/health/sleep-deprivation/effects-on-body.

Weaver, Conrad. 2021. "Documenting the Traumas of First Responders." *National Alliance on Mental Health*, March 12. Accessed on March 26, 2025. https://www.nami.org/frontline-wellness/documenting-the-traumas-of-first-responders/.

White-Gibson, Zuri. 2022. "What Is Secondary Trauma?" *PsychCentral*, July 15. Accessed on March 30, 2025. https://psychcentral.com/health/secondary-trauma.

Witkowski, Kaila, Ryan J. Lofaro, Andrea M. Headley, Santina Contreras, Christa L. Remington, and N. Emel Ganapati. 2024. "Understanding Problematic Substance Use Among First Responders During the COVID-19 Pandemic: A Survey of Law Enforcement, Fire, and EMS Workers in the United States." *International Journal of Drug Policy* 123: 104261. Accessed on March 24, 2025. https://doi.org/10.1016/j.drugpo.2023.104261.

Woodyard, Catherine. 2011. "Exploring the Therapeutic Effects of Yoga and its Ability to Increase Quality of Life." *International Journal of Yoga* 4 (2): 49–54. Accessed on April 8, 2025. https://doi.org/10.4103/0973-6131. 85485

Wright, Hannah M., Dianna Fuessel-Hermann, Myah Pazdera, Somi Lee, Brook Ridge, Joseph U. Kim, Kelly Konopacki, Layne Hilton, Michael Greensides, Scott A. Langenecker, and Andrew J. Smith. 2022. "Preventative Care in First Responder Mental Health: Focusing on Access and Utilization *via* Stepped Telehealth Care." *Frontiers in Health Services* 2: 848138. Accessed on March 24, 2025. https://doi.org/10. 3389/frhs.2022.848138.

ALSO BY YVON MILIEN

The Rhythm of My Life: Tuning into the Rocky Rhythm of Fire

Be Transcendent to Sustain Happiness:
Ethics Philosophical Essays Reduce Miseries and Stresses

THE JOURNEY TO SPIRITUAL WHOLENESS: MAKING SENSE OF BASIC COMMON SENSE

PHILOSOPHICAL ESSAYS

YVON MILIEN

The Journey to Spiritual Wholeness: Making Sense of Basic Common Sense
Philosophical Essays
Copyright © 2025 Yvon Milien

Because of the dynamic nature of the internet, any web addresses or links contained in this book may have changed since publication and may no longer be valid.

ISBN: 979-8-9860364-2-7 (print)
ISBN: 979-8-9860364-3-4 (ebook)

Library of Congress Control Number: 2025904146

Back cover photography by Perspectives Photography Studio

Printed by IngramSpark in the United States of America
Published by Yvon Milien

Visit www.yvonmilien.com

To my beautiful wife, Rose L., who sometimes makes me mad and stimulates me into action, which is good for me. For example, when she notices that I am developing a poor habit, she does not hesitate to command me to take steps to improve. Our life is not easy; we've experienced challenges, such as the frustration of not spending enough time together due to work schedules and long commutes. However, we are patient with each other because we understand how to make sense of basic common sense in our relationships so far. Challenges, like successes, are part of the interlaced fabric of life.

Just as there is no use in medical study unless it leads to the health of the human body, so there is no use to a philosophical doctrine unless it leads to the virtue of the human soul.

— GAIUS MUSONIUS RUFUS, ROMAN STOIC PHILOSOPHER

CONTENTS

Author's Note   xiii

PART I
THE FOUNDATION AND AWAKENING
PROCESS OF THE JOURNEY

1. The Journey toward the Monad   3
Transcending the World's Illusions
2. The Foundation of True Morality and the Journey
of Ethical Responsibility   11
3. The Virtuosity of Virtue   19
A Harmonious Life of Mastery and Spontaneity
4. Life Is a Beautiful Landscape   27
Learning to Navigate Beauty and Hidden Dangers
5. The Importance of Willpower over Intelligence in
Our Development   33
6. The Sovereignty of the Will   37
*A Philosophical Meditation on Destiny and Divine
Alignment*
7. The Sacred Flame and the Vessel   41
Rediscovering the Divine Union Between Men and Women

PART II
THE SPIRITUAL PILGRIMAGE'S
CULTIVATION AND TRANSFORMATION
TOWARD THE MONAD

8. Women's Nature Resembles Fertile Soil, Capable
of Germinating Seeds of Thought   49
9. Rediscovering Our Divine Purpose to Be Whole   55
10. The Blind Path to Peril   59
The Dangers of Ignorance and Misguided Values
11. The Perils of Violent Ambition   63
Disorder, Evil, and the Philosophy of Macbeth
12. The Sacred Electric Fire   69
*The Moral and Philosophical Dimensions of Advanced
Technology*

13. The Relationship Between Impatience and Time   73
When Impatience Makes Time Our Enemy

14. The Blindness to Truth   79
Its Cause and How We Can Cure That Disease or Protect Ourselves from Contamination

15. The Sovereignty of the Spirit Is the Ultimate Triumph of a True Warrior   91

PART III
SELFLESS SERVICE AND HUMILITY

16. Selfless Service Is a Divine Law   99
Forgiving a World That Forgets

17. We Are All Endowed with Divine Potential   105
We Should Choose Humility Over Ego

18. The Folly of Invincibility   111
On Power, Passion, and the Unpredictability of Fate

19. The Illusion of Control of Our Destiny   117
The Foolishness of Believing We Are the Architects of Our Fates

20. We Cannot Cross the Arid Desert of Life Without Carrying the Fresh Drink of Hope Mixed with Faith   123

21. How We Can Cultivate Our Best Spirit in This World of Dualities   127

PART IV
FULFILLMENT AND TRANSCENDENCE

22. Our Fate and the Moral Compass   133

23. The Unbounded Will   137
A Decree of Human Progress

24. False Security   141
The Dangers of Complacency in Our Evolution

25. We Should Be Vigilant About Going Back to the Source   147

Our Spiritual Journey Back toward the Source   151
References   157
About the Author   163

AUTHOR'S NOTE

In writing *The Journey to Spiritual Wholeness: Making Sense of Basic Common Sense*, my intention was not merely to offer another collection of philosophical essays but rather to craft a guidebook for the soul—a nautical chart for those seeking deeper truths in a world that seems eternally shrouded in illusion and material distraction. This book attempts to boil down the timeless wisdom of ancient teachings and blend them with the realities of our contemporary issues. It is a call to be aware that we are traveling on the wrong path, that we should return to our roots and reconnect with the universal principles that have guided humanity across millennia, which we often overlook in our pursuit of fleeting desires.

The concept of common sense, as mentioned in the title of this book, refers to a deeper, more profound understanding of existence and objective reality that has become diluted in modern times. Nowadays, the noise of societal pressures and media influences, as well as the ceaseless pursuit of material gain, has blocked out truths that once made sense.

In these pages, I strive to strip away those layers of distraction,

invite you back to a more straightforward yet profound understanding of existence, and encourage you to open your eyes and
see the truth. This book is a spiritual pilgrimage toward the
Monad, what I consider the indivisible source of all beings. It is a
call to transcend the superficial aspects of life and to rediscover the
deeper, more meaningful essence that resides within each of us.

Throughout this work, you will find echoes of ancient
wisdom from philosophers, mystics, and spiritual leaders who
have shaped human thought for centuries. These teachings are
not relics of the past; they are living, breathing principles that can
transform our lives if we sincerely embrace them. The purpose of
this book is to guide you toward self-mastery and spiritual wholeness and to inspire a return to virtuous living grounded in
universal morals and truths that transcend the boundaries of
culture and time, connecting us to a rich heritage of wisdom.

Each chapter of this book examines a different aspect of the
path of our journey. They explore the pitfalls of unchecked
desires, the dangers of self-deception, and the profound fulfillment in aligning one's life with higher spiritual principles. The
book encourages you to stick firmly to authentic morality and
willpower to develop intelligence and wisdom throughout the
end of your life. I combine philosophical insights with practical
advice to empower you with actionable steps for self-discovery
and self-realization. I also share my observations, reflections, studies, and personal experiences. Like many others, I have grappled
with questions of purpose, morality, the duality of life, the unpredictability of fate, and the nature of existence.

I hope this work revives the wisdom that has faded within
your soul. May it help you cut through the fog of destruction and
illusion, guiding you back to the truth that has always been there,
waiting for us to rediscover it.

This book seeks to illuminate the minds of those interested in freeing themselves from the nonsensical illusionary chains. Nowadays, unenlightened institutions shape our conscious minds to serve their interests—the interests of the dominant—enslaving us in subtle, modern ways. This is not physical enslavement any longer, but a psychological one designed to control our thoughts. The danger lies in the vast number of these "masters of enslavement" that keep increasing geometrically with the development of technology and social media, competing to control our minds, making it increasingly challenging to think independently and educate our will. Their tactics are so deceptive and pervasive that most of us often fail to recognize them, becoming unwitting participants in our subjugation. More than ever, we need authentic guides—wise individuals who do not desire to control us but rather to help us become whole, navigate this world meaningfully, and prepare for our ultimate return to the source of our being. True self-discovery, self-development, and self-realization demand independence grounded in the cultivation of willpower, courage, and knowledge.

This book is about returning to our essence, our most authentic selves, and to the divine source from which we all originate. It is about cultivating a life of hope, virtue, faith, integrity, and profound inner peace amid the modern world's noise, haste, and turmoil. If you gain a bit of or increase your spiritual understanding by reading this treatise, it will have fulfilled its purpose.

The essays in this collection are structured to guide you through a spiritual journey and encourage deep reflection by presenting thought-provoking questions you should carefully consider. Each chapter introduces a fundamental concept or challenge, prompting you to explore your perspectives and beliefs. As the discussion unfolds, the essays provide well-reasoned arguments and insights that offer potential answers, drawing from philosophical, ethical, and spiritual principles. These responses are not merely theoretical, but I designed them to be practical and applicable, empowering you to incorporate them into your daily lives. Through this inquiry, contemplation, and application process, I invite you to engage in meaningful self-exploration and personal growth, ultimately aligning your actions with your highest spiritual purpose.

The organization of these essays follows a structured and progressive journey that guides you on a spiritual pilgrimage toward the Monad, representing ultimate unity, divine truth, or the highest state of being. The sequence of chapters guides you to the path of self-discovery, ethical refinement, and spiritual transcendence, each building upon the previous concepts to deepen your understanding.

The book is divided into four parts:

Part 1 (Chapters 1 through 7): The Foundation and Awakening Process of the Journey. These initial chapters concentrate on establishing the groundwork for the spiritual journey. They introduce essential concepts such as:

- Transcending Material Illusions (Chapter 1): This chapter encourages self-realization and the pursuit of a higher purpose beyond material existence. It emphasizes the need to move beyond illusions and distractions to align with divine truth and achieve unity with the Monad, representing the ultimate spiritual state.
- Ethical Responsibility (Chapter 2): This chapter emphasizes pursuing higher moral principles that transcend cultural, political, and personal biases. It presents morality as an essential tool for self-discovery, societal harmony, and spiritual evolution.

- Mastery and Spontaneity (Chapter 3): This chapter encourages the consistent cultivation of virtues as a path to self-realization, harmony, and inner unity. It emphasizes that embodying virtues is not a passive pursuit but an active and dynamic process that demands effort, dedication, and mindfulness.
- Perception and Willpower (Chapters 4 through 6): This portion encourages you to cultivate discernment and inner strength. Chapter 4 emphasizes the importance of awareness, wisdom, and balance in navigating life's complexities. It presents life as a duality of beauty and danger, requiring vigilance, introspection, and spiritual growth to transcend challenges and move closer to divine unity. Chapter 5 emphasizes the primacy of willpower as the guiding force in shaping human potential and moral evolution. It presents willpower as the key to aligning one's actions with higher principles, transcending intellectual capabilities alone. Chapter 6 highlights the critical role of willpower in shaping one's destiny and achieving divine alignment. It emphasizes that true fulfillment and enlightenment come through the conscious direction of the will in harmony with universal laws.
- Sacred Union (Chapter 7): This chapter emphasizes restoring the sacred unity between men and women. It presents this union as a divine collaboration essential for personal fulfillment, societal harmony, and spiritual progress.

Part 2 (Chapters 8 through 15): The Spiritual Pilgrimage's Cultivation and Transformation toward the Monad. At this stage, the focus shifts toward inner cultivation, where you are encouraged to refine your thoughts, actions, and spiritual intentions. These chapters explore:

- A Road Map for Achieving Spiritual Unity and Divine Alignment (Chapter 8): This chapter presents a vision of unity and spiritual harmony, where men and women can fulfill their purposes and create thriving families and societies by embracing their divine roles.

- Divine Purpose (Chapter 9): This leads you on a spiritual pilgrimage toward the Monad by emphasizing the importance of aligning with sacred purpose and universal laws. It provides a framework for self-discovery and spiritual fulfillment, guiding you through key aspects of your journey.

- Confronting Challenges (Chapters 10 and 11): This portion exhorts you to understand the dangers of ignorance and unchecked ambition. The first chapter identifies the obstacles that hinder spiritual growth and then offers a path toward enlightenment and self-realization. The latter examines the consequences of pursuing noble goals through immoral means.

- Technological Ethics (Chapter 12): This encourages thoughtful and ethical engagement with technology as a means of self-realization and collective evolution. It highlights technology's dual nature—both a potential force for enlightenment and a source of peril —prompting you to cultivate mindfulness, ethical responsibility, and a deeper awareness of your actions.

- Time and Patience (Chapter 13): This offers profound insights into the nature of time and the virtue of patience. It presents time as an impartial, ever-flowing force and highlights how impatience can distort our perception, turning time into an adversary rather than an ally.

- Truth and Protection (Chapters 14 and 15): This portion emphasizes the role of truth in safeguarding the spirit. The first chapter addresses the barriers that prevent individuals from perceiving truth. It explores the societal, psychological, philosophical, and spiritual factors contributing to blindness to truth and provides actionable insights for overcoming these obstacles. The latter emphasizes the importance of inner mastery over external conquests. It provides a road map for achieving true power through moral courage, mindfulness, and self-discipline—qualities that align individuals with their higher purpose and divine truth.

Part 3 (Chapters 16 through 21): Selfless Service and Humility. This part emphasizes humility, service, and the practical application of spiritual insights:

- Forgiveness and Service (Chapter 16): This emphasizes the divine law of selfless service and the transformative power of forgiveness.
- Humility Over Ego (Chapter 17): This chapter leads you toward the Monad by fostering a deeper understanding of unity, purpose, and spiritual humility.
- Understanding Fate and Destiny (Chapters 18 through 20): This portion calls on recognizing divine order versus human illusion. The first chapter

addresses the dangers of pride and the necessity of humility and wisdom. The second addresses the illusion of control and emphasizes surrender to the greater cosmic order. The third guides you from struggle and uncertainty to self-realization and ultimate unity with the divine, highlighting the importance of resilience, faith, and inner transformation.

- Spiritual Cultivation in a Dualistic World (Chapter 21): This addresses life's inherent dualities and emphasizes the importance of conscious choice, humility, and alignment with divine purpose. It fosters inner balance, wisdom, and alignment with the greater cosmic design.

Part 4 (Chapters 22 through 25): Fulfillment and Transcendence. This focuses on achieving a state of spiritual mastery and aligning with the Monad:

- Moral Compass (Chapter 22): This emphasizes the role of conscious choices, alignment with universal laws, and cultivating virtues.
- Boundless Will and Progress (Chapter 23): This guides you from personal empowerment to collective enlightenment, encouraging you to cultivate a strong will, align with divine purpose, and contribute to humanity's spiritual upliftment.
- Avoiding Complacency (Chapter 24): This guides you toward a deeper understanding of yourself and your surroundings, ultimately leading you closer to the Monad by cultivating wisdom, vigilance, and spiritual resilience.

- Returning to the Source (Chapter 25): This guides
  you to align with universal moral laws and return to
  the source of all things in beauty and grace.

This book offers a structured progression of concepts that
guide you on a clear path from awakening to ultimate union with
the Monad. It provides philosophical insights and practical
applications for achieving spiritual enlightenment. Given the
complexities of life and the numerous overwhelming distractions
and psychic challenges one encounters, it is essential to recognize
that, in the words of social psychologist Edgar H. Schein, "Everything refers to everything else," and the journey is cyclical. I
believe we should engage in continuous self-reflection and
renewal to make our spiritual journeys complete.

As you embark on this transformative endeavor, I hope the
insights within these pages will inspire you to explore the depths
of your spiritual potential and align with your highest purpose.
Thank you for embarking on this voyage with me. I sincerely
appreciate your willingness to explore these profound truths. May
your path be illuminated with wisdom, guided by love, and
blessed with the serenity of knowing you are part of something far
more significant than yourself, because you are one of the many
chosen ones.

PART I

THE FOUNDATION AND AWAKENING PROCESS OF THE JOURNEY

1

THE JOURNEY TOWARD THE MONAD
TRANSCENDING THE WORLD'S ILLUSIONS

I n a world where material success and external achievements are often prioritized over inner growth, it is right to ask: What is life's true purpose? Is it to accumulate wealth and status, or is a more profound, meaningful journey awaiting us? Could the true purpose of life go beyond mere success in the material world, guiding us instead to transcend it and rediscover our divine essence?

This essay delves into the concept of the Monad—the divine and indivisible soul—arguing that our ultimate purpose is not to remain trapped in material illusions but to evolve spiritually, fostering virtues that align us with universal laws and timeless wisdom. It explores the ancient wisdom that humanity's ultimate goal is to evolve by moving beyond worldly illusions and reconnecting with our original divine essence—the Monad. In other words, it exposes the path toward self-discovery and ultimate transcendence by examining ancient perspectives and reflecting on our modern institutions. It aims to clarify how understanding and applying timeless moral principles can help individuals overcome destructive illusions and contribute to a harmonious society.

If most humans understood, or even believed, that the purpose of life is to strive toward becoming a Monad—a spiritual entity, a divine and indivisible soul—the world would be a much better place. We would have individuals who grasped the importance of sound judgment, realizing that evil has no rightful place in their own lives or the lives of others, no matter the circumstances. Yet many of us prefer self-deception, engaging in illusions that cause distress and disrupt our lives. This neglect of spiritual growth not only hinders our personal development but also has far-reaching consequences for the harmony of our society.

Ignorance propels us toward the point of no return, blind to the damage we inflict upon one another. We yearn for eternal life, wholeness, and timelessness—a divine existence. Despite this desire, we persist in playing destructive games with ourselves and others, such as waging all kinds of wars—psychological, spiritual, political, ideological, and economic—in the name of love, whether on a small or a larger scale, from family to nation. We also engage in illusions that cause distress and disrupt our lives, as if by destroying one another, we will find happiness. We ignore divine laws, moral principles, and the sense of fairness that could help us achieve our deepest aspirations, only to lament that life is unjust and sorrowful.

To become spiritual, substantial beings, we must cultivate the virtues needed for such growth. This attitude requires self-motivation and the nurturing of self-awareness. Without the conscious sacrifice of our vices and evil passions and the adoption of sound moral principles, neither personal nor spiritual evolution can occur.

According to ancient wisdom, we were all once Monads. We became human when our consciousnesses descended into matter and assumed material forms. As we journeyed through various planes of existence, we inhabited different bodies or vehicles, each overshadowed by our true essence—the universal self that pervades all life forms, whether human, plant, or animal. Our ultimate purpose is to evolve through authentic experience, to transcend these forms, and eventually return to the source—the Monad. In this return, we become whole once more, divine and indivisible, liberated from the influences of evil.

Sadly, the widespread neglect of universal morals has allowed evil to manifest in our world. Our willpower falters in governing the physical body, sensual desires, and the material realm. We lose the ability to discern between genuine and harmful desires because we lack the courage to align with the divine will. Consequently, we become lost souls, abandoning our divine purpose on Earth.

When we reflect on the conditions of the world that obscure higher truths, it becomes evident that our societal institutions have become overly focused on the material. Instead of nurturing the soul's potential for enlightenment, modern, primary institutions such as the family, religion, and the government, and secondary ones such as school, entertainment, peer groups, and politics, emphasize mastery of the material and economic forms, often at the expense of spiritual and moral development. Consequently, as it is not a sin to use material wealth for resources to function in this life, this world—meant to be a growth stage in spirituality for the soul—has turned into a realm filled with moral pitfalls, driven by unchecked desires and vanities.

In contrast, the ancient world had a different vision for institutions. They were considered sanctuaries of development for the soul. Their primary purpose was to guide individuals toward self-discovery, self-realization, and self-mastery because the leaders of these institutions understood that these factors could lead to social harmony. In contrast to the current state of our institutions, the ancient world's vision aimed to build a harmonious society where individuals were guided to develop their inner spiritual growth.

These sanctuaries for soul development can be traced back to several ancient civilizations, each with its own philosophical and educational traditions. The key civilizations include ancient Egypt (ca. 3000 BCE–300 CE), ancient Greece (ca. eighth century BCE–sixth century CE), ancient India (ca. 1500 BCE–500 CE), and ancient China (ca. 1046 BCE–220 CE).

In Egypt, temples served as centers for intellectual and moral enlightenment, integrating spirituality with science. In Greece, philosophical schools like Plato's Academy and Aristotle's Lyceum emphasized the pursuit of wisdom and virtue. Meanwhile, in India, institutions such as Gurukuls and the renowned Nalanda University facilitated self-realization through meditation and knowledge. In China, Confucian and Taoist traditions promoted moral cultivation and societal harmony.

The teachings of these institutions were embedded in individuals' moral codes and society's collective evolution. Leaders of that era, such as Hermes Trismegistus, embodied threefold wisdom: spiritual insight, legislative prudence, and administrative skill. Ancient rulers (pharaohs, Greek kings, Indian emperors, and Chinese monarchs) used philosophy and religious principles to shape moral codes. They recognized that self-governance is the foundation for societal governance and that actual order comes from the inner harmony of individuals.

The ancient institutions, which were divinely inspired, focused on cultivating souls in knowledge and virtue. Their teachings emphasize that it is only through true mastery in life, such as self-control and mental clarity, that we can attune to the inner spirit. By fostering this inner order—spiritual, emotional, and cognitive—social order naturally followed. Self-realization, self-discovery, or self-development, whatever we may call it, was seen as a civic responsibility, aligning individuals with a moral compass resonant with divine laws. It is said that when a person is self-realized, obedience to the divine order, which is the respect of universal laws, even genuine governmental laws, proceeds effortlessly; in contrast, a person who is far from self-realized struggles with obedience, succumbing instead to fleeting desires and chaos.

As most modern institutions have strayed from this ideal of fostering self-realization, society has lost its sense of direction. Instead of helping us evolve, they make our lives a tragedy because they teach us to be more interested in artificial social needs, norms, and values that fail to reflect or nurture our more profound natures. If our culture keeps producing insatiable wants and false beliefs, misinterpreting the material world's abundance as an end in itself, we will never move forward. Our social practices will continue undermining the soul's true purpose and growth potential.

Therefore, to progress, people with knowledge and a position of power must reawaken our educational and social systems to their highest purpose: cultivating the inner life. A resurgence that places self-realization at the core of education and societal development is the only way to restore harmony on both individual and collective levels. This revival is not just a suggestion but a necessary step toward restoring our existence's true purpose and our society's direction.

Consider Hermann Hesse's novel *Siddhartha*. It can be a profound literary reflection of the journey toward self-realization and spiritual transcendence for practice. In this novel, the protagonist, Siddhartha, embarks on a lifelong quest to uncover the true meaning of existence, exploring various paths—from asceticism to indulgence in material wealth and worldly pleasures—only to realize that neither extreme leads to genuine fulfillment. His journey mirrors that self-awareness and adherence to moral prin-

7

ciples are essential for transcending worldly illusions and attaining a more profound sense of purpose. Siddhartha's path illustrates that as souls, we must evolve through authentic experiences, learning to distinguish between transient desires and enduring truths. Throughout his journey, he understands that true enlightenment is not found in external achievements but in the harmony of inner peace, self-discovery, and unity with the divine essence. His transformation highlights the universal truth that spiritual growth requires introspection, discipline, and alignment with higher values, meaning that we must move beyond material illusions and embrace our divine potential. Siddhartha's ultimate realization by the river—where he perceives the interconnectedness of all life—calls for us to remember that the timeless wisdom of personal evolution is an inward journey leading back to the source of all existence, the Monad.

In addition, consider the historical figure Mahatma Gandhi, who exemplified the profound idea of transcending material desires in favor of spiritual and moral growth, illustrating that true fulfillment arises from inner development rather than external acquisitions. Gandhi's unwavering commitment to the principles of nonviolence (ahimsa) and truth (satyagraha) is a powerful demonstration of how aligning with higher moral values can lead to personal transformation and societal progress. Rejecting the allure of material wealth and power, Gandhi chose a life of simplicity, self-discipline, and service to humanity.

At the heart of Gandhi's philosophy was the belief that self-mastery and moral integrity are the foundations for meaningful change. His adherence to spiritual principles allowed him to rise above the material temptations and illusions often dominating human life. In other words, he chose to embrace the higher purpose and evolve beyond worldly distractions. Gandhi's life teaches us that true liberation is achieved not through material accumulation but through self-realization and alignment with universal values such as compassion, honesty, and justice. Moreover, his influence extended far beyond his spiritual journey; his leadership in India's struggle for independence demonstrated how an individual's inner transformation can inspire a collective awakening. By fostering a culture of nonviolent resistance, he urged millions to look beyond their immediate desires and instead work toward a higher purpose—freedom through unity, patience, and moral fortitude. Gandhi's message was that neglecting spiritual growth may result in societal discord, while embracing universal moral principles fosters harmony and progress.

In Gandhi's words, "The best way to find yourself is to lose yourself in the service of others." In other words, true self-discovery occurs when individuals transcend their ego-driven desires and dedicate themselves to the well-being of others. His example serves as a reminder that the path to spiritual growth and self-realization is not isolated but deeply intertwined with social responsibility and collective harmony. Gandhi's life offers a practical, real-world illustration of how humanity can reconnect with its divine essence by embracing moral clarity, self-awareness, and a commitment to higher ideals, meaning that self-realization is essential for both personal and societal evolution.

Having an experience like Siddhartha's or being like Gandhi is not required. Still, we can do our part by turning to mindfulness and minimalism to simplify our lives and focus on our inner well-being rather than material excess. By joining these movements, we may develop the understanding that genuine happiness and purpose lie in self-realization rather than external success and contribute to a better society.

This essay has argued that humanity's true purpose is to transcend the material illusions that dominate our modern existence and rediscover our divine essence as Monads—spiritual beings on a journey of self-realization. It has explored how ancient institutions once served as sanctuaries for personal and societal growth. In contrast, modern institutions have largely lost this focus, emphasizing material pursuits over moral and spiritual development. Individuals can reclaim their divine purpose and contribute to a more harmonious and enlightened world by cultivating virtues such as self-awareness, self-discipline, and alignment with universal laws.

2

THE FOUNDATION OF TRUE MORALITY AND THE JOURNEY OF ETHICAL RESPONSIBILITY

W hat is the proper foundation of true morality? And how can individuals navigate their ethical responsibilities in a world filled with conflicting societal standards? How can we align our moral responsibilities with societal standards while staying true to universal ethical principles?

This essay analyzes the differences and similarities between an individual's moral responsibility and the moral standards of a community. It argues that true morality transcends cultural and political boundaries, leading individuals toward self-discovery, fulfillment, and societal progress. By understanding the balance between duty and freedom, individuals can foster ethical cohesion in society and contribute to humanity's collective evolution. It explores the foundation of true morality, emphasizing the importance of aligning personal moral responsibility with universal ethical principles rather than conforming to the short-term moral codes of specific communities or political agendas.

A practical judgment is that morality should be grounded in what elevates us. It should guide us toward personal and collective growth, fostering a sense of proper conduct rooted in clear thinking and ethical reasoning beyond fear or fleeting emotions.

Propaganda, or the agendas of political or educational elites that only serve a particular group's managerial interests, is far from morality. Morality emerges from universal principles that transcend cultural and political divides. Communities' moral codes do not foster cohesion. Instead, they divide and create tribes in a nation because what one group might consider a good practice might be bad for another. The higher universal morals support humanity's evolution, leading us toward righteousness and inspiring us to act with genuine goodness for the progress of the whole and to be fulfilled and discover ourselves.

When we embrace our moral responsibility, fulfillment and self-discovery automatically arise. As a result, we will be more inclined to be encouraged to take meaningful actions that promote progress and societal well-being. Moral responsibility demands accountability for our choices and acceptance of their consequences. Those who believe in a Creator, such as God, understand that He wants us to evolve because He enabled the animals with instincts so that they could act instinctually. On the other hand, He endowed us with knowledge and a spirit of freedom to discern right from wrong, to shape our world purposefully, and metamorphose into higher beings.

Explaining the difference between an individual's moral responsibility and the community's moral standards is essential. Although different, these concepts are interconnected; ideally, they should align with universal laws. To achieve a genuinely unified society, moral responsibility and community moral standards should be interconnected with universal law. This means that individual moral responsibility should be embedded in the community's moral standards, which, in turn, should align with universal laws. Such an interconnection fosters genuine cohesion within society. However, realizing this interconnection is difficult, as circumstances shape our ethical beliefs and values.

Moral responsibility encompasses the choices and actions we make as individuals based on our understanding of right and wrong, often guided by conscience, personal experiences, and philosophical or religious beliefs. Some key characteristics of a morally responsible individual include personal accountability, autonomy, internalized values, conscience-based decisions, and accepting consequences. Individual moral responsibility includes being faithful in a relationship, making honesty a core value in dealing with others, and speaking out against injustice, even at personal risk.

Conversely, circumstances influence communities to develop ethical beliefs and values, which refer to their communal moral standards. A community's moral standards encompass the collective ethical norms and values upheld by a group, society, or culture. These standards guide behavior and expectations within the community, shaping laws, traditions, and social practices. Some key characteristics of such moral standards are collective agreement, cultural influence, external enforcement, dynamic nature, and social consequences. Examples of community moral standards include prohibitions against theft or violence, social expectations of politeness and respect, and cultural customs regarding marriage, dress code, or gender roles.

Moral responsibility and community moral standards differ in terms of source, flexibility, accountability, scope, enforcement, and changeability. Conflict can arise when individual moral responsibility and community moral standards don't align. Individuals may face ethical dilemmas when their personal beliefs clash with societal expectations. For example, an individual might advocate for conservative social changes, laws, and order that their community resists, or vice versa.

A society can navigate these conflicts through various means. We can utilize critical thinking, dialogue, compromise, and advocacy on the earthly plane. On a higher-consciousness level, we can focus on the vision of becoming Monad, not on life circumstances—a state of unity and oneness with universal laws. Communities and societies should genuinely assist in this transformative task rather than focusing solely on the material circumstances of life.

Focusing on harmony among individual moral responsibility, community moral standards, and universal laws can help build a more cohesive and ethically sound society.

Because of our ignorance and lack of wisdom, we may choose to ignore God's plan, harm others, or compromise our integrity just to feel a fleeting sense of power. However, this path ultimately erodes our character. In contrast, benevolent actions grounded in integrity foster genuine self-worth and create positive influence, making us feel valued and significant.

When we accept our moral responsibility and are aware of our knowledge and freedom, this attitude leads us toward higher standards. In contrast to engaging in evil, acts of kindness and integrity strengthen our personal growth and societal harmony. This harmony is crucial because it can foster a sense of belonging and unity, reminding us of our purpose here on Earth: to evolve through experience and wisdom and connect with our higher selves.

Ethics is the balance between duty and freedom, shaped by universal laws that frame our choices. These universal laws may or may not be officially religious or legal, but principles universally accepted as guiding moral conduct. Aligning ourselves with these laws will help us fulfill the divine purpose, bringing growth while encouraging us to reduce negative impulse-driven behavior. Instead of obstructing truth, institutions should help us manifest goodness, teaching us to discern beliefs that uplift from those who mislead. Immorality often leads to discord, yet some institutions exploit human weaknesses by promoting vices, knowing its appeal to weak-willed people over virtue.

A classic example of guiding moral conduct is the Golden Rule: "Treat others as you would like to be treated." This principle is universally accepted as a moral guideline across cultures and philosophies. In Christianity, it is, "So in everything, do to others what you would have them do to you, for this sums up the Law and the Prophets" (Matt. 7:12, *New International Version*). In Islam, it is, "None of you truly believes until he wishes for his brother what he wishes for himself" (*Sahih al-Bukhari*, Book 2, Hadith 12). In Buddhism, it is "Hurt not others in ways that you yourself would find hurtful" (*Udānavarga* 5:18, in Ross 1960). In philosophy, Immanuel Kant formulated a version of the Golden Rule within his deontological ethics, stating that one should act only according to principles that could be universally applied. Confucius stated in *The Analects*, "Do not do to others what you do not want done to yourself."

The Golden Rule encourages empathy, fairness, and respect in interactions, regardless of whether it is rooted in religious beliefs or legal frameworks. For instance, in a workplace setting, applying this rule means respecting colleagues' opinions, communicating honestly, and offering support when needed. It promotes fair treatment of employees and customers. In legal systems, concepts of fairness and justice often align with the Golden Rule's emphasis on reciprocity and respect. These examples demonstrate the universal acceptance of the rule as a guiding moral principle across different domains of human life. Even without formal policies, this principle fosters a positive and ethical environment.

When we understand the lasting fulfillment of moral strength —that is to say, the feeling of deep contentment that comes from living a life that is aligned with our ethical values, genuine passions, and the universe's purpose—succumbing to temptation warrants a demerit, as it reflects a conscious choice. Adults who behave like children without this understanding face the consequences through social or legal means. For the individuals or institutions who have power and foster corruption for their gains or pleasures, sooner or later, consequences as cosmic justice ultimately will prevail because they understand the repercussions. Cosmic justice refers to the idea that the universe, or a higher power, will eventually ensure justice is served, even if it may not be immediately apparent in our human experience.

The civil rights movement of Dr. Martin Luther King Jr. is a classic example of aligning personal moral responsibility with universal moral laws. He was an advocate of justice, equality, and nonviolent resistance in the face of the dominant community's and government's moral standards of systemic oppression. His congenial sense of moral responsibility, his belief in the dignity and worth of every individual, inspired King's actions to be driven by the universal moral principles of fairness, respect, and compassion—values that transcend cultural, religious, and political divides. His actions, obviously influenced by the Golden Rule, urge individuals to treat others as they would like to be treated, as well as by religious teachings emphasizing love and forgiveness.

King's commitment to nonviolent resistance embodied ethical principles that resonated across diverse belief systems. His civil rights movement is a living testament to the power of moral responsibility to inspire collective action to positively influence society. When we develop a strong moral responsibility, hostility and death threats cannot affect our convictions or integrity. The movement demonstrates the power of moral responsibility to drive change for the better. When individuals appeal to universal ideals of justice and human rights, they will successfully build a movement that unites people across racial and cultural lines; they will show that ethical values can transcend individual and community interests to promote a higher moral good when consistently applied. When individuals are determined to advocate for what is right, even when it conflicts with prevailing societal norms, they will succeed. King's efforts, such as the Montgomery bus boycott and the 1963 March on Washington, highlighted that. His philosophy that we should judge individuals by the content of their character rather than superficial differences reinforces that true morality is grounded in universal principles of equality and justice. So aligning personal moral convictions with universal ethical values can lead to meaningful societal transformation.

This essay argues that true morality is not dictated by cultural or political influences but by universal principles that guide humanity toward righteousness, self-discovery, and self-development. It emphasizes the importance of aligning personal moral responsibility with higher ethical standards while recognizing the challenges posed by societal norms and expectations. By embracing moral accountability and striving for ethical consistency, individuals can foster societal harmony, achieve self-development and self-realization, and contribute to the collective good.

3

THE VIRTUOSITY OF VIRTUE
A HARMONIOUS LIFE OF MASTERY AND SPONTANEITY

I t is pure self-destruction and the road to misery when we seek shortcuts to happiness, success, or moral excellence because of our fast-paced, convenience-driven world. Yet it is possible that the true path to a fulfilling and harmonious life lies not in instant solutions, deceit, and exploitation but in a deliberate and disciplined cultivation of virtues. Can a life of true integrity and fulfillment be achieved by cultivating virtues with discipline and spontaneity? Should we cultivate virtue like mastering an art to realize a harmonious and fulfilling life? What does leading a life of true fulfillment and integrity take and give?

This essay explores how the harmonious integration of virtues —disciplined practice and spontaneous action—leads to a life of integrity and fulfillment. It explores the role of virtues in shaping our personal and social lives. Because the central theme is the parallel between mastering a craft or art form and mastering virtues, it emphasizes that virtues should not be compartmentalized but should permeate every aspect of our lives, much like a musician who masters their craft through continuous refinement and inspired expression. It argues that virtues are abstract ideals and living principles that require structured discipline and spontaneous adaptation. Therefore, much like practicing a melody leads to beautiful music, practicing virtues can shape the foundation of a meaningful life and generate health, prosperity, and serenity.

To live a stable, happy, and meaningful life, we must consistently apply virtues to every part of our existence. We cannot afford to compartmentalize our morality but should strive to embody virtue in all we do. Only then can we experience the proper fulfillment of a life of integrity.

Virtues are living principles that we must embody in our actions. We must not think of them as merely abstract ideals. For instance, honesty can be practiced by always speaking the truth, even when it is difficult. Achieving this requires moving beyond mere knowledge; we must aim to become virtuosos of virtue, just as musicians refine their craft to perfection. Like an accomplished musician who constantly performs great concerts, playing gracefully and precisely despite the moment's pressure, so must we perform gracefully with precision when facing difficult situations, thanks to our practice and understanding.

Because we are humans, sometimes we may experience doubt, so instead of looking for external guidance, we should draw upon our inner qualities such as determination, tenacity, and resilience. We should use our creativity and imagination, which can allow us to envision the benefits of overcoming our doubts, even when that seems unattainable. We should summon our enthusiasm and optimism to help us positively engage ourselves and others while focusing on our purpose. We should be committed to grounding our actions in something higher. These qualities are essential for finding the courage to persevere.

To foster a coherent social unity, we must strive to develop many virtues, including self-awareness, honesty, integrity, patience, humility, gratitude, forgiveness, compassion, discipline, mindfulness, courage, purposefulness, and resilience. These are foundational for building harmonious relationships; without them, our personal, communal, or professional connections remain fragile and prone to conflict. But first, we must attain unity in ourselves, and this demands a great deal of resolution. Through this process, we can only nurture authentic, lasting relationships grounded in trust, respect, and shared values. The path to harmony demands a deep, inner commitment and continuous effort because there are no shortcuts or quick fixes.

In our pursuit of becoming virtuosos of virtue, we might be tempted by shortcuts or strategies that promise relief without hard work. However, such strategies only deepen our struggles. We cannot force or fabricate the truth. It should be aligned with reality; how we live and interact with others should reflect it. When we embody these virtues, we align ourselves with reality and move closer to inner and outer unity.

In Shakespeare's *Julius Caesar*, the quote, "The fault, dear Brutus, is not in our stars, but in ourselves," spoken by Cassius, can be interpreted as our destiny being shaped by our inner character and moral choices, not external forces, which means that virtue is not granted by fate. It is something we must actively cultivate. Pursuing virtue requires discipline, tremendous effort, a touch of artistic flexibility, and versatility in morality. Virtues are developed through resoluteness, practice, and intelligence; mastering them is similar to learning an instrument. We need basic training, as a musician trains in classical music and jazz. The classical musician's training is oriented toward being meticulous, while the jazz musician thrives on spontaneity and improvisation, much like virtues such as kindness and generosity spontaneously develop when we are in harmony with our inner selves. Yet both need to cultivate patience, be consistent in the rhythm of the music, and try to play it well. It is a process of refinement through effort to develop our skills, enjoy our development, and make others happy.

The formation of virtue is grounded in deliberate practice and structure, yet its true manifestation emerges in the artful, unpremeditated responses of a well-ordered soul. Consider the relationship between performers and their instruments: If they do not learn to play the instruments, they will never perform. Likewise, dancers must be balanced to reflect the beauty of music in fullness. If dancers deliberately refuse to follow a rhythm, they will not respond authentically or perform adequately.

In nurturing virtue, we must follow both the slow, methodical shaping of habit and the spirited dance of our soul in moments of grace. Musicians practice scales to discipline their fingers to beautifully play musical masterpieces. To play our lives beautifully, we must follow a similar strategy: the rehearsed rhythms of prudence, temperance, justice, and courage in our actions.

Developing virtues plays an essential role in our journey toward self-realization. Virtues are for self-realization, much like an artist needs certain talents or skills. Just as artists hone their skills to create beautiful art, we must cultivate virtues to create a beautiful life. Rare and refined talents require deliberate nurturing, like students that shine through dedicated effort and perseverance. Ordinary talents serve practical purposes but might not guide us toward profound growth. It is the same for virtues. Therefore, it is up to us to choose which skills or virtues to cultivate more because we know our weaknesses very well.

Aiming to reach the stars, we must elevate ourselves through discipline and dedication. Distractions like indulgence in alcohol or drugs only cloud our potential.

To become virtuosos of virtue, we must understand that

developing virtues requires patience, effort, and a willingness to toil. Fate will not give us virtues. This understanding can help us rise to our fullest potential, living a life guided by integrity and enriched by the virtues we have cultivated.

Before summarizing, let's consider these two examples: a virtuous entrepreneur and a dedicated teacher.

First, consider entrepreneurs who create prospering, innovative businesses and personify virtues such as honesty, resilience, and adaptability. What will happen when citizens like that maintain a steadfast commitment to ethical practices, even when facing tempting shortcuts or challenging circumstances? Because they focus only on helping their communities, countries, or nations, and not just during difficult circumstances, their honesty fosters trust with clients, employees, and partners, laying the foundation for sustainable growth. The focus on their vision gives them the strength that will enable them to navigate setbacks and uncertainties, allowing them to let innovation propel their business forward through changing market demands, much like the wind moves a sailboat on the sea.

The structured balance of discipline and spontaneous flexibility exhibited by such entrepreneurs reflects this essay's analogy of classical and jazz musicianship. The linkage of the structured discipline of consistency to ethical practices represents the classical approach; the inclination to embrace change and adapt with spontaneity in responding to unforeseen challenges aligns with the improvisational nature of jazz.

The practice of these virtues in business to benefit others exemplifies how, with genuine dedication, virtues can create a successful business that profits everyone.

Second, imagine that in the heart of an underfunded high school, a dedicated teacher with diverse talents and degrees chooses to act with resolute compassion and purpose to make a difference in the lives of his students, even though most of his friends say he could have found a more lucrative job. He believes that teaching is a noble profession. Faced with limited resources in addition to students experiencing personal struggles, he refuses to let these external obstacles discourage him and influence his work. Instead, he makes the philosophy of his teaching practice commitment, patience, creativity, respect, and integrity. His patience allows him to meet each student where they are, recognizing that growth and learning take time. Rather than succumbing to frustration when progress seems slow, he celebrates small victories, encouraging his students to believe in their potential verbally and with his positive behavior. He understands that not every student is always ready to learn—circumstances and challenges can stand in the way. Progress, even in small steps, takes time. He sometimes feels frustrated, but he reminds himself that learning is a journey he cannot control alone. Actual growth comes when students are engaged and curious.

He makes every effort to inspire his students' curiosity and interest each day, with unwavering enthusiasm and dedication to engage them in learning. Rather than forcing learning, he creates a space where it can flourish. In his practice, he balances empathy and compassion with wisdom, guiding students while respecting their paths.

He uses innovative methods to teach his students, even with limited tools. His efforts yielded some outcomes. Some struggling students show a little progress, and some discover talents they never knew they had. His classroom becomes a sanctuary where they feel seen, valued, and empowered to develop their skills. Beyond academic success, his influence instills virtues—endurance and resilience.

This teacher exemplifies how virtues, when practiced consistently, even though they may not be 100 percent able to overcome the most daunting adversity, can make a slight difference in a challenging setting. At least he transforms some lives in the process. He demonstrates that while extreme external circumstances may limit resources or discourage students from focusing on learning, they cannot ultimately limit the transformative power of character and intention because he focuses on his vision for his students, not the external circumstances. May this example inspire others to live virtuously, rise above challenges with compassion and resolution, and continue helping students face challenging situations.

In conclusion, this essay has argued that achieving a life of integrity and fulfillment requires us to become virtuosos of virtue —balancing discipline with spontaneity in our moral choices. Virtue is a concept that needs to be cultivated to have a stable, meaningful, harmonious life. Please, make no mistake: It is not easy; pursuing virtue demands tremendous effort and patience. But by cultivating virtues through continuous practice and sincere commitment, not only will we align our actions with reality and common sense, but by nurturing meaningful relationships based on trust and respect, we will be delighted and enjoy serenity. Just as musicians refine their craft over time, we, too, must refine our character through deliberate effort and reflection. Ultimately, living a virtuous life is an ongoing journey that enriches ourselves and the world.

4

LIFE IS A BEAUTIFUL LANDSCAPE
LEARNING TO NAVIGATE BEAUTY AND
HIDDEN DANGERS

U ndeniably, life is a beautiful, breathtaking landscape. Yet even a scenic landscape can hide land mines beneath its surface in a war zone. Our lives similarly are filled with hidden dangers—emotional struggles, toxic relationships, envious people, hackers who want to cripple us financially, and self-inflicted wounds. How do we successfully navigate this reality planted with fears, unresolved traumas, and the negative influences of others without succumbing to its traps?

This essay examines how we can enjoy and embrace life's beauty and remain vigilant against its hidden perils, developing self-awareness, emotional intelligence, and the wisdom to recognize potential hazards. In addition, it argues that we can succeed in this endeavor by acknowledging the hidden emotional and psychological land mines that can shatter our lives. This essay uses three real-world experiences from literature to ground and illustrate the struggle between life's beauty and its hidden dangers.

Camouflaged by the landscape, these land mines blend in with no apparent signs of danger; they remain hidden until a misstep detonates them. Naively, we are unaware of this fragile terrain, navigating unseen dangers that can alter the course of our lives in an instant. Yet we can reshape our personalities and polish our inner negativity rather than nurture it, presenting a kind, caring version of ourselves.

For years, some of us may carry hidden emotions like land mines until someone special comes along—a person whose gentle nature transforms us—by the grace of God to save us. Their kindness disarms those inner mines, offering us hope and a path to overcome our destructive tendencies to make life safe for us and others.

What triggers these transformations remains a mystery, but something about the truly kind person seems to smooth the rough edges of our turmoil. Emotional psychology is powerful. Social and environmental factors shape our thoughts and behaviors, but we can resist unpleasant forces and strengthen our minds.

We must learn to trust our intuition. By sharpening it through knowledge and experience, we can recognize and avoid "land mine" people unwilling to change and who might sabotage us or themselves.

Encountering these individuals requires wisdom to navigate without harm. Even if we survive contact, we may not emerge unscathed. The wounds left behind may be psychological, emotional, or spiritual, leaving parts of us trapped in the aftermath of each unseen explosion.

Many ask, "If God loves the world, why would He allow these land mines in our path?" The answer might lie in divine action and our choices.

Shakespeare wrote in *Julius Caesar*: "The fault, dear Brutus, is not in our stars, but in ourselves." We should not blame God or our fate for the problems others create and place in our path to destroy us for their evil will, ignorance, ill desires, and bad decisions. The difficulties lie in ourselves. We hold the power to choose rightly; we have the free agency to choose between good and evil. God gives us the intelligence to recognize what will destroy us or sustain our lives. When blinded by ignorance, we create most of our problems and try to provide them with a glamorous look to make them attractive. In other words, we disguise the very problems we have created by dressing them in charm and appeal, concealing their true, destructive nature.

In a world filled with these self-made problems, we often admire the surface beauty of life while ignoring the dangers beneath. The mechanisms of consequence and morality require us to look deeper, yet we often turn a blind eye, trapped by our spiritual apathy.

The landscape has no power to change by itself. It is our responsibility to examine it clearly before adventuring through it. In such a situation, we need to develop sound knowledge. We cannot simply admire the beauty while ignoring its dangers. We should not let fear prevent us from moving forward in such a situation; yet we must be cautious and vigilant.

The key is to develop our intelligence first and then explore with an awareness of risk to successfully navigate the beautiful yet dangerous landscape. This balance provides a steady guide as we engage with the world.

Constant awareness is one of the necessary tools to successfully navigate this existence filled with hidden dangers and potential pitfalls. With such a strategy, we can protect ourselves in a world where risks are often unseen.

Life is undeniably beautiful, yet its allure is intertwined with traps and hidden perils. The dangers are real but so is the magnificence of existence. We cannot separate beauty from danger; we must learn to live with both—that is life's essence.

We must remain vigilant as we navigate this stunning yet

treacherous landscape, filled with people and situations resembling hidden land mines. Unfortunately, we cannot avoid all dangers in life, but we can avoid many pitfalls by recognizing them for what they are.

Make no mistake, these "land mine" individuals exist in every field—politics, love, relationships, and business. They might even be our neighbors. Yet we should enjoy the landscape, being mindful and careful in our steps.

Life's beauty and dangers are intertwined to make our experience exciting. We must embrace both and explore the heart of existence while being aware of the risks.

Life's dangers serve a vital purpose, like shadows in a painting, which is to give form, depth, and dimension by revealing where light is obstructed. Yet to fixate solely on the shadows is to lose sight of the beauty they help define. No matter how masterfully an artist crafts a painting, we cannot appreciate it if our gaze remains bound to the darkness alone. Likewise, to truly enjoy the beauty of life God and we have crafted, remember that we are cocreators because we have the free will to add color, light, and shadow according to our tastes and desires. One must acknowledge the shadows of life without becoming consumed by them. Only then can we appreciate the interplay of light and dark that makes existence a work of art.

To illustrate our struggle between life's beauty and its hidden dangers, consider Pip, the protagonist in Charles Dickens's *Great Expectations*, a realist novel that depicts the social milieu of nineteenth-century England. Pip is initially blinded by wealth and social status, believing them to be the key to happiness. However, from his journey, he learns that chasing social status and misplaced trust, driven by ambition, are hidden dangers that eventually lead to destruction. This situation ultimately teaches him that true fulfillment lies in authenticity and kindness.

Next, consider Oscar Wilde's philosophical fiction and gothic horror novel *The Picture of Dorian Gray*. The protagonist Dorian's primary obsessive drive to pursue beauty and pleasure, ignoring the danger of his moral decay, leads to his downfall. He indulges in a life of self-serving pleasure and cruelty, which he can't bear to confront, resulting in his eventual suicide. So admiring the surface beauty of life while ignoring the more profound consequences can be disastrous. His story illustrates that we must constantly be aware of life's hidden perils to enjoy life's beauty. Similar to Dorian's experience, at another level, how often do we enter a love relationship because of physical beauty such as the height of the person, their blue or green or brown eyes, and ignore the individual's character, then later experience deep regret about our choice?

Finally, consider *Of Mice and Men* by John Steinbeck. This tragic realistic novel illustrates that the dream of owning a farm represents hope and beauty, but the harsh realities of life—including betrayal and the consequences of misunderstanding—shatter this dream, emphasizing the unpredictable dangers of human nature.

These examples illustrate that beneath the beauty of life, which includes tempting pleasures, fascinating dreams, and physical beauty, lies a world of deceit, betrayal, regret, self-deception, and trauma that can destroy us in the blink of an eye. But we must move forward and enjoy life despite these dangers, the evil of others and ours.

Life is a reality that combines beauty and peril, offering moments of joy intertwined with hidden threats. Navigating it requires both appreciation and caution, as this essay has explored. Ignorance always leads to disaster. Therefore, we must recognize when we disregard or refuse to understand that, despite the indisputable beauty of life, there are unseen dangers planted around us, which make us vulnerable. Self-awareness, emotional intelligence, and wisdom are potent abilities, attributes we can use to avoid the land mines threatening our well-being and preventing us from enjoying the beauties of life. Rather than being paralyzed by fear, we must engage with life fully—embracing its beauty while remaining vigilant against its dangers. Such a genuine, balanced attitude can transform life's challenges into lessons enriching our journey, allowing us to move forward with caution and courage.

5

THE IMPORTANCE OF WILLPOWER OVER INTELLIGENCE IN OUR DEVELOPMENT

We often encounter people with exceptional intelligence who struggle to make ethical choices or achieve meaningful lives while others with average intellect but strong determination reach remarkable heights. Is intelligence—our ability to acquire and apply knowledge—truly the most critical factor in pursuing fulfillment, or does willpower play a more crucial role? This essay argues that willpower, which directs our intentions and actions rather than intelligence, determines our progress, happiness, and moral integrity. The analysis of the role of willpower in our lives shows why strengthening the will is the key to leading a meaningful and successful existence.

In our quest for personal growth and progression, we should focus more on the development and education of our willpower than the development of our intelligence to have a more meaningful life and be able to help others. Willpower is the essential foundation for our growth. It guides the orientation of our desires, tendencies, and purposes. If we develop robust and genuine willpower, our actions will be good. Positive willpower will encourage us and steer us from stagnation or negativity. As humans, we are not meant for laziness but engagement with the world, embodying an active energy-driving progress. This potential for growth and development through willpower is truly inspiring.

While intelligence is valuable, it operates according to our chosen intentions. Misdirected intelligence will not align with truth, and evil may lead even the brightest minds astray, using knowledge to deceive or cause harm rather than uplift. Many historical figures had high intelligence, but their ill-aligned will impaired their intellect. As a result, they caused a lot of suffering in this world because they lacked the broader vision to foresee the consequences of their actions. This idea highlights the supremacy of will as the driving force in shaping our lives—determining our progress, happiness, or regression.

It is will that determines our choice between good and evil. The internet is a case in point. It offers both beneficial and destructive information, good and bad entertainment. However, due to insufficient willpower training, even educated individuals often need help to make wise decisions. In this way, the internet mirrors the symbolism of the ancient Egyptian tarot card's "Door of the Occult Sanctuary," where a seated woman is flanked by two columns: one representing the spirit's ascent and the other the captivity of the spirit. Similarly, the internet holds both good and harmful knowledge, and without a disciplined will, we risk making choices that harm rather than heal.

Ultimately, true happiness does not lie in intelligence but in the guidance of our will. Intelligence follows whatever our will directs: If we lean toward darkness, darkness manifests; if toward light, then light emerges. True peace and happiness come from aligning our will with justice and truth. Many historical figures who did not have exceptional intelligence but a healthy will have led prosperous lives and contributed positively to humanity's evolution. This understanding can guide us toward more fulfilling and meaningful lives.

While willpower and intelligence are both necessary, willpower is more essential. It is the first faculty that institutions should prioritize in education. They should teach how to develop our will to desire justice and health, to act against evil, and to avoid the passivity that leads to stagnation. This passivity, the lack of will to act and make positive changes, can halt our personal growth and development. When we align our will with justice and truth, we develop our true potential, achieving the happiness and peace we seek.

Before summarizing this chapter, consider Thomas Edison's life example. He is regarded as one of the most famous inventors of all time because of his contributions to inventions such as the incandescent light bulb, the phonograph, and the motion picture camera. He famously failed more than a thousand times before inventing the light bulb. While he did not lack intelligence, his relentless willpower made him succeed after so many attempts.

Our ability to acquire and apply knowledge in the affairs of life is essential, but willpower plays a more crucial role. Will directs our lives and determines our success, ethical choices, and contributions to society. Intelligence may deceive us, for it can lead to harmful outcomes under a weak or misaligned will, whereas strong, genuine willpower fosters resilience, growth, and a commitment to justice and truth. By prioritizing the development of willpower in education and personal growth, we can cultivate individuals who acquire knowledge and use it for the betterment of themselves and others. Thus, true fulfillment and progress lie in aligning our will with good intentions rather than relying solely on intellectual ability.

6

THE SOVEREIGNTY OF THE WILL

A PHILOSOPHICAL MEDITATION ON DESTINY AND DIVINE ALIGNMENT

I s our fate predestined, or do our choices shape the trajectory of our lives? This essay contends that while external conditions may influence our journey, the ultimate determinant of our character and fulfillment is our will—the conscious direction we give to our actions and intentions. It discusses how aligning our will with higher principles such as truth, justice, and compassion leads to harmony while surrendering to corruption, turning toward darkness, and injustice leads to destruction. Furthermore, it briefly explores how our moral and existential choices define our individual lives and our place within the grand order of the universe.

Our success or failure, happiness or unhappiness, rests upon the direction we give to our will. It is not external circumstances that define our lives; it is the deliberate choices and intentions that we cultivate. We shape our essence; our personality results from how we wield our will. Most of us are unaware that we are the architects of our character. The unfolding of our lives directly reflects the path chosen by our inner volition. When our will aligns with higher principles—such as compassion, truth, and justice—it gains a profound strength and influence over life's vicissitudes. When we orient our will in the right direction, harmony exists that transcends adversity, a deep-seated joy that persists even through trials. Such inner alignment, however, does not come easily; it requires a process of inner collection, silencing the lower passions and desires that often obscure the voice of higher wisdom. For this divine whisper to continue speaking in our lives, we must quiet the flesh's noise and clamoring instincts.

Conversely, if our will turns toward corruption—embracing perversion, violence, injustice, and darkness—we set ourselves on a path of self-destruction. This is a moral lapse and an existential choice against our well-being. A sure way to initiate a form of spiritual suicide, binding ourselves to the forces of death rather than life, is to choose evil deliberately. A will that turns toward darkness becomes enslaved, cut off from the higher realms of existence and its true purpose. The consequences of such a choice are dire, leading to a life devoid of light and joy, a life that is a mere shadow of what it could be.

According to the ancient teaching, when our will rebels against the eternal laws that govern existence, it conflicts with the universal order, subject to the reproof of an unyielding, eternal reason. These universal laws, such as the law of cause and effect, the law of karma, and the law of balance, are the guiding principles of the cosmos. The cosmos gives us these laws but gives us free agency to obey or disobey them. God provides us with the freedom to test our will. There is nothing arbitrary in this plan. The freedom is a holy trial. It is an essential aspect of our spiritual journey. God, or the divine source, grants us this freedom to discern our true nature and see if we can return to a higher state of unity. A sure way to reach enlightenment and fulfillment in our spiritual journey is to deliberately align our will with these universal laws.

The trials we encounter and our choices within the circle of universal law are the crucible of our evolution. In this space of freedom, we are given the chance to refine our will, to choose light over darkness, truth over deception, and love over hate.

The power that propels us either upward toward enlightenment or downward into the void of despair is nothing else but our will. It has the potential to be both the instrument of our salvation and the seed of our undoing. In such a case, we are not simply making a choice—it is the act of self-creation, shaping our destiny.

Ultimately, our life mirrors the path our will has carved. The true test of our existence is not found in our circumstances but in the integrity and direction of our will—in other words, how we use it to act. As we navigate the moral landscape of our choices, we sculpt our essence, determine our fate, and find our place within the vast, eternal order of the universe.

Consider *Les Misérables* by Victor Hugo. This novel illustrates how the will can reshape destiny when redirected toward virtue. The protagonist, Jean Valjean, undergoes a profound transformation after serving a lengthy prison sentence for stealing a loaf of bread to feed his family. Initially hardened by injustice, he chooses redemption and selflessness, aligning himself with compassion and truth. In Fyodor Dostoevsky's *Crime and Punishment*, Rodion Raskolnikov's descent into darkness through a will bent on justification of evil shows the consequences of moral corruption. His existential crisis reveals the self-destruction that follows when the will is divorced from higher principles. Finally, C.S. Lewis's allegorical novel *The Great Divorce* illustrates how choices toward light or darkness determine the soul's fate.

Ultimately, the will is both the architect of our character and the force that determines or plans the direction of our lives for good or bad. Our deliberate choices, not fate or external circumstances, define our character and destiny. If our will is in harmony with higher principles, we will develop the power to foster an elevated inner life and fulfillment. A will that turns toward corruption, injustice, and evil leads to self-destruction and existential despair, such as a low life. Our journey is shaped by our ability to refine, direct, and elevate our will, making it the central force in the moral and spiritual evolution of our being.

7

THE SACRED FLAME AND THE VESSEL

REDISCOVERING THE DIVINE UNION BETWEEN MEN AND WOMEN

Since the beginning of life on Earth, to survive, man and woman have had to unify in a matrimonial relationship to face the natural dangers and rivalry from others that threaten their lives. Men's role was to hunt to provide for their partners and children and protect them while women cared for the family. So men's and women's relationships were built on the foundation of unity, a partnership that fosters harmony, purpose, and social stability for the benefit of the whole.

Over time, human beings created civilizations, and they thrived on such sacred relationships. However, due to such factors as moral decay, lust, greed, and jealousy, this balance has eroded in the modern era, giving rise to discord in relationships, weakening family structures, and contributing to societal fragmentation. How has the growing division between men and women impacted the stability of families and the fabric of society, and what can be done to restore the sacred unity that once defined human relationships?

This essay explores the consequences of this growing divide and examines how ancient wisdom—such as the teachings of the

Hindu deity Rama—can serve as a guide for restoring the sacred partnership between men and women.

Throughout history, humanity has drifted away from an ideal of unity between men and women: one designed to foster harmony, purpose, and the flourishing of families. In our time, this sacred bond has often deteriorated into discord. Many women seem uninterested in forming a partnership with men and working together to fulfill a shared purpose, and many men have failed to inspire the spiritual qualities needed to cultivate this union. As a result, a profound division between men and women is growing in all societies. The drift from the ideal of unity between them not only impedes personal relationships and erodes marriages but also affects our society's fabric. Consequently, this leads to issues like giving rise to dysfunctional or broken families and societal deterioration. The urgency of this issue cannot be overstated, and immediate action is needed to restore this sacred bond if we want to see our world evolve.

Looking back to ancient civilizations, we see how corruption eroded the institutions intended to uplift humanity—rather than guiding with wisdom and compassion, priests, rulers, and judges often prioritized their power, neglecting their duty to foster unity and respect. This failure corrupted the family, the cornerstone of a thriving society. In response, female seers emerged, prophesying in search of a more excellent vision. But as with many human endeavors, the desire for power and revenge corrupted this calling, leading some female seers to engage in rituals of cruelty rather than healing. However, amid this, there was also great harmony and unity in a few civilizations where men and women worked together in sacred partnership, each fulfilling their unique roles. This balance and mutual respect led to the flourishing of families and societies. This is the ideal we should strive to restore.

Amid this turmoil in that era arose Rama, a visionary inspired by a divine calling. As a result, he became one of the Hindu deities. He recognized that true social harmony depended on reuniting men and women in sacred partnership. Rama taught that man and woman embody complementary aspects of divinity: man, as the bearer of the divine flame, and woman, as the vessel of life and love. They could bring forth a radiant harmony that elevated both and sanctified their bond when joined with mutual reverence. This shared respect is not just a nicety but a necessity for restoring unity. It is the cornerstone of our journey toward harmony.

Yet even today, as we are more connected and technologically advanced, the ideal of unity has drifted further, leaving us questioning whether this kind of progress has brought us closer or merely highlighted our differences. Regarding relationships between men and women nowadays and technological progress, genuine connection requires more than just technology—it demands empathy, understanding, and action.

Economic development and the rise of individualism have deepened the divide, and the roles once revered are misunderstood or dismissed. For instance, many women no longer see themselves as life-givers, as the societal focus has shifted toward career and personal achievements, thereby competing with men, their partners, or their husbands. Similarly, many men are interested in pursuing self-centered pleasures, abusing their partners, using them for pleasures or economic profits, and neglecting their children rather than embodying the qualities of guidance and support essential to family life.

There is nothing wrong with economic development, just as there is nothing wrong with a knife. The problem is how we use the tool. It depends on our level of understanding, the level of our mind's evolution, and especially our will. Suppose our will is not genuinely educated to focus on using any tools, whether technology, wealth for our progression, or improving our relationships to improve our society and the world. In that case, we will use it to destroy us as well as the world.

Rather than envisioning marriage as a shared spiritual purpose, the once-clear vision of divine partnership has grown clouded, leading to a focus on material ambitions, exploitation, and the pursuit of deviant pleasures.

To heal this division, men and women must renew their understanding of their roles. They need to sincerely recognize their union's higher purpose—a sacred bond designed to create life, foster responsibility, and contribute to a peaceful society. They can achieve this divine mission only when they work together, each bringing forth their unique gifts. Men and women need to be united. Consequently, they will embody the flame and vessel to complete each other and fulfill their purpose; divided, they risk losing the very foundation of their shared destiny and be damned. But there is hope; God is merciful. With a renewed understanding and commitment, we—morally responsible educators, leaders, institutions, and governments—can restore the unity between them and, with it, the harmony and purpose that it brings. This hope for a better future should inspire us all, throughout all nations.

Before concluding this chapter, let's clarify the concept of sacred union and lawful marriage. It is essential to distinguish between sacred union and lawful marriage in modern society. These two concepts are fundamentally different. Historically, men and women did not require a priest or an official to validate their union. Instead, they took vows in nature—perhaps in the woods, in their simple homes, or before God—sincerely pledging themselves to each other from the depths of their hearts, minds, and souls. Some may have had witnesses, but the essence of their union was their mutual commitment. Due to life's challenges, they remained faithful, providing for and nurturing their families.

An English astrologer, Alan Leo, emphasized that a valid marriage is aligned with astrology and the stars. He observed that many legally married couples later separated and formed more profound, more lasting unions with others. Despite having children with their lawful spouses, some individuals found true love and stability only after parting ways. This suggests the real issue lies in the absence of authentic unions between men and women today. The confusion between sacred marriage and so-called lawful marriage is a significant dilemma. What truly matters is the intention behind the union. The marriage will ultimately deteriorate if the intention is not pure—with no sacred vision or meaningful purpose.

Numerous studies have examined modern marital trends and the phenomenon of family disintegration. In the United States, research shows that traditional two-parent households have declined, with increases in divorce, remarriage, and cohabitation. Factors such as shifting societal norms, economic challenges, and evolving attitudes toward marriage and family structures contribute to these trends. A 2015 Pew Research Center report revealed that only 46 percent of US children lived in a household with two married parents in their first marriage—a significant drop from 73 percent in 1960.

Given these findings, additional studies on the instability of unmarried or unlawfully married parents at the time of their child's birth may hold some validity. However, despite their initial close relationships, many legally married parents face significant challenges over time, leading to instability. The root of the problem is not the legal status of the marriage but the lack of moral responsibility, sacred vision, and shared ideals. Many couples fail because they do not understand the true meaning of family and union.

Today, men and women often marry legally for practical reasons, such as financial security and inheritance. Legal marriage serves an important function but should be entered authentically, with genuine commitment. Otherwise, it becomes a legal transaction—an arrangement for material wealth rather than a sacred partnership dedicated to raising a strong family and contributing to society.

Ultimately, marriage is sanctified by the individuals who take the vows, not by a priest, an officiant, or the grandeur of a ceremony. Rituals and legal formalities cannot make a marriage last—only the couple's understanding, moral responsibility, and sincere dedication to their shared vision can ensure its success.

This essay argues that the division between men and women has weakened relationships, broken families, and caused social instability after exploring the significance of sacred unity between men and women. Drawing on historical wisdom, spiritual teachings, and scientific studies as examples, it emphasizes that only through a renewed understanding of their roles and responsibilities can men and women restore harmony. With moral guidance and a commitment to a higher purpose, societies can flourish again by fostering meaningful, cooperative partnerships between them.

PART II

THE SPIRITUAL PILGRIMAGE'S CULTIVATION AND TRANSFORMATION TOWARD THE MONAD

8

WOMEN'S NATURE RESEMBLES FERTILE SOIL, CAPABLE OF GERMINATING SEEDS OF THOUGHT

Because women can nurture and bring forth seeds of thought planted in their minds, we can liken them to fertile soil—that is to say, much like fertile soil rich with potential. Their innate capacity for growth and cultivation transforms ideas into reality, illustrating their profound strength and influence. But what determines whether this soil—like the womb of thought—is capable of nurturing not only life, but also entire worlds of meaning, and whether it fosters what is good or what is destructive? How does women's ability to nurture and bring the ideas planted in their minds to life shape relationships, families, and societies? Women possess a unique ability to germinate and nurture the seeds sown into their minds and hearts, whether for good or ill.

This essay explores that how they are treated—whether with love, respect, wisdom, neglect, cruelty, or deception—significantly impacts their lives and the harmony or disharmony of families and communities. It examines the impact of this nurturing capacity, drawing on spiritual archetypes, everyday narratives, and modern realities to illustrate how women's nature shapes the world around them—either for creation or for its downfall.

When a loving man honors and respects his partner, he inspires her to bloom, creating an environment where joy and growth thrive. Together, they can form a sanctuary of love—a home and a community filled with vitality and purpose. On the other hand, a man devoid of wisdom who treats his partner with disrespect and cruelty risks transforming her into a reflection of his neglect. She will magnify what he sows into her, whether for creation or destruction.

Women are not merely nurturers; they are divine projects entrusted with the sacred power to bring life into form. God created men to embody wisdom and channel the spiritual into the earthly experience through their actions. To form a divine partnership, we should understand that men's and women's roles are complementary. Their partnership must reflect the harmonious balance and unity in the sacred, in heaven. In this partnership, men plant seeds of love, and women nurture and mold these seeds into reality. As a result, their unity creates a harmonious radiance that fulfills their shared destiny.

Men typically function at the conscious, rational level, which often limits their ability to directly access divine truths. Women, by contrast, are more attuned to their emotions and the subconscious. Such skill gives them a unique gift: the capacity to communicate with the divine more effortlessly. This interplay is beautifully depicted in the sixth Major Arcana of the tarot, "The Lovers." The card shows a man and a woman standing beneath a guiding angel in the sky. The man gazes at her while she looks toward the angel—a metaphor for their connection. In this metaphor, the man represents the conscious mind; the woman, the subconscious; and the angel, the divine.

The man gazing at the woman symbolizes that he must rely on her to understand the divine in addition to his rational mind. The woman gazing at the angel symbolizes that she is endowed with the natural ability to connect with the divine, provided she is worthy. This card in the tarot highlights that men and women, with their unique strengths, can form a harmonious relationship and develop together.

The story of Adam and Eve provides further insight. The serpent represents cunning and deception. It seduced Eve because it understood her unique capacity to germinate seeds within her. Throughout history, this truth is evident: Those seeking to elevate or corrupt humanity, a family, often begin by controlling women, knowing their impact will ripple outward.

This type of cunning and deception can also be observed in modern examples. For instance, corrupt individuals, such as pimps, manipulators, or fake preachers, exploit women, abusing, degrading, and mocking them to further destructive agendas, knowing how this will negatively influence families and communities. Unfortunately, they always, and will always, find naive women who do not understand who they are and their divine power, enabling these evil disciples to succeed. These individuals merely are manifesting an evil agenda in this world. But, in truth, in the Lord's terms, they will have their rewards at the end of the day; check the history record.

Conversely, a man rooted in wisdom and love can inspire a woman to build a strong, nurturing family and transform her environment for the better. Imagine that most men are determined to fulfill their roles as wise partners, and most women, in turn, develop a genuine will to nurture families with integrity and care. Such a world would radiate harmony, with flourishing families and thriving societies.

Note that when evil partners contaminate women in a previous relationship, there might be a disaster. Their powerful virus has one mission: Destroy other men in the next relationship, even their children, consciously or unconsciously. A sacred, heavenly union would be practically impossible to form between them. They may pretend for a while. It may be possible if the grace of God allows it or if He has a definite plan for them to show the world His power, provided they have the goodwill to make the relationship work.

The sacred union of men and women is not merely a partnership but a profound spiritual collaboration. They should embrace themselves to complement their roles and develop their partnership to a higher level. Through unity, they can achieve their highest potential, creating a legacy of love and wisdom and manifesting their divine purpose here on earth. They have no choice but to close their ears to deceiving and misleading spirits to nurture each other's spiritual growth and contribute to a more harmonious relationship for their evolution.

The cycle of love and trauma in families' lives is a consequence of our choices. Note that when we experience trauma, sometimes it may be the consequence of a bad choice because we were not looking for genuine love. We often see women who have been mistreated in relationships struggling to form healthy bonds later. A woman who finds a loving man, not because she was lucky or privileged but because of her sincere desire for authentic love, becomes nurtured with love and respect and builds a strong family, fostering kindness and stability in children. Conversely, we often see some women who pick the wrong guys, be it for fame or wealth or power or because of their naivete, enduring emotional abuse and perhaps unknowingly pass trauma forward, affecting future generations.

This essay has argued that women are not just nurturers but powerful amplifiers of what is sown within them. Whether in relationships, families, or society, they magnify love, pain, wisdom, or folly, depending on how they are treated. This essay discussed how women who receive love and wisdom create substantial homes and inspire social progress. However, when subjected to deception and cruelty, they may unintentionally perpetuate cycles of suffering. Some of us may rightly note that this principle also extends to men—for when men are wounded by betrayal or harshness, they, too, can become vessels of further pain. The human soul, regardless of sex, tends to echo what it has received. Yet women's unique relational and generational influence, particularly within the formative spaces of the home and heart, gives their role as amplifiers a particular gravity. Thus, how we treat women is not a private matter—it is a matter of legacy, of the kind of world we are sowing for those who come after us.

9

REDISCOVERING OUR DIVINE PURPOSE TO BE WHOLE

W e learn from history that most humans have sought fulfillment through wealth, power, and personal ambition, often feeling empty despite outward success. What is the true source of human fulfillment, and how does aligning with our divine purpose lead to wholeness?

This essay discusses how genuine happiness is not something we can manufacture; rather, it is a by-product of living by the purpose for which we were created.

No amount of material wealth, titles, or awards can substitute for the joy that comes from aligning with our destiny and living in harmony with universal laws. If we want to discover and fully develop ourselves, we must embrace the divine design.

Blinded by ignorance and the influence of misguided forces, many stray onto paths that lead them away from their true calling. Tragically, this awareness often dawns too late after we have ventured too far from the way meant for us. We were not born to live in conflict or to embrace evil, for God created us in His image. When we act contrary to that image, we experience deep dissatisfaction, for we are at odds with our nature.

Humanity suffers when we reject cooperation and unity under God's laws. This rejection is not just a personal choice. Still, it is a collective responsibility. Cooperation requires more than working together—it demands that we respect the unique roles we were created to fulfill. When we envy or attempt to usurp the purpose of another, we abandon the complementarity meant to bring us together as a whole.

Deviation from our divine roles is not only a betrayal of God but also of ourselves. Without self-love, rooted in understanding and acceptance of our purpose, we cannot love others. And without love for one another, we resist God's decrees, setting ourselves against eternal reason. Ancient wisdom teaches that opposition to divine will bring both chastisement and a profound sense of loss and emptiness. This is not from cruelty but from the immutable justice of eternal truth.

Observe those who have chosen to fight against God's reason. They may appear happy, but their inner void and lack of fulfillment expose their facade. True happiness cannot be manufactured. Happiness can emanate from living by the divine purpose. We will be chastised by eternal reason when we choose to live otherwise. So we will never enjoy the peace and fulfillment that come from loving God, ourselves, and one another.

We should ask ourselves this straightforward question about the present state of our lives: Will we choose the path of wholeness, or will we persist in the emptiness of resistance? Let us reflect profoundly and realign ourselves with the source; only then can we find true happiness and meaning.

In real life, in the news or in literature, individuals are depicted as searching for fulfillment in the wrong places, only to realize that true happiness comes from embracing a higher purpose. We have seen or heard about many celebrities who chase material success, status, and love, believing they will bring them happiness. Yet despite their wealth, they remain deeply unfulfilled; they marry and remarry many times and get involved in many relationships in their quest for happiness, but in vain, symbolizing the emptiness that results from seeking purpose outside of moral and spiritual truth.

This essay has argued that true happiness is not found in material success, competition, or self-serving ambitions but in embracing our divine purpose. When we reject our true calling, we experience deep dissatisfaction and suffering, individually and collectively. It has been argued that we can realign ourselves with the source of true fulfillment by trying to recognize that cooperation, self-understanding, and adherence to God's laws are essential for wholeness. The question remains for each of us: Will we choose the path of wholeness or persist in the emptiness of resistance?

10

THE BLIND PATH TO PERIL

THE DANGERS OF IGNORANCE AND
MISGUIDED VALUES

M any of us, perhaps because we did not have the opportunity to be influenced by enlightened institutions during our formative years or because of our own willful choices, have become blind—carrying a heavy load of misguided ideas and values that are far removed from universal morality. The peril is right before us, as menacing as a crocodile and more significant than a dinosaur, jaws wide open, waiting for us to walk straight into its maw. Despite the warnings from those who still see clearly, we march headlong toward danger, ignoring the signs and the voices urging us to stop. Unenlightened peers, institutions, and culture often influence our choices, which may shape our destinies. Yet, too, usually because of our naive compliance, we fail to question whether these choices align with universal morality.

This essay seeks to answer a crucial question: Can we awaken from our blindness before we fall into the abyss of ignorance and self-destruction? In addition, this essay highlights why it is essential to pair discernment with conscious decision-making in shaping a meaningful and fulfilling life by examining the dangers of misguided values. Furthermore, it discusses reclaiming our discernment to lead more meaningful and fulfilling lives.

The predicament outlined above arose because the institutions that should be educating us about the nature of good and evil have instead enslaved us to the forces of ignorance and error, rendering us ignorant to the truth. But we must remember that we have the power of discernment. We can choose to listen to the wisdom of those who attempt to warn us of the impending dangers. Do we have the courage to open our eyes and ears to the truth to seek a life guided by universal morality? If we can do that, such realization should empower us to take control of our journey and avoid the unseen threats that lie in wait.

Life is a beautiful gift, a precious opportunity to explore and grow. Yet there are hidden dangers that threaten to derail our destiny. One such danger is the influence of peers. Some powerful institutions also have convinced us that life is too short, so we should waste it on pleasures of all kinds; in other words, enjoy it. They promote a lifestyle of superficial pleasures, leading us to believe that endless parties, drugs, and reckless behavior are the only ways to make the most of our time on Earth. But we should ask: In what way do frivolous pleasures help us make good use of our time toward our progression in this life? Empty pleasures cannot help us to see the beauty of life and develop the potential for more profound, more fulfilling experiences. Self-discovery, self-development, and self-realization require activities beyond these superficial distractions. Thinking about realization should inspire us to seek a more meaningful existence.

While there is nothing inherently wrong with entertainment, it must be wholesome, uplifting, and in harmony with the values that elevate our souls. God created us to work hard and to enjoy the fruits of our labor, but we must choose amusement that nurtures our spirit, not one that drags us into the depths of misery and hinders our spiritual evolution. Any form of enjoyment that does not bring us into communion with the universe and the divine is, in essence, a destructive act.

When we partake in harmful pleasures, we create "ghosts"— manifestations of our unresolved errors and regrets—that haunt our lives. These ghosts give rise to "vampires," symbolic of the forces that drain our spirit and bind us in a cycle of despair. Ancient wisdom teaches us that whoever surrenders to error becomes its prey, caught in a trap of his or her own making.

The dangers we face are external and rooted in our choices and the institutions shaping our understanding of good and evil. We must open our eyes and ears to the wisdom of those who warn us and seek a life guided by universal morality. Only then can we avoid the open jaws of the metaphorical crocodile and forge a destiny that aligns with the higher principles of life and creation.

Several literary and real-life examples illustrate the dangers of ignorance and misguided values; for instance, consider the contemporary example of the impact of social media culture. Many young people today are influenced by trends promoting superficial pleasures—obsessing over material wealth, viral fame, or reckless lifestyles—only to feel empty, anxious, or depressed. The rise of influencers, heavily encouraged by their fans by their likes to show their sick admiration, who later regret their past reckless behavior is a classic case in point.

Undeniably, blind adherence to societal influences, misguided values, naivete, and unwillingness to use our discernment will automatically lead us toward perilous and unfulfilling, sterile spiritual lives. In other words, when we fail to question the unenlightened values of institutions, societies, or our peers, we often face disastrous consequences. However, we are not powerless—we can discern truth, reject destructive influences, and seek a life guided by universal morality. The challenge remains: Will we choose to open our eyes before it is too late, or will we continue marching toward the jaws of peril, unaware of the danger ahead?

11

THE PERILS OF VIOLENT AMBITION
DISORDER, EVIL, AND THE PHILOSOPHY OF MACBETH

Throughout history, ambition has been a defining trait of great leaders and visionaries, yet Shakespeare's *Macbeth* warns of its perilous nature when pursued through immoral means. Using violence inherently corrupts ambition and leads to chaos, disorder, and the demise of those who wield it.

This essay examines a central philosophical question: Can noble ambitions ever be genuinely realized through violence, or does seeking good through evil corrupt the intended goal? Through the tragic descent of Macbeth and Lady Macbeth, Shakespeare illustrates that violence is not merely a tool of power but a force that inevitably breeds disorder and self-destruction. The play serves as a warning, demonstrating that pursuing power through bloodshed does not secure greatness but enslaves the individual to chaos, guilt, and moral decay.

Desiring good through violence is as unjust as desiring evil. Furthermore, violence leads to disorder, which is the root of all evil. This perspective provides a fitting lens through which to interpret the tragic arc of Shakespeare's Macbeth. In this play, he makes Macbeth and Lady Macbeth symbolize the dangerous allure of achieving noble ends through ignoble means. Their actions illustrate a fundamental philosophical principle: Violence will corrupt the essence of the intended goal, even in the pursuit of good. Our actions will lead to chaos, suffering, and the erosion of moral integrity. Violence, in this context, becomes not a tool of justice but a catalyst for self-destruction. Any influential people's will that takes this direction is a perverse one that ultimately enslaves its perpetrators to their downfall.

In the opening act, Macbeth is introduced as a noble warrior admired for his loyalty and bravery. Yet the witch's prophecy awakens a latent ambition within him—a desire not merely for power but for what he perceives as a rightful, good end: the throne of Scotland. Macbeth has a clear awareness of the inherent danger in forcing the prophecy's fulfillment through violent means:

"If chance will have me king, why, chance may crown me / Without my stir."

This line reflects a brief adherence to the fact that acting violently for the sake of good undermines the very virtue we seek to attain. Macbeth's hesitation shows his fleeting grasp of the paradox that violence, even in the service of a noble cause, will have consequences of disorder and moral decay. Indeed, having ambition is not wrong, but it should always be guided by wisdom. Once planted without the guidance of discernment, the seed of ambition will decay sooner or later, overshadowing good intentions.

Lady Macbeth's influence tips the scale, persuading Macbeth to abandon reason in favor of a perverse will. She embodies the inversion of natural order and morality. Her invocation of dark spirits to "unsex" her reveals her willingness to abandon feminine tenderness and moral restraint to achieve her goals. In urging Macbeth to murder Duncan, she exemplifies the philosophical notion that a perverse will—the desire for good through evil acts —is the beginning of self-inflicted ruin. Her famous plea— *"Look like th' innocent flower, / But be the serpent under 't"*—encapsulates the fundamental deception at the heart of their plan. Lady Macbeth and Macbeth attempt to defy the natural and moral order by masking their violent intent with a veneer of virtue. Yet as philosophy teaches, disorder bred from violence cannot remain hidden; it seeps into the very fabric of the psyche, creating a dissonance that leads to self-destruction.

Macbeth's descent into moral chaos is evident in his soliloquy in act 1, scene 7, where he acknowledges that his only spur is "vaulting ambition." He realizes that to pursue the throne through murder is an act of self-sabotage:

"I have no spur / To prick the sides of my intent, but only / Vaulting ambition, which o'erleaps itself / And falls on th' other."

Here, Macbeth articulates a central philosophical truth: When ambition vaults beyond the bounds of moral restraint, it inevitably collapses under its weight. In choosing violence, he enslaves himself to a course that leads not to the good he desires but to a progressive erosion of his humanity. His decision to murder Duncan marks the moment his will becomes perverse. And his perverted will set in motion a chain of events that lead to his suicide. Macbeth kills his moral self by taking another's life for personal gain, a prelude to his physical demise.

Once the line is crossed, Macbeth's actions exemplify the philosophical assertion that violence creates disorder, and disorder is the principle of evil. The murder of Duncan, a king chosen by divine right, symbolizes a direct assault on the natural order. When the natural order is assaulted, unnatural events may follow

—horses eating one another and the sky darkening in the middle of the day. Any assault on the cosmic harmony can produce corresponding bad omens or anomalies.

Macbeth's actions create ghosts and give birth to vampires because he indulges in violence and becomes its prey. This descent into disorder is mirrored in his psychological turmoil. Macbeth's hallucinations, such as the vision of the bloody dagger and Banquo's ghost, represent the internal manifestation of the chaos he has wrought in the external world. His mind becomes a battleground of guilt and paranoia. He becomes the prey of his violent actions and enslaves himself to a perpetual state of fear and unrest. The more he attempts to secure his position through further acts of violence, the more profound his internal disorder becomes, illustrating the inexorable link between external tyranny and internal disintegration.

When our will is perverted and we inspire others to act evilly, it does not matter if we are not the one who executes the evil action: We will suffer the appropriate consequences. That is why Lady Macbeth, who once seemed impervious to the moral qualms that plagued her husband, eventually succumbs to the same fate. Her descent into madness, marked by the famous sleepwalking scene, reveals the ultimate price of her perverse will. As she compulsively tries to wash away the "damned spot" of Duncan's blood, she confronts the inescapable reality of her actions:

"What, will these hands ne'er be clean?"

This line sadly captures the symbolic truth that we cannot physically clean the stains of violence because they are the permanent marks of an infected soul to the core. Lady Macbeth's unraveling mind is the final testament to the self-destructive nature of desiring good through evil acts. Her eventual suicide serves as the literal manifestation of the philosophical assertion that a perverse will is the beginning of suicide—she becomes the architect of her demise, unable to live with the disorder she has unleashed.

In the final act, Macbeth's realization of the futility of his violent quest encapsulates the play's philosophical message. As he faces the collapse of his empire and the death of his wife, he muses on the meaninglessness of his achievements:

"Life's but a walking shadow, a poor player / That struts and frets his hour upon the stage / And then is heard no more."

These lines express Macbeth's regrets about rejecting his dear moral principles under the evil influences. They made him foster violent ambition, which he believed would grant him ultimate power, but instead led him to a state of existential despair. Evil turned his desire for good—a stable and robust kingship—to a dark path, obliterating any true purpose or fulfillment. Like Macbeth, sooner or later, we realize that any violent acts have the potential to enslave us to a fate worse than death: a life devoid of meaning, consumed by chaos and disorder.

Shakespeare's *Macbeth* teaches us to avoid becoming prey to violence. We must always make wise decisions and never seek good through violence. The play's tragic curve affirms the philosophical principle that brutality is not a neutral tool but a force that inherently corrupts the desired ends, transforming noble ambition into destructive chaos. A perverse will is the beginning of suicide, and Macbeth and Lady Macbeth, in their pursuit of power, exemplify the self-destructive nature of such perverse will. Their choices lead not to fulfilling their desires but to the disintegration of their souls and the unraveling of the social order they sought to control.

Macbeth is a philosophical exploration of the consequences of violent ambition. The play demonstrates that when we attempt to achieve noble ends through ignoble means, we will not attain our desired success but instead become victims of our actions.

Macbeth and Lady Macbeth's pursuit of power through murder leads to psychological torment, moral corruption, and, ultimately, their downfall. The play affirms that violence disrupts the natural and moral order, causing those who wield it to suffer under its weight. In the end, *Macbeth* warns that ambition must be guided by wisdom and morality, for to desire good through evil is to invite self-destruction.

12

THE SACRED ELECTRIC FIRE
THE MORAL AND PHILOSOPHICAL
DIMENSIONS OF ADVANCED TECHNOLOGY

Today's highly advanced technology can be seen as a "sacred electric fire" set forth by the universe's intelligence, inspiring scientists to develop it in the service of humanity. Like any mighty force, it will serve those who master it and may unleash its destructive potential against those who abuse it. Because humanity faces a profound ethical dilemma in an age where technological innovation accelerates at an unprecedented pace, how should we balance the power of technology with our moral and ethical responsibilities to ensure it serves humanity rather than harms it?

This essay investigates how we can harness innovation responsibly while safeguarding human dignity, autonomy, and well-being. It evaluates how technology impacts privacy, mental health, social connections, and existential self-realization by examining utilitarian and deontological ethical frameworks.

Individuals, corporations, and governments have held an immense responsibility to wield the sacred fire of technology development with wisdom. The far-reaching impacts of technological progress necessitate a foundation in moral philosophy to guide its ethical use and development.

Whom should technology serve the most? From a practical perspective, for instance, the authority must achieve the greatest good for the most significant number. In other words, for an action to be correct, it should be helpful to the majority or benefit the majority, which can be applied to technological innovations. However, the potential for technology to inflict harm also necessitates the consideration of deontological ethics, which emphasizes duties and individual rights.

From a deontological perspective, ethical technology use requires respect for individual privacy, mental health, and autonomy, even when the broader benefits are substantial. The tension between utilitarian goals (such as enhanced security) and deontological principles (such as the right to privacy) becomes apparent in the debate around surveillance technology.

How far should we pursue technological advancements if they infringe on individual freedoms or dignity? Is developing potentially destructive technologies, such as autonomous weapons, morally acceptable if their misuse could result in catastrophic consequences? Here, we are more focused on the potential of technology to affect our self-realization.

There is no question that in this age of advanced technology, we have an ethical problem that needs to be solved. We have seen that technology has extended our capabilities. We have unprecedented access to the information it offers; the connection is fantastic, and the innovation improves our lives a great deal. At the same time, we have to deal with the risks of diminishing essential aspects of our moral and social fabric, such as empathy, face-to-face interaction, and genuine connection, which is hindering our progress on the path of evolution.

We need to exercise prudence and temperance in our technological endeavors. Restraint can help ensure that technology becomes a force for good rather than a destructive tool.

The notion of technology as a sacred electric fire invokes the image of Prometheus bringing fire to humanity—a gift that brings both enlightenment and potential peril. Technology is like a knife; it has a dual aspect. A knife can be used for good or evil purposes; it depends on the moral value of the user. So just as we educate people to use a knife for beneficial purposes, we should motivate citizens to use technology for their advancement. This task can be done by elevating our collective consciousness, shared awareness, and understanding of the moral implications of our actions and moral wisdom, which involves making ethical decisions based on this shared understanding. Our civilization cannot afford for technology to lead us into more profound ethical and existential quandaries.

The psychological implications of technology are profound, shaping how we think, feel, and interact with the world. Not only does research indicate that the overuse of social media can raise the level of depression, anxiety, and loneliness, especially among young people, but many of us who are not science-savvy can notice this in our lives. This paradoxical effect—where technology designed to connect us may also contribute to feelings of isolation —highlights its complex influence on mental health. The list of ways technology can hinder the conditions of being human can go on and on; it can destroy our relationships, reduce our capacity for deep, reflective thinking, diminish our authenticity, and increase pressure to conform when we become heavily dependent on it.

A careful examination of technology's effects suggests that while it offers convenience and access, it also comes with significant problems. Cultivating mindfulness and self-awareness in our digital interactions becomes essential to prevent being burned from this powerful sacred fire.

It is imperative to educate users to see its benefits and dangers. Rather than approaching it merely as a tool for progress, we can see technology as a sacred gift that demands careful, thoughtful stewardship.

Consider the example of Facebook and the Cambridge Analytica scandal to illustrate the ethical dilemmas surrounding technology. This was a major data privacy breach that emerged in 2018, revealing how the data analytics firm Cambridge Analytica improperly accessed the personal information of over 87 million Facebook users without their consent. The firm used this data to build detailed psychological profiles, which were then exploited for targeted political advertising during major events like the 2016 US presidential election and the Brexit referendum. The scandal exposed serious ethical concerns about privacy violations, data misuse, and the role of big tech in influencing public opinion.

This essay has examined the dual nature of technological progress—its immense potential for human advancement and its profound ethical risks. We have explored how misused technology can infringe on privacy, erode mental well-being, and diminish authentic human connections by analyzing utilitarian and deontological perspectives—real-world examples of serious ethical concerns. Ultimately, the challenge of the twenty-first century is not merely advancing technology but ensuring it aligns with moral principles that protect individual dignity, autonomy, and societal well-being. As we stand at the crossroads of innovation, the true test of progress lies in whether we can temper our technological ambitions with moral wisdom, ensuring that this sacred electric fire illuminates rather than consumes us.

THE RELATIONSHIP BETWEEN
IMPATIENCE AND TIME

WHEN IMPATIENCE MAKES TIME OUR
ENEMY

I n contemporary society, time is often seen as our most limited resource—something to be managed, conserved, or even conquered. We meticulously plan our lives around it, striving to maximize productivity and efficiency. But do most of us ever consider the role of impatience in this practical approach to time? Impatience can transform our time from a neutral continuum into a relentless adversary; that is to say, our impatience can distort our perception of time.

This essay explores how a lack of patience weaponizes time against us, making it not merely a passive dimension but an active force of resistance. It is noticeable that, from our experiences and those of others, impatience does not make us powerful or productive in any endeavor. Instead, it creates frustration and failure, while patience allows us to harmonize our efforts with the natural flow of time. Although patience might appear like inaction, at the end of the day, when we achieve our goals, it becomes the highest form of energy.

Time, in its essence, is impartial. It is an ever-present river, flowing continuously, unaffected by our wishes or concerns. As the Greek philosopher Heraclitus noted, "No man ever steps in the same river twice, for it is not the same river, and he is not the same man." Time constantly changes, moving forward without pause, and our perception shapes our experiences. When we approach time with patience, it becomes a canvas upon which we can carefully and thoughtfully paint our lives. However, when we approach it with impatience, we experience tremendous anxiety; we may have an angry outburst because we cannot perform under such circumstances, making time feel like an unyielding barrier rather than an open horizon.

Philosophical traditions such as Stoicism and Taoism have long emphasized the importance of patience as a guiding virtue. The Stoics, particularly Marcus Aurelius, argued that aligning oneself with the universe's natural order requires accepting the flow of time with stability. In *Meditations*, Aurelius writes, "Time is like a river made up of the events which happen, and a violent stream; for as soon as a thing has been seen, it is carried away, and another comes in its place, and this will be carried away, too." One way to deal with the tyrant of impatience and stop it from persecuting our time is to adopt the Stoic approach that teaches us to embrace the present moment and accept what comes with patience rather than trying to rush or force outcomes.

Similarly, Taoism offers wisdom on the natural flow of time. We are more likely to fail when we hurry or rush a project. In the *Tao Te Ching*, Lao Tzu encourages us to use the virtue of effortless action, which involves aligning one's actions with the universe's rhythms. In this view, patience is not passivity but an active attunement to the natural unfolding of events, the attitude, and the state of mind to let everything unfold in its turn. Working with time means developing patience. Developing impatience is working against time, and such an attitude will negatively alter our experience. In our rush to achieve immediate results, we distort the temporal dimension, making it seem like an oppressive force. The philosopher Søren Kierkegaard described this phenomenon in his analysis of anxiety and despair. Kierkegaard argued that impatience is rooted in a deep existential discomfort with the present moment. We become so fixated on a desired future that we lose sight of the present, experiencing it only as a series of delays or obstacles. Time appears to conspire against us in this state, stretching forever as if mocking our inability to control it.

Modern culture glorifies speed and efficiency, equating faster outcomes with better results. However, as the French philosopher Henri Bergson argued in the essay "Time and Free Will," there is a difference between "clock time" (measurable, linear time) and "lived time" (our subjective experience of duration). When we become impatient, we live in clock time, obsessively measuring and counting movements. We lose the sense of lived time, where moments are filled with meaning and presence. Ironically, when we are trying to accelerate the process and cannot wait to see a result, we waste time because we make more mistakes, overlook details, and fail to appreciate the gradual progress of our work.

Patience requires deliberate work. We need to leave room for the slow by cutting back on instant gratification, the longing for quick results, and instant rewards that have the power to exacerbate our impatience, making time feel even more adversarial. As the philosopher Byung-Chul Han notes in *The Burnout Society*, our culture of speed and hyperactivity leads to a "crisis of temporality," where we lose the ability to engage deeply with time. We become overwhelmed, unable to tolerate any delay, and thus, we make time our enemy.

If impatience makes time an enemy, patience can reclaim it as an ally. Patience is an active, intentional practice that allows us to slow down, focus on the process, and find satisfaction in incremental progress. The French Jesuit priest Pierre Teilhard de Chardin captures this sentiment beautifully in his prayer: "Above all, trust in the slow work of God. We are quite naturally impatient in everything to reach the end without delay." These words remind us that patience is a form of trust—in time, in the process, and in our unfolding.

We align ourselves with the natural pace of life by embracing patience. A greedy mentality sees time as a scarce resource to be put in the bank, like money, or conquered like a city to find gold. We should start viewing it as a companion on our journey. The development of this state of mind will transform our experience of time. It will become a space for reflection, growth, and the organic development of our projects and dreams.

Ultimately, time is not our real enemy—our impatience is. Our internal battle is against our restless desires and inability to be present fully in the moment. Cultivating patience does not mean that we are passively waiting. It means we are engaging deeply with the present. We are allowing time to work for us rather than against us. Some of us may believe or feel that patience slows us down, but it does not—instead, it liberates us from emotional tyranny, turning a potential adversary into our greatest ally.

In any crucial situation, we need to choose patience over impatience. By doing so, we align ourselves with the flow of time and practice our trust in its silent wisdom. Paraphrasing Confucius, patience is one of the key virtues that, when developed, will enable us to abide long in a condition of poverty and hardship or enjoyment. When we develop patience, time becomes the gentle guide, allowing us to enjoy our lives with harmony and grace.

To illustrate how impatience can backfire and make time our worst enemy, consider this example of impatience in a typical workplace that leads to outcomes contrary to genuine intentions. Imagine an employee eager for a promotion who rushes through tasks to showcase their efficiency. Consequently, this haste results in overlooked details and errors. At the end of the day, the rush delays progress, damages the professional reputation of that employee, and causes them to lose the job.

Next, imagine an individual starting a fitness regimen but expecting quick results. When immediate changes aren't visible, that person becomes discouraged, abandons the routine, and then quits; consequently, they never experience the long-term benefits. This reflects how impatience can undermine our goals, whereas patience and persistence are essential for personal growth.

When we force outcomes, we open our doors to mistakes, stress, and unfulfilled aspirations; we disturb the natural flow of events. Patience is not mere passivity but an active and intentional practice that allows us to align with time rather than fight against it. If we do not open the door to patience, we also do not open ourselves to clarity, resilience, and appreciation for the process. To grow, adapt, and achieve meaningful success in our endeavors, we must embrace time as a guide, not an obstacle. To master it, we must develop our ability to slow down, trust the process, and allow life to unfold at its own pace. Doing so turns time from a relentless force into a powerful ally, leading to a more harmonious and fulfilling life.

14

THE BLINDNESS TO TRUTH

ITS CAUSE AND HOW WE CAN CURE THAT DISEASE OR PROTECT OURSELVES FROM CONTAMINATION

W hy do some people fail to see or accept the truth, even when it's plainly in front of them? Is it a matter of intelligence or education? This blindness is often a consequence of deep-seated psychological tendencies, social conditioning, ideological influences, and moral shortcomings. Blindness to the truth, a dangerous disease, can be spread by the media's manipulation of information and other institutions and the ego's resistance to change. Various forces shape our perceptions and obscure reality. Through the lenses of sociology, psychology, moral philosophy, and spirituality, this essay examines the causes of truth blindness. It explores ways to cultivate critical thinking, intellectual humility, and spiritual discernment to cure that disease. Understanding these obstacles is crucial for reclaiming clarity of thought and authentic engagement with reality in this world of illusion where so many so-called authorities hide behind beautiful masks of deception and their selfish agenda and spread misinformation and ideological bias.

The truth may be before our eyes and close to our noses for us to see and smell, but for some reason, we cannot detect it. Those of us who are fortunate enough to do so may find it difficult to understand why other people cannot.

Losing our sense of the truth can significantly impact our quality of life. It can greatly affect our emotions, making us incapable of participating adequately in any debate. That is to say, we get so angry that we become disrespectful instead of using sound sense. Do we need support, in such a case, to function well? Yes. A more critical question is, why can some of us not know the truth, even when it is right in front of us?

This question cuts to the heart of philosophical inquiry, revealing deep-seated psychological biases, social conditioning, and ethical shortcomings. Let's attempt to briefly explore the issue of blindness to the truth through several perspectives to open some people's eyes.

1. Sociology: The Power of Social Conditioning and Media Influence

Our blindness to truth can be attributed to the social frameworks that shape our perception of reality. According to the social construction theory of reality, we consider what is "real" not an objective truth, but a socially constructed narrative influenced by culture, institutions, and language.

- Media Influence: The media uses manipulation tactics to influence public perception to align with a political ideology. It prioritizes information that aligns with its political, social, psychological, or economic agendas, depending on the media outlet. Media that leans liberal will only push information that promotes liberal ideas, and vice versa. The media can construct reality and limit our understanding, creating a myopia that shapes our worldview without us realizing it.

- Cultural Hegemony: Italian philosopher Antonio Gramsci's concept of cultural hegemony is also relevant here. We are prone to accept as "common sense" the ideas the political elites and our education system promote, especially when the media reinforces these specific ideas. These automatically become the dominant cultural narratives. This ideological dominance closes our eyes to alternative perspectives, making it difficult to see beyond our constructed reality. Days and nights, we are fed a constant stream of specific information that may be supported by preexisting beliefs, which as a result reinforces our biases. This informational environment creates a cultural prison, which makes breaking free from these ideological constraints harder.

2. Psychology: Cognitive Biases and the Tyranny of the Ego

Cognitive biases, emotional attachments, and the ego's need for validation interact complexly. This interplay may be another problem that prevents us from recognizing the truth.

- Cognitive Dissonance: When confronted with evidence contradicting our beliefs, we experience cognitive dissonance. It is an attitude that plays a crucial role in guiding us in resolving inconsistency that creates psychological discomfort when we encounter information that conflicts with or contradicts our beliefs. Rather than accepting the new information, we reject it or rationalize ways to alleviate the discomfort. For example, people deeply invested in a particular ideology may ignore facts that challenge their worldview because the emotional cost of accepting the truth is too painful.

- The Ego's Defense Mechanisms: Carl Jung makes an essential distinction between the ego and the self (or should I say, instead of the lower and higher selves). Our personality, the ego, is concerned with maintaining its current identity, even at the expense of truth. So to protect our lower self, or personality, from feelings too difficult to process or admit a fact that contradicts our beliefs, we tend to construct defense mechanisms like denial, projection, and rationalization. The higher self, however, places its interest in truth and integration, pushing us toward growth and self-awareness. If we operate at the level of the higher self, it becomes easier for us to accept the truth. When we prioritize the ego's comfort over the expansion of the higher self, we become blind to deeper truths.

- Confirmation Bias: We tend to lean toward information that confirms our beliefs. When defending our interests, we seek information that only confirms our opinions; this is called confirmation bias. In other words, we further entrench our blindness. We use this bias to filter out truths that do not align with our views, beliefs, and political or social agenda, making it difficult to objectively analyze and accept new information.

3. Moral Philosophy: The Ethics of Truth-Seeking and Intellectual Integrity

Philosophically, having a genuine disposition to find the truth is imperative. Without moral responsibility, we cannot detect the truth. Only people with good faith, not bad faith, can recognize the truth when they encounter it.

- The Virtue of Intellectual Humility: According to Aristotle, virtues lie between extremes. In the case of truth-seeking, the key virtue is intellectual humility, the willingness to admit when we are wrong and to revise our beliefs accordingly. This requires a lot of courage and humility to overcome the arrogance of the lower ego, our personality, which clings to certain traits even in the face of reality.
- The Moral Imperative for Truth: Socrates emphasized the importance of the examined life in his search for wisdom. Only those of us willing to live in ignorance refuse to seek the truth. We should train our will to strive to develop genuine knowledge. Once we understand that, it will become easy to recognize the truth. We should not accept anything at face value. Instead, we should question everything, including values and ideologies, before accepting them. We may use our intuitive faculties added to our reasoning power that God endowed us to develop a nicely balanced mind capable of great power to discriminate between truths and lies. Such faculties will always help uncover deeper truths, challenge assumptions, and dismantle false beliefs.

4. Spiritual Awareness: Transcending the Ego's Illusion

In spirituality, the ego—our personality fabricated by this illusory world—is the primary barrier to seeing reality. In Hindu philosophy, the veil of illusion, or Maya, symbolizes the deceptive layer of perceptions that obscure the more profound truth of our existence. It is indeed deceptive. If we do not see it that way and rely on the media, especially the unenlightened ones, for the truth, we will never truly see it.

- The Path of Mindfulness: Mindfulness practices in Buddhism and modern psychology offer a way to transcend the ego's illusions. It becomes easy to see the truth when we cultivate our awareness, develop our observation ability about ourselves and world patterns, and control our thoughts and emotions to avoid becoming entangled with them. This practice can help us see through the thick veil of the stories we tell ourselves and the narratives imposed on us by society.
- Awakening to the Higher Self: Once our higher self is awakened, a state of consciousness transcending the limited lower perspective, we will be able to vibrate at a higher level or frequency. Then we can access a deeper level of awareness to help us see the truth.

To avoid falling prey to ideological blindness, we must develop a multifaceted approach:

1. Critical Thinking: It is crucial to train our minds to cultivate skepticism of any information or knowledge, especially when it comes from powerful institutions,

the media, social media, and even religious leaders. Because we are human, creatures full of bias, we must rely on our genuine intuition to confirm or discard the information, using common sense to question the source, motives, and validity of the ideas we encounter.

2. Spiritual Discernment: Use spiritual discernment, engage in mindfulness and meditation to quiet the mind, and detach from the ego's narratives. We need to first seek alignment with the higher self, which is more attuned to truth and inner wisdom, to recognize the truth when we see it. Here, it is worth making the distinction between intuition and discernment. Intuition is the soul's whisper, an unshakable feeling that something is wrong even when all appears beautiful, perfect, or reasonable. It is that gut feeling, the internal nudge that always warns us that something is wrong, urging us to look deeper for the truth. This is where discernment should take over. Like a sharp blade of wisdom that cuts through deception, its function is to reveal to us the hidden motives and veiled agendas lurking beneath the surface. Its job is to analyze, see patterns, refine, and recognize the more profound truth behind the illusion. While intuition senses the storm behind the calm, discernment unveils the architect, the blueprint of the illusion. One warns; the other reveals. For instance, intuition might whisper, "Something isn't right here," while discernment confirms, "Here's why it's not right." Note that their marriage will give birth to true wisdom—the ability to feel the falsehood and to identify its source, to navigate a world where

beauty can be a mask and truth is often concealed beneath layers of manipulation.

3. Moral Courage: Even when it makes us uncomfortable or challenges our beliefs, we should be committed to seeking truth. As a result, a genuine calm will underlie our turmoil and give us the foundation on which to live a peaceful life. Recognize that personal growth and collective well-being depend on our willingness to accept reality and reject lies.

Institutions are impersonal, meaning they neither harm nor benefit anyone. It is the actions and attitudes of citizens—its human members—that make institutions appear biased. According to Dutch philosopher Baruch Spinoza, emotions and external circumstances drive our actions, and we often do not fully understand our emotions. He explained that emotions such as fear, anger, and jealousy often stem from misunderstandings of ourselves and the world around us.

These emotions are natural, but they can trap us in bondage, limiting our ability to express our higher, or divine, selves. For example, the unenlightened media often fails to present the truth to its audience because its members are influenced by emotional bondage—fears of being canceled by managers, anger toward political figures or personalities they dislike, and jealousy of successful, prominent individuals.

Most of us lack both the will and the interest to explore our emotions and the external forces that influence us. This lack of understanding makes it difficult for us to manage our emotions or present the truth as it is. Consequently, we lose the ability to genuinely help our audience improve their lives.

Consumed by the demands of competition, our hectic schedules, and our personal issues, we rarely find moments of solitude to appreciate beauty, discover our true selves, or embrace the freedom of authentic expression. Without this foundation, we cannot cultivate the intuition necessary to seek and reveal the truth. When we are trapped in our own emotions and life circumstances, can we truly be free to help others escape their ignorance and challenges? Is that a reasonable question we should ask?

Suppose the unenlightened media members want to help us escape our ignorance. In that case, it is straightforward: Make a genuine effort to acknowledge their emotional problems and understand the causes behind their emotions and the laws governing them. Spinoza said that emotions are natural reactions with predictable patterns, like any other part of the universe; by studying these patterns behind our reactions, we can learn to manage them, finding peace and stability instead of being upset by every passing feeling and making others' lives miserable. According to Spinoza, our emotions, such as anger, fear, hate, and jealousy, which are passions, cease to be passions as soon as we form a clear, distinct idea of them. Once we sincerely understand that, internalize this theory, and apply it in our daily lives, we can improve our lives and society. The media's role in this process is crucial. They will no longer have the will to contaminate their audience with their viruses because they will be free from them. In Spinoza's terms, we would be able to practice ethical living, which involves understanding our place in the larger order of the nation and the world, and we will have a cohesive society.

Our passions can strongly affect us, and unless a higher purpose inspires us to cultivate a strong and enlightened will, we cannot free ourselves from fanaticism, anger, hate, fear, and jealousy. These passions can have a destructive impact. Cultivating a strong and enlightened will requires us to meditate to reflect on our emotions and desires, developing a vision that aligns with universal moral values. Those of us who are influenced by untrustworthy media, politicians, and popular songs promoting toxic messages, toxic families, and friends may become increasingly consumed by these negative passions over time.

We need to prioritize our well-being by discriminating information. If it does not sound healthy, discard it. But first, we need to develop the necessary skills to identify trustworthy sources of information. We need to develop critical-thinking skills by cross-referencing news from multiple reputable sources, reading good books, and being aware of potential human biases.

We must protect ourselves in this world where information is becoming more discordant and toxic, encouraging us to participate in increasing the noise level to make us deaf about the real issues of life. Our mental equilibrium is not just a part of us but the core of our well-being. When we let people play with our emotions, we will lose our peace of mind, which we should make nonnegotiable because our mental health is our wealth, our capital for prosperity and serenity.

To protect our mental health from toxic information, we should establish boundaries with media consumption. Do the same with families and friends who keep sharing information across social media that does not make any sense and prioritize sharing uplifting content.

The discussion above underscores the importance of developing critical thinking, spiritual discernment, moral courage, and the intuition to scan deception. Your educational level is irrelevant —unenlightened media personalities will always lie to their audiences. It is our responsibility, as the audience, to sharpen our intuition, enabling us to instinctively discern lies.

Our inability to detect the truth is a choice influenced by unenlightened institutions, psychological tendencies, social conditioning, and moral attitudes. To cure it, we must reclaim our vision and take responsibility for our awareness. This first requires spiritual growth, a commitment to intellectual honesty, and the courage to live authentically in the light of truth.

Our blindness to truth is multifaceted; social structures, psychological biases, unenlightened moral attitudes, and lack of spiritual awareness influence that blindness. Media manipulation, cultural conditioning, cognitive dissonance, and our ego's resistance contribute to the development of this condition. To be free from social and psychological biases, unenlightened moral attitudes, and lack of spiritual development requires consciously questioning our assumptions, embracing intellectual honesty, and prioritizing truth over comfort. Only then can we truly see the reality that has always been before us.

15

THE SOVEREIGNTY OF THE SPIRIT IS THE ULTIMATE TRIUMPH OF A TRUE WARRIOR

W hat does it truly mean to be powerful, and how does the sovereignty of the spirit define the essence of a true warrior? Nowadays, power is often equated with external conquest, material wealth, status, or dominance over others.

This essay explores how true warriors achieve greatness or develop genuine power as exemplars of self-mastery. In addition, it argues that it is through an internal transformation that we can create authentic power. A true warrior's ultimate triumph lies in the spirit's sovereignty and the pursuit of the truth. Drawing upon philosophical traditions, psychological insights, and real-world examples, this discussion explores how true warriors culti-vate inner strength to navigate life's challenges with integrity and wisdom to inspire others to improve this world. This inward journey can shape the world's individual and broader moral fabric.

Control of the world, conquering territories, or amassing wealth does not mean we have real power; true power belongs to those who command the sovereignty of the spirit. Such individ-uals possess an inner light, an enlightened state of being that illuminates the profound mysteries of life. This mastery means a profound command over oneself, achieved through moral courage, rigorous judgment, the will of action, intelligence, mindfulness, and a disciplined psyche; it is not about control over others. It is the essence of the true warrior's journey—a path defined by morality, responsibility, and cultivated inner awareness.

Moral courage forms the bedrock of the warrior's path. When faced with fear, uncertainty, or social opposition, the will inspires us to act according to our moral principles. A true hero or heroine always acts, in Marcus Aurelius's words, and lives in alignment with one's values, regardless of external circumstances. Moral courage is not impulsive bravado but a deliberate, thoughtful boldness tempered by wisdom. It empowers the individual to confront life's challenges with a resolution for the glory of God, to manifest what is above here, on this plane, on Earth: truth and justice.

Aristotle's concept of courage as a virtue highlights its role as the mean between recklessness and cowardice. The true warrior embodies this balanced courage guided by reason and ethical conviction. In today's world, this virtue is exemplified in those who stand up for justice, speak truth to power, and act against wrongdoing, even when the cost is high. The American psychologist Rollo May viewed courage as the foundational virtue from which all other virtues spring, as it enables the individual to confront the anxiety of existence and make meaningful choices.

We must develop a disciplined mind capable of rigorous judgment and unwavering rectitude to become warriors. The ancient Confucian concept of Yi, or righteousness, embodies this principle: the commitment to act according to what is morally right rather than practical or self-serving. This world needs genuine role models of living righteousness, the internal compass. Most of us need guidance in our decisions to ensure we are aligned with a higher ethical standard. We should not leave such a sacred task to unenlightened people, such as entertainers. They cannot guide us to become warriors because their lives lack genuine continuous reflection, moral courage, wisdom, and a willingness to challenge their biases to discover themselves. Why do people who do not know who they are guide us in our quest for self-discovery?

For the true warrior, morality does not simply mean following rules but also cultivating an inner sense of justice that transcends personal interests. Immanuel Kant's emphasis on the categorical imperative reflects a similar ethos: the necessity of acting in a manner that could be universally willed as a law. This alignment with a higher moral order becomes the foundation for integrity and authenticity in action.

Courage and righteousness provide the foundation, but the will to act propels us forward. The will to act here is similar to Nietzsche's concept of the will to power, the drive to actualize one's potential and bring one's vision into reality. However, unlike the blind ambition of those associated with power, our will must be guided by ethical considerations and supported by mindfulness to become genuine warriors. The warrior's path should be paved with the disciplined application of effort toward meaningful goals aligned with the greater good.

In psychology, Viktor Frankl's logotherapy highlights the importance of purposeful action as a source of fulfillment and meaning. As true warriors, we should not act out of compulsion but out of a deliberate choice fueled by a sense of mission and responsibility. When this attitude is grounded in conscious intent, we can transform genuine ideals into reality.

The excellent life in this world belongs to those who possess the sovereignty of the spirit; those warriors develop their intelligence beyond mere analytical capability. Their intelligence involves a holistic awareness that integrates rational thought, emotional insight, and intuitive understanding. The ancient Greeks referred to this as *phronesis*, or practical wisdom, the ability to make sound decisions in the face of complexity. Intelligence, however, must be paired with moral responsibility. We should never forget that knowledge and power come with an ethical duty to use them to advance humanity. Such should always be the state of mind of warriors.

This sense of responsibility is echoed in Albert Schweitzer's concept of reverence for life when he urges us to act with compassion and respect for all living beings, regardless of their social/political/economic background. It is not the background of the individuals that is important but the soul's progression in this world. If we never understand this, wars will never end and sufferings and miseries will always be this world's shadow. We should not focus on training warriors for wars and destruction but on ending miseries, unnecessary sufferings, the genuine advancement of humanity, and the plan of the Almighty. Every action has consequences, which can be good or bad, so exercising power must be tempered with humility and empathy to achieve such a goal.

Mindfulness is fully present in each moment, an essential aspect of the warrior's journey. In the Eastern tradition, mindfulness is central to the teachings of Buddhism, where it is seen as a path to enlightenment. The warrior gains clarity and inner peace by cultivating awareness of thoughts, emotions, and sensations. This practice can allow us to develop a deliberate and measured response to life's challenges.

The psychologist Jon Kabat-Zinn, a pioneer of mindfulness in the West, emphasized its role in reducing stress and enhancing emotional regulation. Mindfulness should be a calming tool for us and for developing a state of mind that allows for greater self-awareness and alignment with our deeper values. It is the silent observer within, the inner light that guides the way forward.

As warriors in this world, we must use visualization, too; a powerful technique we should practice to harness the creative potential of the mind. Such practice calls for consistent focus on success with clarity, intention, discipline, and objectivity. Even though it may seem impossible to achieve, we should keep focusing on our visualization, no matter what. We must strive to align our subconscious mind with our conscious goals, paving the way for actualization. When we visualize our success in advance of our endeavors, we increase the power to help the mind connect vividly imagined scenarios and authentic experiences. In psychologist Albert Bandura's terms, visualization can enhance our beliefs and capabilities, thus increasing the likelihood of success in our endeavors. True warriors must use visualization not as escapism but as a practical method of preparation, envisioning the steps necessary to reach their objective—self-realization—and, at the same time, inspire others to follow this path.

Living should be a balance between rights and duties. Our actions must be guided by an inner sense of duty, not out of obligation but from recognition that our strength and abilities must serve a greater purpose.

The sovereignty of the spirit is the ultimate triumph of the true warrior, a mastery that transcends the material and touches the essence of existence. The warrior gains true power through the inner state of mastery, not by conquering the world or accumulating wealth. We gain true power by developing moral courage, rigorous judgment, the will of action, intelligence, mindfulness, and disciplined visualization. All we can carry is the achievement of the mastery of our inner state; we cannot carry anything from the external world. The development of our highest potential is the embodiment of the universal truth.

Nelson Mandela, who, after spending twenty-seven years in prison, led South Africa through a peaceful transition from apartheid to a democratic society, is one of the greatest examples of how inner strength, moral courage, and commitment to justice without personal gain exemplify the virtues of a true warrior. Another powerful example is Mahatma Gandhi, whose life was defined by nonviolent resistance. His ability to overcome external struggles with internal strength and moral conviction led to India's independence and influenced global movements for civil rights.

This essay has argued that true power does not lie in wealth, territorial conquest, or external dominance but in the sovereignty of the spirit—the mastery of one's inner world through moral courage, discipline, and wisdom. Drawing from philosophy, psychology, and real-life examples, we see that the greatest warriors cultivate integrity, act purposefully, and align their actions with universal truths. Whether in the moral leadership of Mandela or Gandhi's nonviolent resistance movement, the path to true power is an inward journey. By embracing this philosophy, individuals can navigate life's challenges with clarity, strength, and an unwavering commitment to justice and truth.

PART III

SELFLESS SERVICE AND HUMILITY

16

SELFLESS SERVICE IS A DIVINE LAW
FORGIVING A WORLD THAT FORGETS

S elf-interest can overwhelmingly overshadow generosity and appreciation, making it difficult for most of us to be grateful for a genuine, loving gesture from loved ones, friends, or colleagues, causing us to respond with ingratitude. So when our acts of kindness and service are met with thanklessness, how should we respond to that?

This essay explores altruism or selfless service as a divine law, emphasizing that we should serve others without expecting gratitude. Our motivations for helping others should not have anything to do with seeking appreciation. Our purpose should be serving others for the sake of goodness itself. When others respond with ingratitude to our good deeds, we should respond with forgiveness; we should adjust our expectations and understand that ingratitude is an inevitable part of life. As a result, we can cultivate inner peace and remain steadfast in our commitment to doing good.

In the vast, silent expanse of the universe, a noble law governs the most dignified human actions: to dedicate ourselves to others without any expectation. For instance, apple trees, mango trees, peach trees, and avocado trees produce fruits to eat and do not expect anything in return. This is the divine, the universe's law—a summons to selflessness that surpasses personal gain or recognition. This inspires us to live as vessels of goodness, emanating compassion and extending kindness, even when the world responds with indifference, ingratitude, or cruelty.

To serve others with a pure heart is to align ourselves with this higher moral principle. But how likely are we to find others willing to repay our service? How often do we find our acts of goodwill met with ingratitude? Despite our best intentions, it is an undeniable reality that the world may remain blind to the sacrifices we make. Ingratitude, however, should not deter us from our sacred path of serving others. Instead, we should look at that response as a tool of motivation to broaden our understanding and develop our compassion to practice forgiveness because we will always encounter ignorant people. To deal with ingratitude, we should remind ourselves of why we are serving in the first place, which is to serve God and deepen our resolve.

A suggested strategy to deal with ingrates is to readjust our expectations. When we anticipate gratitude from others, we are acting in a subtle form of self-interest. When we insist on acknowledgment of our goodness, we dilute the purity of our actions, reducing them to mere transactions. Genuine selflessness demands that we detach ourselves from the outcome of our deeds. We should serve others for nothing in return, even for applause, just for the sake of God and the serene joy of knowing that we have contributed to their welfare.

But what about the pain of ingratitude? Yes, it may pierce our hearts like a sharp thorn and leave us disheartened and disillusioned if we are not strong and detached. The best response in moments like these is to forgive. Forgiveness is the most significant act of liberation. To forgive the ungrateful is to free ourselves from the corrosive grip of bitterness. It is a profound release, a declaration that will prevent us from being imprisoned by the expectations we once held. When we hold on to resentment, we just stab our hearts repeatedly, inflicting wounds that only we can feel, dwelling in the dark solitude of our making while the ungrateful move forward with their lives.

Stop torturing yourself for the sake of self-pity; refusing to forgive ingrates is merely a form of self-punishment that drags us into an abyss where we become captives of our unforgiving spirit, haunted by the shadows of those who failed to appreciate our kindness. We should continually strive to remember that forgiveness is a light that illuminates our path, guiding us from the dark waters of resentment toward the calm shores of inner peace. Such a strategy is difficult to implement, but we should try it for our serenity and peace of mind. Understand that God wants us to make love and compassion our rewards when we serve others. The only way to transcend the shallow tides of worldly recognition and anchor ourselves in the profound, abiding truth of divine law is to forgive. This attitude is merely common sense. To solve most of our problems, we need to make sense of common sense. Strive to make sense of God's laws and integrate them into your actions. That is what is called observing divine law; any other attitude is observing evil law.

As we approach the twilight of our lives, the moments of ingratitude we experienced may weigh heavily on our hearts if left unforgiven. It is a sin to miss the peace that forgiveness offers, to die burdened by bitterness. It does not make sense to expire in the cold grip of resentment; we should unburden our minds from our bitterness when others do not show gratitude toward us. So, learn and practice to release bitterness every day. When we serve the public, we'll often encounter ungrateful people, even in our inner circle. Embrace the warmth of a forgiving spirit. In doing so, we will cleanse our hearts and prepare them for the quiet, eternal rest that awaits us. Peace of mind is impersonal and nonpartisan; it serves everyone who merits its blessings without discrimination.

Life is too short to spend it in bitterness. Instead, we should enjoy the rest of our lives serving without expectation, forgiving without hesitation, and loving without condition like the father in the biblical parable of the prodigal son (Luke 15:11–32) who welcomes his wayward son with open arms despite the son's reckless choices and initial lack of gratitude. His unconditional love mirrors the idea of selfless service—he gives without expecting anything in return, demonstrating the power of forgiveness even in the face of ingratitude. Another example is Mother Teresa, who devoted her life to helping the poor, the sick, and the dying without any expectation of recognition. She embodied the principle of serving with love and detachment from worldly approval.

How many of us have witnessed that many parents often sacrifice their time, energy, and resources to provide for their children, who may not fully appreciate these efforts until later in life? Some children never understand their mother's and father's efforts. Even when they create their own families, their parents as grandparents often babysit for them or give them money when needed. They do so because something in themselves whispers to their souls that genuine service is provided without expectation and ingratitude should be met with understanding rather than resentment.

One of our tasks in this life is to abide by the divine law of selfless service. Our worth is measured by the sincerity of the love we give the world to help people progress. People's ungrateful attitudes are merely tests of our conviction in helping others. When we serve others, we fulfill the highest calling of our existence, living as instruments of a greater, unspoken truth that binds us all.

To sum up, we have seen that selfless service is a divine law, urging us to give without expectation of gratitude and to forgive those who fail to acknowledge our kindness. We must have serenity and enjoy a healthy life till our deaths, the transition to the other world where ingratitude may not exist. This essay has highlighted that detachment from recognition is a necessity to preserve inner peace and resentment only harms the giver. Through real-life examples, including religious parables, historical figures, and everyday life experiences of parents, we see that true service transcends personal validation. Ultimately, by embracing forgiveness and understanding the nature of human ingratitude, we can live a more fulfilling life and remain steadfast in serving others.

17

WE ARE ALL ENDOWED WITH DIVINE POTENTIAL

WE SHOULD CHOOSE HUMILITY OVER EGO

What happens when we let ego dictate our perceptions of others' potential rather than recognizing the divine order that assigns individuals their unique purpose? Some of us may be blinded by arrogance and our ego, refusing to understand that the spirit of God blows where He wants. We are all destined to fulfill a specific role in this life to advance the work of the Almighty. Influenced by our lower personality and arrogance, we believe we can determine who deserves particular roles. We appoint ourselves God by trying to obstruct others rather than recognize their purpose.

This essay highlights the importance of humility in recognizing the divine purpose bestowed upon each of us. It argues that our roles in life are not self-determined but instead granted to us by a higher power and rejecting this truth results in societal discord and personal dissatisfaction. Our limited perceptions do not dictate greatness. Still, by a more significant, divine design, it is important to humble ourselves to be free from arrogance and the lower ego to let the true nature of destiny take its course.

The Creator endowed us with infinite possibilities, giving us unique combinations of talents meant to contribute to God's purpose on earth. The world is like threads woven into a vast tapestry, each of us playing a distinct role according to our abilities for the sake of God. Our lower self refuses to understand that fact. It blinds us, leading us to believe that we have the right to determine who is entitled to positions of prestige. This mistaken belief stems from our personality, the part of us that seeks power and recognition at the expense of truth and humility.

Our talents are intended to guide us toward fulfilling a specific role aligned with the world's needs and the universe's higher plan. However, when dominated by ego, we misinterpret this. Instead of understanding the spirit of the Lord chooses whomever He wants to fulfill a position based on the talent He endowed us, a great majority of us, due to our ambition and jealousy, resist that. We insist that we can do the job of destiny for another person. As Hindu monk Paramahansa Yogananda said, we all cannot be kings or presidents. Another group of people always judges others on their countenance to determine who can fulfill a prestigious role, such as a leadership position. Others believe their inner circle only has the right to occupy significant positions. This delusion leads us to think that others lack the right or the worthiness to occupy such roles. We might even boldly declare that some individuals will never rise to a particular status or achieve greatness simply because they do not fit our narrow, biased expectations.

When we declare that someone else will never achieve a specific goal, we place ourselves in a divine position, as if we possess omniscient insight into the future. This is a grave misunderstanding of our place in the universe. We are not God; we do not have the power to dictate the destinies of others. At best, we might succeed in discouraging those who lack strong will or self-belief. Yet we cannot deter individuals who are firm in their purpose and confident in their abilities. History has shown us countless examples of people who rose above the dismissive judgments of others, achieving what was deemed impossible.

Consider the countless historical figures whom many said would never amount to anything. Abraham Lincoln was deemed unfit for politics, yet he became one of the most revered US presidents. Helen Keller, who was blind and deaf, was told she would never lead a meaningful life, yet she became a symbol of triumph over adversity. Paul Revere Williams, orphaned at four and raised in Los Angeles, surmounted racial prejudice to become a pioneering architect. Despite being told white clients wouldn't hire a Black man and Black clients couldn't afford his work, he earned his license in 1921 and became the first African American member of the American Institute of Architects in 1923. Williams designed over three thousand buildings, including the Beverly Hills Hotel renovation, the Los Angeles County Courthouse, and the iconic Theme Building at Los Angeles International Airport. Renowned for his elegant style, he created homes for stars like Frank Sinatra and Lucille Ball.

Consider Joseph's story in the Bible: Consumed by jealousy, Joseph's brothers attempted to prevent him from fulfilling his divine destiny. They sold him into slavery in Egypt to Potiphar, an officer of the pharaoh (Genesis 37:12–36). After Potiphar's wife, who unsuccessfully tried to seduce him, falsely accused him of rape, Joseph was imprisoned (Genesis 39:19–20). Despite that, he rose to become an influential leader in Egypt. The inconsiderate actions of his brothers and Potiphar's wife were significant in making Joseph fulfill his destiny; God let them act like evil creatures to show us He has the power to work mysteriously. So any human attempts to control destiny are futile in the face of divine purpose.

The above people's stories remind us that no human has the right or authority to determine another person's potential limits. We will never succeed or fulfill our purposes when we let others define our potential. We are the ones who know who we are, not others. When we lack self-confidence and do not know who we are, it is easy to fall into the dangerous trap of aligning ourselves with those who believe they can decide who is worthy of specific roles.

It is a sin to interfere in the paths of others because the spirit of God blows where He wants. God will make sure He disappoints those of us who exhibit such arrogance and obstruct the natural flow of destiny. If some people are meant to fulfill specific roles that can advance the collective good, our attempts to sabotage or discredit them are futile. We may employ deceit, manipulation, or other underhanded tactics to stop people destined to fulfill a specific role, but these efforts will only lead to our disgrace. In trying to limit someone's potential, we reveal our insecurities and fundamental misunderstanding of the divine order. Ultimately, we will disappoint ourselves because we cannot change what someone is meant to be.

Such a low attitude will only make us miserable. The best attitude is to be free from arrogance, meaning we should always choose humility over our lower personality. It is not our duty to decide who can or cannot fulfill a high position when the person exhibits merit; we must accept that each person has a unique role crafted by a higher power. We should support and encourage each other to contribute to a more harmonious world. Such action will make others feel free to explore their talents and fulfill their purposes in life, and everyone will benefit.

Shifting our perspective to a higher one would be a helpful and practical act for our development that will help advance our nation and the world. We will create a positive ripple effect when we uplift rather than belittle others and foster an environment where creativity, innovation, and growth can flourish. We must relinquish our false sense of superiority and see others as equal participants in humanity's unfolding story.

We are all part of a more outstanding design, each with a role to play according to the gifts we have been given. This is a simple truth, common sense, but very difficult for some of us to accept because we still need to have the capacity to make sense of common sense. If our tasks were to hinder or limit others, God would have never endowed us with different talents or abilities to fulfill specific roles. When we abandon our negative mentality and support others to fulfill their destinies, we open ourselves to a deeper understanding of the interconnectedness of all life.

Our task is to support each other and use our talents to thread the beautiful woven tapestry representing our world. By embracing this attitude, we will uplift others and find our proper place within the sacred order. It is crucial to unburden ourselves from judging others, stop trying to play God, and become cocreators in a world where everyone can fulfill their potential. We can contribute to a shared destiny that is more significant than any of us alone.

This essay has argued that humility, rather than ego, should guide our perception of others' potential. When we assume the right to judge who is worthy of fulfilling a specific role, we misunderstand our place in the divine order, and such an attitude tries only to obstruct the natural course of destiny. We will not succeed most of the time. History and literature provide countless examples of individuals who defied human judgment to accomplish their purposes. We should have the courage to recognize that God assigned every person a role in His grand design. We should not let our arrogance mislead us. By listening to our ego and rejecting humility, we foster a world where people cannot pursue their true calling, leading to a more unjust and unharmonious society that can bring turmoil.

18

THE FOLLY OF INVINCIBILITY
ON POWER, PASSION, AND THE UNPREDICTABILITY OF FATE

C an believing in our invincibility lead to our downfall? How can we navigate power with wisdom rather than arrogance? In asking these questions, we must consider how people in authority should display their power, meaning they should always strive to be aware of its impermanence. Because of our ignorance and lack of spiritual development, we often mistake authority for invulnerability. From emperors, queens, and presidents to corporate leaders, many have succumbed to the illusion that their influence makes them immune to the forces of fate. However, time and again, history reminds us that unchecked ambition and arrogance invite one's downfall.

This essay discusses the folly of invincibility, the consequences that will inevitably follow, and the necessity of humility in facing fate's unpredictability. It argues that true strength lies in wisdom, humility, and understanding our limits.

An enduring conflict between the will and our darker, baser passions marks human history. In moments when we allow ourselves to be enslaved by ultimate greed and pride, prone to misuse and overestimating our power, fate has a way of erupting violently, like a dormant volcano suddenly awakened. It is in these unexpected eruptions that our prudence is laid bare and our well-crafted plans disintegrate. The ancient philosophers warned us that unchecked desires are the seeds of destruction; yet time and again, we fall prey to the illusion of control. We believe we are the masters of our destiny, yet we fail to recognize that fate is not a servant but an untamed force that humbles even the most powerful among us.

When we rise to positions of influence—whether in government or the private sector—a peculiar arrogance often takes root. We develop the folly of invincibility; such arrogance stems from a delusion that our power shields us from the consequences of our actions. We mistake the trappings of authority for invulnerability and indulge in excess, using our power to satiate our lowest desires. We become like the towering oak tree, standing proudly and seemingly invincible. The oak is not immune to a sudden strike of lightning, no matter how strong we believe it is and how much reverence we give it. Lighting can reduce it to fragments in the blink of an eye. Its formidable exterior is an illusion that masks its fragility.

This oak tree image is a fitting metaphor for humanity's hubris. In a position of power, we often perceive ourselves as unassailable, provoking others and standing firm against the winds of change and the storms of fate. Yet it is precisely this attitude—this belief in our strength—that leaves us vulnerable. It is not power that protects us but wisdom; it is not the sheer size of our achievements that safeguard us but the humility to recognize the limits of our control. The notion that we can withstand any shock and are impervious to the unforeseen is a dangerous fallacy. Such arrogance results from minds that cannot form a clear idea about who they are and cannot distinguish between the path that leads to their downfall and the one that leads to their glory. Their destruction is the fruit of their pride and imprudence or their voluntary mistakes due to their passions, for which they do not have a clear and distinct knowledge about how dangerous they can be when they do not control them. It is the height of madness to believe that we can anticipate every turn of fate or shield ourselves from every calamity.

Life's unpredictability is its great equalizer; it can modify the frequency of any of the passions we thought were unmodifiable and powerful because the rationality of the universe sees that they no longer serve our highest and others' good. The well-known aphorism "Man proposes, God disposes" expresses the idea that no matter how meticulously we plan, how shrewdly we strategize, or how tightly we hold the reins of power, God has a way of reminding us of our limitations.

How can we live in harmony with the unpredictable nature of existence? We need to learn to temper our passions and curb our desires. The Stoics, in their meditations on fate, gave this golden advice. When we let our passions run unchecked, we become like vessels adrift in a storm, at the mercy of forces beyond our control.

Throughout history, we see many leaders, entrepreneurs, and influential figures who succumbed to the intoxicating belief in their infallibility. Some notable examples include military genius and self-made emperor Napoleon Bonaparte, ideologue and genocidal dictator Adolf Hitler, authoritarian president and kleptocrat Ferdinand Marcos, aviator-industrialist and paranoid recluse Howard Hughes, entrepreneur and convicted fraudster Elizabeth Holmes, evangelist and cult leader Jim Jones, and science fiction writer and religious founder L. Ron Hubbard. They recklessly pursued their desires, mistaking the temporary stability of their positions for a permanent shield against fate. Their lack of knowledge about the cosmic law governing the universe atrophied their minds against reality. Their ambitions shattered because of their arrogance. History is littered with their ruins—empires that crumbled, corporations that fell, and leaders who were toppled instantly. The lesson is clear: The higher we rise, the more vigilant we must be against the creeping arrogance that whispers we are untouchable.

True strength lies not in power or position but in the discipline of the will. It lies in the capacity to resist the seductive pull of passion and the wisdom to acknowledge that our control is limited. In addition, most of the time after rising in power, our ambitions follow the structure of our lower self; we think we are invincible and separate from the universe. We must recognize the impermanence of our circumstances and approach our successes with humility, understanding that they can be swept away at any moment by forces outside our grasp. In Buddha's words, when we refuse to learn that, we are merely ignorant and will never be free from suffering. Remember that the oak tree is mighty, but its strength does not make it immune to the sudden strike of lightning.

Ultimately, it is not the shock of unforeseen disasters that ruins us but our refusal to prepare our minds for the inevitability of the unexpected we put in motion by our ill will. Our madness in believing we can dictate the terms of fate leads to our downfall. We should be humble and embrace life's uncertainness with equanimity when in a position of power. We should strive to understand that to live well is not to control every outcome but to learn to navigate the unpredictable with grace and prudence. This is called the right attitude. Only when we temper our passions and humble our sense of invincibility do we stand firm against the vicissitudes of fate.

This essay has argued that believing that we are invincible when in a position of power is folly that blocks our reason regarding the unpredictability of fate. The examination of historical figures and the towering oak tree metaphor illustrates how arrogance and unchecked ambition lead to destruction. True strength comes not from power but from the wisdom to recognize our limitations and the humility to accept uncertainty. Undeniably, history has testified that those who refuse to be reasonable and acknowledge their vulnerability are destined to fall. To navigate power wisely, we must abandon the folly of invincibility and instead embrace prudence, self-awareness, and adaptability in the face of life's ever-changing nature.

19

THE ILLUSION OF CONTROL OF OUR DESTINY

THE FOOLISHNESS OF BELIEVING WE ARE THE ARCHITECTS OF OUR FATES

W hereas the previous chapter addressed the folly of invincibility—the arrogance that so often accompanies power and blinds us to the limits imposed by fate—this essay turns its gaze to a subtler yet no less dangerous delusion: the illusion that we are the sole architects of our destiny. While Chapter 18 explored how power can lead to ruin when paired with unchecked pride, here we confront a universal temptation that afflicts not only the powerful but all who believe that willpower and planning can override the currents of the universe.

The distinction is significant. The folly of invincibility is the hubris of the already powerful; the illusion of control is the mistaken belief that any human, by sheer force of will, may seize the reins of fate. The former is a tragedy born of pride at the summit of success; the latter is a quiet despair masked as ambition, a modern faith in self-determination that often leads us into internal conflict and disillusionment. From the dawn of our consciousness, humanity has sought to carve its fate, to paint the universe with its aspirations and ambitions. Do we truly control our destiny, or is our belief in control just an illusion that leads to internal conflict and suffering?

This essay will explore how such belief is a dangerous illusion that blinds us to the forces of chance, circumstance, and the natural order of existence. We are far from the architects of our lives, but merely participants in a vast, uncontrollable cosmic order. God is the great architect; for instance, He plans to come here on Earth when we must exit this world to move on. The essay demonstrates that true wisdom lies not in struggling against fate but in surrendering to or executing the natural plan God designed for us, following the currents of life with humility and acceptance.

We have long believed that our destiny lies firmly within our grasp and that we can mold the world according to our desires with enough resolve and effort. It is merely an idea to comfort us —a myth of power and autonomy. To believe we genuinely control our destiny is to reach the height of madness. In this illusion of control, we become trapped by the conflict of lost forces, sowing the seeds of internal and external destruction.

It is misleading and scary to think we have absolute agency, for such an idea closes our eyes to the complex interplay of chance, circumstance, and forces beyond our reckoning. When we envision ourselves as the masters of our fate, we silently struggle against the universe. It is a rebellion not against oppressive chains but against the very nature of existence; therefore, it is a battle doomed from its inception. Our minds become battlegrounds, racked by rivalries between our genuine self, the self we imagine we could be, or the self the world assigned or suggested to us we should be. In striving to dominate our destiny nowadays with all the technology and information available to us, we unknowingly split ourselves into fragments, each vying for supremacy, each doomed to failure.

A life driven by unyielding ambition cannot be peaceful; it must be a life of turmoil. We have the right to set high goals and be propelled by the conviction of sheer willpower, but that does not mean we have the right and power to bend reality to our desires. Yet with each step in our plan, we may encounter resistance from the universe: unforeseen obstacles, random misfortune, unnecessary suffering, and the limits of our capabilities. Instead of accepting these setbacks as part of a broader, uncontrollable tapestry, or specifically, in Spinoza's words, seeing them as part of a larger rational order that wants to correct the system, we rail against them. Such attitude is the beginning of folly. We interpret these misfortunes as betrayals of fate, as injustices inflicted upon us. And so, a bitter rivalry unfolds within us—a rivalry between our expectations and reality. This conflict, born from our belief in control, breeds only ruin.

Ambitions struck by lightning and hopes aborted before they bloom—such is the fate of those who believe they hold the reins of destiny. Like Icarus soaring toward the sun on wings bound by wax, we are bound to falter when we rise too high on the currents of our delusions. Our powers, seemingly vast in moments of triumph, melt away like snow in the sun when the cold winds of reality blow. Then we realize that we have been hammering at our loss all along, our labors not leading to our flourishing but to the hollow fruits of our pride.

Pride, imprudence, and the willful fault will design our downfall like architects do. Pride convinces us that we are invincible, that our inner strength alone can overcome the chaos of the external world. Imprudence closes our eyes to the lessons of humility, deafening us to the whispers of caution. And our willful faults—the stubborn refusal to acknowledge our limits—become the final nails in the coffin of our ambitions. The more we press against the boundaries of destiny, the more violently they push back. The universe does not bend; it only shatters what dares to oppose its current.

To live under the illusion of control is to live a spiritually sterile life. It is a life spent in vain attempts to conquer the unconquerable, to impose order where only chaos reigns. Instead of finding peace in the ebb and flow of existence, we exhaust ourselves in futile struggle, sapping our vitality for illusions. When the dust settles, what remains? Ruins—ours and others— are left in the wake of our reckless pursuit of control. Relationships falter, dreams dissolve, and we find ourselves stranded, wondering how it all unraveled. We might start drinking or doing drugs to escape our failures.

Ultimately, the forces we sought to command proved to be our undoing. We did not see that the ambitions we pursued fervently initiated conflict, nurturing inner rivalries. As a result, we were left with the wreckage of aborted hopes and a life that, for all its striving to achieve something, turned out to be a complete failure. The irony is that in trying to control our destiny or give it a direction, we were not aligned with the reality of the universe and its plan, and we forfeited our chance at true fulfillment. We lost sight of the beauty in surrendering to the currents of life, of embracing the mystery and uncertainty that define our existence by attempting to grasp the reins of fate.

The actual height of wisdom lies not in seeking control but in relinquishing it and having faith in God. The universe, or whatever we might call this force, wants us to realize ourselves by abiding by the laws. The only way to find peace in the uncontrollable, the universe in which we are merely a part—the interconnected whole, according to Spinoza—is by allowing the universe to unfold as it will. Surfing it with grace and humility may be the only way to escape the madness of self-imposed conflict. When we release our grip on the illusion of control, we make space for a different kind of power: the power of acceptance, flexibility, and true inner harmony. In this letting go, we may find that we have gained more than we ever lost and that our true strength lies not in dominating our destiny but dancing with it.

Consider the life of Apple cofounder Steve Jobs, a visionary who seemed to control his destiny. However, despite his success, he faced significant challenges in his life: childhood struggles, a divorce, being fired from Apple and eventually returning to the company, experiencing depression and anxiety, battling pancreatic cancer, and ultimately realizing that specific forces were beyond his control. Despite his billions of dollars and intelligence, he died at fifty-six. His story exposes the illusion of being the architect of our lives and the necessity of embracing uncertainty.

This essay has argued that believing we have absolute control over our destiny because we might enjoy some power and intelligence, earn a couple of titles, and have material wealth is a harmful illusion that breeds internal conflict and suffering. Any attempt to force reality to conform to our desires will lead to frustration, disappointment, and self-destruction. The story of Jobs and the philosophical insights developed in this essay make it evident that true wisdom lies not in trying to control our fate, because we have no power to do that, but in embracing the unpredictability of life with humility and acceptance. Instead of clinging to the illusion of control, we should seek harmony with the natural flow of existence, recognizing that surrendering to life's uncertainties is the key to true fulfillment.

20

WE CANNOT CROSS THE ARID DESERT OF LIFE WITHOUT CARRYING THE FRESH DRINK OF HOPE MIXED WITH FAITH

T here are days when life sometimes unfolds like a journey across a desert, where we face hardships that seem endless and insurmountable. In such a journey, we encounter moments of desolation where hope seems like a distant mirage. The relentless sun beats down on us, and the dry earth stretches endlessly before us, offering no sign of respite—no trees, shelter, or oasis in sight. Such is the nature of our most difficult days: Stripped of comfort, we must stand exposed to the raw elements of existence. All of us will, at some point in our lives, experience such extreme situations. In such circumstances, we must ask ourselves: How can we find the strength to move forward when everything around us feels desolate and hopeless? Yet in these moments of emptiness, we have no choice but to summon the essence of hope for survival. Hope, the daughter of faith, is the only thread that can carry us through such lonely situations.

This essay explores how faith and hope work together as essential virtues that sustain us during difficult times. The metaphor of the desert represents our life's struggles. This essay argues that overcoming hardships requires carrying the "fresh drink" of hope, strengthened by faith, to endure and transcend life's struggles. These virtues are not merely abstract concepts but essential forces that sustain us. Our spiritual and personal transformation depends on our perseverance guided by a belief in a better future.

Hope is the dew that lingers in the early morning, a fragile and precious presence that sustains us through the arid landscape of our trials. As our supporting star, hope will give us the courage and stamina to continue crossing until we reach the end. It will emerge as the divine poetry to elevate our gaze from the dust beneath our feet to the skies above to remind us over and over not to focus on the arid wilderness of life's hardships but to see only the grassland. These virtues must be our constant companions along the way. Their function is to give us a glimpse of the future, a vision of the fertile grasslands beyond the desert's edge. Just as dew refreshes the parched earth, hope and faith can keep us alive by infusing our minds with the strength to endure and persevere.

Yet the path to the promised land of fulfillment and peace is challenging. We must eliminate our destructive passions, those burdens that weigh heavily on our spirits and prevent us from moving forward. Otherwise, we will perish under the relentless heat of the desert. This unloading is necessary to make it easier for us to travel during the journey. Only when we unburden ourselves from our fears and the mirages created by the desert can we open ourselves fully to the wisdom that the desert imparts. The knowledge we gain from these trials is not acquired through books or teachings alone; it is a deeper, more intimate understanding forged through experience and suffering.

Once we have faith, it becomes the bedrock upon which hope can build a resilient foundation. Hope can transform our perspective and open our vision to see beyond the immediate barrenness of the desert to the lush, verdant future that awaits. Through our understanding of these virtues, we will become aware that the difficulties of the present moment are but a necessary passage, a rite of transformation. We should avoid thinking about the desert as a permanent place of exile but as a crossing stage on the journey to a more prosperous, more abundant life. In the crucible of the desert, our souls are refined, much like gold is purified by fire.

As we progress through this landscape, hope must constantly intertwine with faith. We should never let our hope falter in the presence of the enormity of the desert's difficulties. It needs faith as its companion—faith in a higher purpose, in the existence of a greater plan that we might not yet fully comprehend. Faith is the compass that directs us toward the unseen destination, giving us the courage to take each step forward even when the path is unclear. Faith assures us that we will cross the desert to the other beautiful, serene side and stimulates our minds to believe that a place of refreshment and renewal lies beyond the scorching heat and desolate sands.

We have the power of our will to create a powerful force to move us forward in uniting hope with faith. Faith anchors hope, giving it a more profound, more enduring quality. Under the harsh sun of despair, faith certainly will prevent hope from withering. Faith will nourish hope, allowing it to flourish even in the most inhospitable conditions. Together, they form a harmonious duo: Hope provides the vision of what could be, while faith supplies the conviction that this vision is attainable.

We should not see the journey's trials in the desert as a punishment for being in the wrong place at the wrong time. It is a spiritual trial to test our intention. This journey is an opportunity for profound transformation, a chance to shed the old skin of our former selves and emerge renewed.

We must be encouraged to cross the desert to reach the fertile grasslands of a fulfilled life. Symbolically, the desert, far from being a place of hopelessness, is in fact the proving ground of our spirit. It is a place to learn to rise above difficulties and see beyond the immediate pain to the promises of the future.

We must carry the unwavering belief that the desert is not our destination as we continue our journey across this arid land. It is a temporary passage, one that prepares us for the abundance that lies ahead. Each step must be guided by the intertwined forces of hope and faith, forming a fresh drink as we draw closer to the fertile grasslands—a place where the trials of the desert will be but a distant memory and where the soul, purified and transformed, will bask in the light of true happiness.

Let's draw an example from the Bible to illustrate how faith and hope sustain people in challenging times. Consider the story of Moses and the Israelites. According to the Bible, the Israelites journeyed through the desert for forty years, led by Moses, after escaping slavery in Egypt. They faced many hardships but ultimately reached the promised land (Exodus 15:22–27). The Israelites' journey in the desert mirrors this essay's metaphor of life's struggles. Their faith in a higher purpose sustained them despite hardships, much like this essay argues that faith and hope guide us through personal trials.

This essay argues that life's struggles resemble a burdensome journey crossing a desert to the promised land or heaven, where survival depends on hope and faith. Hope is the vision of a better future, the abundance that lies ahead, and faith is the conviction that this future is attainable; it is the compass that guides us. Together, they serve as forces that help us endure hardship and ultimately emerge transformed. The story of Moses and the Israelites illustrates how those who maintain hope and faith during difficult times persevere and, ultimately, thrive and survive. The desert is not our destination—it is merely a passage that refines us, preparing us for a more abundant and fulfilling life.

21

HOW WE CAN CULTIVATE OUR BEST SPIRIT IN THIS WORLD OF DUALITIES

Throughout history and across cultures, people have been confronted with the challenge of choosing between paths that either elevate the human spirit or lead to moral and personal decline. The world is not a neutral space—it is a battleground where action or inaction tilts the balance between good and evil. In this world of dualities, we all face this crucial choice: to align ourselves with growth and virtue or succumb to vice and malevolence.

This essay seeks to answer the question: How can we cultivate a life of purpose and virtue where forces of good and evil, success and failure, action and inaction are constantly at play? This essay will explore how we can transcend victory and foster inner harmony by inquiring into the necessity of active moral engagement, the dangers of pride, and the importance of humility and balance.

Our lives are presented with two fundamental choices: one that leads toward fulfillment, growth, and harmony, and another that spirals into failure, dissolution, and chaos. These paths are not arbitrary; they embody the eternal conflict between good and evil. There is no neutral territory in this arena. We must choose, and in our choice, we must act, for indecision is itself a decision— a silent consent to the encroaching tide of evil. To abstain from action is to allow the weeds of neglect to overtake the field of virtue. Just as thorns and brambles soon consume an untended plot of land, so, too, does the spirit falter when we fail to nurture it in a matter of what is right. Our existence is suspended in a delicate equilibrium between these opposing forces, and it is through the exercise of our will, guided by sound judgment, that we tip the scales toward the good.

The wisdom of the ancients asserts that to refrain from willing, to abstain from action, is as pernicious as the deliberate doing of harm. Our lives should not be passive states of being but fields of potential waiting to be tilled by intention. In this light, the path of righteousness is not a mere suggestion but a mandate—a call to continuously enact good in the world, thereby aligning ourselves with divine purpose.

Victory is not the ultimate aim, as it is commonly perceived. Many of us equate success in life with the attainment of victory, but this is a limited view. True victory lies not merely in winning but in establishing harmony, the balance of forces we set into motion. The universal law of reciprocity teaches us that every action, whether triumph or defeat, elicits a corresponding reaction. Therefore, we must humble ourselves, learn to temper our desires, and anticipate the inevitable jealousy from others that may push them to sabotage our success.

Pride and ego are the great pitfalls of this journey. They whisper the illusion of superiority, seducing us into the fallacy that we stand on equal footing with the Creator. Be aware of excessive pride that always leads us astray, transforming our victories into hollow triumphs that sow the seeds of future calamity. When we elevate ourselves above the divine order, we unwittingly become agents of the forces we seek to overcome. Actual progress is thus marked not by the vanquishing of opposition. We will maintain our victories when we master our inner lives, allowing us to act wisely and humbly to serve the greater good.

The task is to navigate the duality of life with vigilance and discernment, to choose deliberately and act decisively. We can fulfill our roles in the cosmic design and partake in a victory that transcends mere conquest only through the active cultivation of the good and the mindful restraint of our baser impulses. This victory embodies the enduring work of the divine within us.

Many historical figures have grappled with similar moral dilemmas discussed in this essay yet aligned themselves with growth and virtue—for instance, Dr. Martin Luther King Jr. and Nelson Mandela. King's active resistance to injustice exemplifies the argument that failing to act is equivalent to allowing evil to flourish. He chose to pursue nonviolent resistance despite knowing the dangers, embodying the idea that one must actively cultivate virtue and righteousness in the face of oppression. Despite being imprisoned for twenty-seven years, Mandela did not let resentment or hatred consume him. Instead, he cultivated wisdom, patience, and forgiveness, leading South Africa toward reconciliation rather than revenge. His journey aligns with the idea that true success is not about conquest but creating lasting harmony.

Many literary characters also have grappled with similar moral dilemmas yet aligned themselves with catastrophe—for instance, Victor Frankenstein (from *Frankenstein* by Mary Shelley) and Jay Gatsby (from *The Great Gatsby* by F. Scott Fitzgerald). Frankenstein serves as a cautionary example of unchecked ambition and pride. His desire to surpass natural limits leads to destruction, illustrating this essay's warning about the dangers of excessive pride and the illusion of superiority over the natural or divine order. Gatsby's relentless pursuit of success and recognition ultimately leads to his downfall, reflecting the dangers of allowing ego and pride to dictate one's path. His story underscores this essay's caution against seeking personal triumph at the cost of moral clarity and inner peace.

This essay has explored the necessity of conscious moral effort in a world where forces of good and evil, order and chaos, are constantly at play. It has been argued that passivity is not neutrality but a silent surrender to chaos, urging us to act with intention and wisdom. Moreover, it has warned against the perils of unchecked pride and the illusion of superiority, emphasizing that true success lies not in mere victory but in achieving harmony with oneself and the greater moral order. By examining historical and literary examples, this discussion has demonstrated that cultivating virtue requires vigilance, humility, and a commitment to enacting good in the world. Ultimately, the path to true fulfillment is not in conquering others but in mastering one's inner life.

PART IV

FULFILLMENT AND TRANSCENDENCE

22

OUR FATE AND THE MORAL COMPASS

F ortune or misfortune, not determined by good or bad luck, is an experience we will go through according to the principles we adopt. To what extent does our moral compass shape our fate, determining whether we experience fortune or misfortune? This essay examines the idea that the orientation of our morals primarily determines our destiny. It argues that aligning with virtue brings prosperity in our lives while following vice leads to downfall. This discussion will highlight how ethical decision-making plays an important role in shaping our destiny by considering real-life examples and philosophical perspectives.

We are more likely to experience misfortune when we choose the evil path; on the other hand, if we take the righteous path, we are more likely to experience good fortune. So, most of the time, unless providence for a higher purpose wants to interfere in our lives, fortune or misfortune is generated by our choices. We rise or fall by aligning with virtue or vice, guided by our decisions between good and evil. Based on our chosen path, fate will elevate or humble us. This realization empowers us to make conscious choices that lead to a more fortunate life.

To embrace the blessings of good fortune, one must aspire to live in the pursuit of what is faithful; in other words, we must obey the law of the universe. In addition, we must develop the courage to strive for what is possible to achieve and be tempered by patience to endure the journey's trials. For some of us, patience may be seen as a sign of weakness, not as a testament to our resilience and determination. We must eliminate this attitude to increase our chances of good fortune. This understanding can illuminate our destination and the road ahead through the sharpened blade of intelligence.

A positive will, assisted by a firm resolution, is an excellent strategy for maneuvering toward the righteousness God wants us to achieve. It will help us enjoy the fortune we desire. The education of our will is not just a process but a journey of enlightenment that guides us toward the right path. Only then do we align ourselves with the flow of fortune, bending the arc of fate toward prosperity and fulfillment.

Consider these examples from literature (Charles Dickens's *A Christmas Carol* and Victor Hugo's *Les Misérables*) and history (Mandela) to highlight how ethical decision-making is vital in shaping our destiny. In *A Christmas Carol*, Ebenezer Scrooge begins as a greedy and selfish man and suffers emotional isolation and dissatisfaction. However, his fate drastically improves after changing his ways and embracing generosity. His transformation from vice to virtue illustrates how moral choices affect our fortune or misfortune. In Victor Hugo's *Les Misérables*, Jean Valjean, initially an ex-convict burdened by misfortune, experiences redemption and a better fate when he chooses righteousness. He finds peace and prosperity by helping others and committing to goodness—his moral choices as an ex-convict shape his destiny. Imprisoned for decades, Mandela remained steadfast in pursuing justice and reconciliation rather than revenge. His adherence to virtue despite adversity eventually led to his role in uniting South Africa, demonstrating how moral perseverance can lead to a fortunate outcome.

This essay has argued that fortune and misfortune are not simply products of chance but are greatly influenced by our moral decisions. By aligning with virtue, we increase our likelihood of experiencing health, prosperity, glory, and serenity, while choosing vice often leads to our downfall. Through the examination of a few pieces of literature and one historical event, we see how figures like Scrooge, Valjean, and Mandela illustrate this principle. Ultimately, this perspective empowers us to embrace moral responsibility to shape our fate as cocreator with God by making conscious, ethical choices that align with universal moral laws.

23

THE UNBOUNDED WILL

A DECREE OF HUMAN PROGRESS

I f we look closely at our civilization, we may grapple with
what defines true progress nowadays. Is it material wealth,
societal advancements, or something deeper within a human or a
nation or the world's spirit? What is the true measure of human
progress, and how will our strength determine our ability to reach
our highest potential?

This essay argues that progress is not merely an external affair
but an internal procedure driven by the courage of our will. It
explores the essential role of human will in achieving it, arguing
that unwavering determination, moral integrity, and the willingness to uplift others are fundamental to personal and collective
advancement. True advancement is achieved when individuals
commit to a continuous state of personal evolution, guided by
virtue, perseverance, and a sense of duty to help others ascend
alongside them. The discussion developed in this essay will
examine the power of inner resolve, its role in human progress,
and why genuine wisdom must be shared rather than hoarded.

The ascent of our destiny knows no limits beyond those we

impose with the weakness of our will. When our resolve is fortified and unwavering, set on the task of inner evolution, there is no
force, no obstacle disturbing enough to halt our advance. This
inner strength, this unwavering resolve, is our greatest asset in the
labyrinth of life. It is an uncontested fact that every remarkable
ascent begins on firm ground. We must first lay the foundation of
noble virtues and unwavering moral principles to have a prosperous, serene life—this bedrock should become the launchpad of
our journey.

When we establish a genuine moral ground as we complete
our mission on this plane, God will recognize our sincerity and
grant us the silent mandate to persevere. We can only carve a path
toward progress through the sharpness of our motives and the
tenacity of our efforts. And we should never make victory merely
a destination in our journey but instead a continuous state of
becoming, an endless pursuit of overcoming. The idea of a
perpetual growth journey should be our inspiration and motivation to constantly strive to discover more about ourselves, like the
universe always expanding, knowing there is always more to
achieve and become.

In this noble pursuit, we should always believe we are called to
a divine duty beyond the lower self to share the fruits of our
wisdom. It would be a selfish act if we did not share our experience. What value does our ascent have when we climb alone,
leaving behind those who could rise with us? True wisdom
demands its propagation; like the sun, it should illuminate the
path for others. Once we become wise due to the development of
a salutary will, we must turn our journey into a beam of hope and
a testament to the boundless power of the human will. By helping
others to realize themselves, we not only uplift ourselves but also
contribute to the growth and enlightenment of others, fulfilling
our responsibility to the collective human journey.

Consider a couple of historical figures. In Helen Keller's *The Story of My Life*, we learn how a woman who was deaf and blind as a child overcame significant adversity. Keller learned to communicate and became a renowned writer, political activist, and advocate for people with disabilities through persistence, determination, and the guidance of her teacher, Anne Sullivan. Her story is an inspiring example of the boundless power of the human will and that true progress comes not from external circumstances but from an unwavering inner resolve.

Mandela's life exemplifies that progress is not a fixed goal of attaining a permanent presidential title—despite his popularity, he declined a second term—but an ongoing pursuit of advancing justice and combating poverty through his charitable foundation. Despite spending more than a quarter of his life in prison, he emerged with a vision of unity and forgiveness, dedicating his life to dismantling apartheid and fostering reconciliation in South Africa. His resilience and moral strength highlight that perseverance and virtue lay the foundation for true progress.

Beyond historical figures, the argument in this essay applies to everyday life. For instance, students who overcome academic struggles, single parents who work tirelessly to provide a better future for their children, or entrepreneurs who rise after multiple failures—all embody the principle that inner willpower fuels human progress.

This essay has argued that human progress is fundamentally an internal pursuit driven by the strength of our will and our commitment to moral integrity, justice, and cohesion to make this world a better place. By fortifying our resolve and continuously striving for self-betterment, we transcend limitations and contribute to the collective advancement of humanity. True wisdom is not achieved in isolation but must be shared, illuminating the paths of others. Through real-life examples, from historical figures to everyday experiences, this discussion has demonstrated that the boundless potential of the human will is the key to unlocking a life of purpose, resilience, and profound impact.

24

FALSE SECURITY

THE DANGERS OF COMPLACENCY IN OUR EVOLUTION

I n our lives, there are moments when everything appears to be moving in the right direction, as if we are in God's favor. We feel untroubled, convinced that we are no longer dealing with dark, unseen perils such as deceit, envy, or betrayal that once crept into our path. As a result, we may lower our defense systems and enjoy peace and well-being. But is this belief in safety always justified, or does it blind us to lurking dangers? How does false security lead to personal and social vulnerability, and why is vigilance essential for personal growth? We might let ourselves be rocked by praise and flattery, believing that hostilities have disappeared and that the smiles and celebrations of those around us are genuine. And yet beneath this surface of apparent goodwill lies a more profound, more indirect danger—something we fail to recognize until it is too late. This state of careless contentment is called false security.

This essay explores how the illusion of security can make us complacent, why discernment is crucial in human relationships, and how awareness can protect us from unseen threats. False security is a dangerous and deceptive attitude born from a failure to recognize that not everything is as it seems. Some people who smile at our success might secretly harbor resentment toward us. Their applause may cover envy, and their admiration may conceal a burning desire for our downfall. This is not to say that we should be constantly suspicious of others but that we should maintain a healthy level of trust while being aware of the possibility for hidden agendas.

We succumb to false impressions when we let our guard down, and in that instant, we become vulnerable to unseen threats intent on our destruction. However, this is not a fate we must accept. False security is not merely a lack of awareness but a failure of basic common sense, a vital misjudgment of human nature. Not all of our friends who celebrate our victories are sincere. The absence of open hostility does not mean that there is no conflict. Any assumptions of this kind imply that we need to understand the complex dynamics of human relationships. But with vigilance, we can regain control and protect ourselves from these hidden dangers.

Success can breed jealousy and deep resentment regardless of how it is achieved or deserved. Despite our hard work, there are always those who watch us with envy and quietly wish for our downfall and who, under the appearance of friendship, may conspire against us. But we are not powerless. We must remain vigilant, even if it is in our moments of triumph that we must exercise prudence.

Our vigilance is not just a shield but a tool for personal growth, meaning that we should do our best to protect our lives and use our time for self-discovery, self-development, and self-realization. In addition, understanding what governs human relationships helps us see beyond the surface and grasp the dynamics at play. Discernment and carefulness must be exercised to fulfill our duty to ourselves and our continuing self-development. Such an attitude does not mean we cultivate paranoia but nurture a healthy awareness. Again, basic common sense and experiences teach that true wisdom lies in understanding that not all smiles are sincere, not all praises are genuine, and not all who stand beside us are on our side. The evolution of our character and consciousness depends on our ability to see beyond the facade. We should not solely trust people's words; an inquiry through observation of the underlying intentions of others is crucial. During our lifetime, we must constantly strive to develop the skills necessary and maintain the genuine awareness to safely navigate the traps of human interactions with greater clarity to avoid being destroyed by those who may secretly wish us harm. This attitude is essential for us to develop to unlock the truths beneath the surface, making us wise and insightful in our relationships.

Note that the false security we experience is a test of our discernment and an opportunity for growth in this life. If we work on that sincerely, such challenges will refine our common sense. We will see through the superficial and grasp the social reality of the world more profoundly, which is often veiled by conventionally accepted truths. Being aware of false security is not just a challenge but a duty and an opportunity for growth and the development of understanding of human relationships, which can instill a sense of optimism and hope in our life's journey.

Maintaining constant awareness will protect us from the ambushes of deceitful spirits and jealous minds. This vigilance is not a mark of distrust but a commitment to our evolution. We must defend or preserve ourselves to develop. In this adventure that is life, we may sometimes be too lazy to see the external threats that are the most dangerous due to our negligence in judgment. But with our vigilance, we can see these threats coming, and we can protect ourselves.

It is an understanding that in life's journey, the most significant dangers often come not from external threats but from our lack of judgment and our willingness to believe in safety that does not exist. To be on the safe side and for our progress, we must consistently build awareness, balancing our optimism with a realistic understanding of human nature. We are creatures of emotions and external circumstances that drive our actions most of the time, according to Spinoza. Our responsibility, especially for those of us who have the will and the determination to evolve, is to ensure that our growth is not stunted by complacency and that illusions of false security do not derail our progress. Only then can we continue our path of evolution, guided by an accurate and clear vision, unclouded by the deceptive comfort of unearned trust.

Several literary works and historical events illustrate the dangers of false security. In *Julius Caesar* by Shakespeare, we see that Caesar ignored multiple warnings, including the soothsayer's "Beware the Ides of March," as well as signs from his wife and close advisers. His belief in his untouchable position led to his betrayal and assassination by those he trusted. In *The Great Gatsby* by F. Scott Fitzgerald, we see that Gatsby believed his wealth and charm would win Daisy Buchanan back, ignoring the social realities and Tom Buchanan's dominance. His misplaced trust in an idealized version of love led to his tragic downfall. In the story of the Trojan War from Greek mythology, the Trojans believed the Greeks had retreated and left the giant wooden horse outside the gates of Troy as a peace offering. The Trojans let their guard down and brought the horse and its hidden Greek soldiers into their city, only to be ultimately destroyed. In *The Wizard of Lies: Bernie Madoff and the Death of Trust* by Diana B. Henriques, which is based on interviews with Madoff while he was in prison for his Ponzi scheme, many investors trusted his financial empire, believing in its stability. Their complacency prevented them from questioning inconsistencies, leading to financial ruin when the scheme collapsed.

This essay has argued that false security is a deceptive and dangerous state that makes us vulnerable to betrayal and unseen threats. People often fail to recognize the hidden dangers in their relationships and business dealings by assuming that peace or success guarantees safety. However, the sure way to protect ourselves and continue our evolution is by cultivating awareness, discernment, and vigilance. True wisdom lies not in paranoia but in maintaining a balanced understanding of human nature—acknowledging that not all smiles are sincere, this world is filled with deceiving souls and people with no sense of moral responsibility, and that genuine growth requires ongoing self-awareness and careful observation of the world around us.

25

WE SHOULD BE VIGILANT ABOUT GOING BACK TO THE SOURCE

I n our journey on Earth, we are not exempt from the choices that shape our moral destiny. Some of us begin our journeys with virtue but later fall into complacency or corruption. In contrast, others start on an unsteady path and have a lousy moral life, yet redeem themselves through steadfast effort. How can we ensure our lives conclude in moral triumph and we return to the source with integrity and grace?

This essay examines the significance of unwavering moral purpose, the dangers of moral compromise, and the necessity of fortitude in pursuing a virtuous life. It will examine how perseverance in virtue determines the ultimate fulfillment of human existence by reflecting on philosophical insights and real-world examples.

We must strive to live with unwavering integrity, dedicating ourselves to lives of purpose and virtue. Our ultimate aim should be to culminate this journey in a blaze of glory, returning to the source, the essence of all that is good and pure, in beauty and grace. A life loses its meaning if it does not end in moral triumph. If we begin well in our pursuit to return to the source and later let our will become corrupted and sow harm, the previous good we did at the beginning will be undone. No amount of past virtue can redeem the abandonment of morality in the pursuit of fleeting peace or selfish comfort. Such betrayal causes us to fall from grace, severing our connection to God, the source.

The path to fulfillment is demanding but simple. All that is required is to be steadfast. Success or failure depends greatly on the degree of our resolution. If we develop a strong, unyielding will focused on the higher goal, we will ensure a life that concludes in a glorious return to God. Even a life that begins poorly can be redeemed through sincere effort and transformation. However, persisting in wrongdoing and ending without redemption is squandering the gift of life entirely.

Through the perfection of our will, we gain clarity of vision and understanding of the path. It is better to endure suffering in this life than to exchange our grace for the fleeting pleasures of vice. Pleasures dissipate quickly, leaving the soul impoverished and burdened. Wicked, influential people might destroy our lives; for instance, we might lose our jobs. But this is not a loss but the highest form of advancement, a noble fight when we go ahead of unpleasant situations for moral development to eventually reunite with the source. Such an attitude is a testament to our commitment to integrity and virtue.

Using Spinoza's terms, since we are interconnected, virtue is not merely a series of isolated actions but a way of harmonizing with one another. It involves living like rational human beings, not like depraved humans or savage animals. Virtue calls us to act in ways consistent with moral universal laws. By doing so, we align our lives with the rational structure of the universe, reaching the elevated side of our nature as a precondition for returning to the source.

We should develop a steadfast will in addition to vigilance and fortitude to return to the source. Remember that our ultimate goal is to return to the source in beauty and grace. Such is the focus that should guide our actions and decisions and ensure we live a life of integrity and moral purpose.

Mandela's life serves as a compelling example of steadfast moral integrity. He endured many years of imprisonment for his role in South Africa of opposing apartheid, a system of legalization of racial segregation and discrimination, without compromising his commitment to justice and reconciliation. Even when faced with the opportunity for personal benefit through negotiations that would betray his principles, he remained resolute, ultimately leading South Africa to a more just future. His story illustrates that suffering for righteousness is not a loss but a higher form of fulfillment.

In *Man's Search for Meaning*, Viktor Frankl, a Holocaust survivor, describes how those who found purpose and moral clarity in extreme suffering could endure. At the same time, those who abandoned their inner resolve lost the will to live. His experience proves that external suffering is far less significant than the moral strength with which one faces adversity.

The Bible's parable of the prodigal son illustrates that some of us may begin poorly in life or not be proud of ourselves for applying virtues. Yet we can find redemption after a 360-degree turn later, like the son who squandered his inheritance in reckless living but ultimately repented and returned to his father. This story illustrates the possibility of moral restoration if one realigns with virtue.

Many whistleblowers, whether in the public or private sector and even religion, risk their careers and reputations to expose corruption. They choose integrity over personal comfort. For instance, figures like Edward Snowden or Frances Haugen exemplify individuals who, despite facing backlash, decide to prioritize truth over fleeting security. Such action shows that moral stead-fastness is not abstract.

This essay argues that the ultimate purpose of life is to main-tain unwavering moral integrity and return to the source in a state of grace. A meaningful life is not defined by temporary successes or comforts but by the steadfast pursuit of virtue. While some might begin on a righteous path and later falter, and others might struggle early on but redeem themselves, the key determinant of fulfillment is perseverance in moral purpose. Through historical, philosophical, and literary examples, this discussion has shown that integrity is the highest measure of human success in the face of adversity. Ultimately, we must cultivate vigilance, fortitude, and an unyielding commitment to virtue to ensure our journey culminates in a triumphant return to the source.

OUR SPIRITUAL JOURNEY BACK TOWARD THE SOURCE

DEVELOPING INNER STRENGTH THROUGH EXPERIENCES AND THE PATH TO WHOLENESS

Life often seems to be a series of random occurrences when facing its challenges, especially when others are voluntarily or involuntarily doing malevolent things to us we did not expect, in addition to all the other events that might put our lives in challenging situations. But when we start thinking, we can see that it is more than a series of random occurrences; it is a guided journey toward self-realization and spiritual evolution. Every challenge we face is an opportunity to break through the illusions that bind us to lower vibrations of existence. But what is the purpose of these trials? Are they mere sufferings or serve a greater function in our spiritual transformation?

This essay examines the nature of human struggles as necessary catalysts for growth, arguing that they are divinely designed to refine our consciousness, dissolve our attachments, and lead us back to our highest state of being—the ultimate reunion with the divine source. Suppose we have the gut to develop the courage to try to understand the deeper meaning behind life's adversities. In that case, we can embrace our experiences with greater awareness and move toward our wholeness with purpose.

In the grand account of existence, life can often seem like a continuous series of events, challenges, and experiences that shape our perceptions and beliefs. Yet beyond the mundane cycle of everyday struggles lies a profound philosophical truth that most of us refuse to understand: Our ultimate purpose in this life is to evolve, grow, and transcend the very material world, the illusion that binds us. At our core, we are seekers on a path of return—a return to the Monad, the singular divine source from which we all emanate.

We should expect to encounter many challenges or trials in our lives. Difficulties are not roadblocks but prompts for the success of our evolution; in other words, they are stepping stones. The universe and God have intricately woven them into the fabric of our existence to foster spiritual growth. Challenges compel us to confront our limitations and break the illusions that keep us chained to lower vibrations of existence.

In this context, growth is not merely about accumulating knowledge or achieving success by worldly standards. It is about the deep, often painful process of shedding old patterns, dissolving the lower ego, and aligning with our higher self. This process is not passive; it requires authentic experience—real moments that test our moral fiber and stretch the boundaries of what we believe is possible. Through these authentic experiences, we integrate wisdom at the core of our being, transcending the superficial to access a more profound truth.

Transcendence is a challenging path. It requires courage to face our shadows and surrender our attachments. The illusions that hold us—fear, greed, pride, and attachment—are manifestations of what many traditions call evil. In this context, *evil* does not necessarily refer to malevolent forces but rather to the negative influences that hinder our spiritual growth. We should not fear these manifestations because they are reflections of the separation from our divine origin. Being transcendent involves escaping these influences and understanding their role in our journey. When we develop sound intelligence, we will understand that they serve as signposts, marking areas where we need to heal and grow.

Returning to the source, or the Monad, does not mean that our life will revert to the state of origin; rather, it signifies a transformation, a progression. We return to God transformed, accumulating genuine experience, bearing the fruits of our journey through countless lifetimes and lessons well learned, meaning that we pass the class of life on Earth. The return to the source symbolizes a state of wholeness where we are no longer fragmented by the illusions of separateness. So we are transformed into a divine state and indivisible, liberated from the influences of evil that once held sway over us.

To be whole is to be aware of our true nature, see beyond the illusions of duality, and recognize the unity underlying all existence. This awareness, vision, and knowledge developed is basic common sense. To be whole is a liberation not bound by external circumstances but realized through inner transformation. The journey back to the source is, in essence, a journey back to ourselves, who we are—to the realization that we are, and always have been, part of the divine fabric of the universe.

In our modern world, losing sight of this ultimate purpose is easy with all the distractions, unenlightened media that inform and entertain us, false ideologies, and technology that can be misused or abused. We are often distracted by the noise of material desires and societal expectations, leading us away from the path of inner growth. Yet the daily trials serve as gentle reminders (or sometimes harsh awakenings) of the more profound work we are here to do. They beckon us to pause, reflect, and ask ourselves the fundamental question: What is the true nature of our existence? Wouldn't God be a joke, a hoax, if He had made the ulti-mate purpose of our lives here only to have as much superficial fun as we can, partying, drinking, and accumulating material things?

When we begin to see our challenges as opportunities for growth, we shift our perspective. We no longer view hardships as obstacles but as necessary steps in our spiritual evolution. Shifting our perception from having good times and seeing life as walking in an amusement park to embracing our challenges to growth as the essence of transcendence—this alchemical process transforms suffering into wisdom and darkness into light.

The ultimate realization is that the journey itself is the desti-nation. The trials, the growth, the transcendence, and the return are all parts of a divine dance. It is a process of remembering who we truly are: divine beings temporarily experiencing separation so that we may appreciate the profound beauty of unity.

As we evolve and transcend, we contribute to the evolution of the collective consciousness. Every individual's return to whole-ness brings a ripple of healing and light that touches others, helping them awaken to their path of return. In this way, our journey is not solitary but a shared journey—a collective move-ment toward realizing the divine on Earth. We are all part of this beautiful, interconnected web of spiritual growth.

Our ultimate purpose is not a distant goal to achieve in some far-off future but a present reality unfolding through each authentic experience. Our spiritual journey back toward God is a journey home, a return to a state of wholeness and divinity that transcends the influences of evil and reunites us with the Monad. The whole purpose behind all the turbulence is to develop inner strength through experiences to become whole and evolve to the highest state of being.

May we all embrace this journey with open hearts and minds,

knowing that every step brings us closer to realizing our divine nature and the ultimate return to the source.

This essay has argued that our challenges are not arbitrary but vital to our spiritual development. By embracing hardships as necessary lessons, we break free from illusions, cultivate inner strength, and transcend lower states of being. Our journey is not merely about surviving but evolving—shedding our attachments, refining our understanding, and returning to our divine source transformed. True wisdom lies in recognizing that our trials are not punishments but opportunities for enlightenment, and through them, we rediscover our innate connection to the divine.

REFERENCES

Altekar, Anant Sadashiv. *Education in Ancient India*. Varanasi: Nand Kishore & Bros, 1965.

al-Bukhari, Muhammad ibn Isma'il. *Sahih al-Bukhari*. Translated by Muhammad Muhsin Khan. Accessed October 10, 2023. https://sunnah.com/bukhari:13.

Aristotle. *Nicomachean Ethics*. Translated by Terence Irwin. Indianapolis: Hackett Publishing Company, 1999.

Assmann, Jan. *The Mind of Egypt: History and Meaning in the Time of the Pharaohs*. Translated by Andrew Jenkins. Cambridge, MA: Harvard University Press, 2003.

Aurelius, Marcus. *Meditations*. Translated by Gregory Hays. New York: Modern Library, 2002.

Berger, Peter L., and Thomas Luckmann. *The Social Construction of Reality: A Treatise in the Sociology of Knowledge*. New York: Anchor Books, 1966.

Bergson, Henri. *Time and Free Will: An Essay on the Immediate Data of Consciousness*. Translated by F. L. Pogson. London: George Allen & Unwin, 1910.

Branch, Taylor. "The Moral Example of Martin Luther King Jr." *The Atlantic*, January 18, 2018. www.theatlantic.com/magazine/archive/2018/02/martin-luther-king-moral-leadership/552551/.

Buddha. *The Udana & the Itivuttaka: Two Classics from the Pali Canon*. Translated by John D. Ireland. Kandy, Sri Lanka: Buddhist Publication Society, 1997. Accessed January 27, 2025.

Cadwalladr, Carole, and Emma Graham-Harrison. "Revealed: 50 Million Facebook Profiles Harvested for Cambridge Analytica in Major Data Breach." *The Guardian*, March 17, 2018. https://www.theguardian.com/news/2018/mar/17/cambridge-analytica-facebook-influence-us-election.

Chomsky, Noam, and Edward S. Herman. *Manufacturing Consent: The Political Economy of the Mass Media*. New York: Pantheon Books, 1988.

Cone, James H. "Martin Luther King Jr. and the Legacy of Justice." *Harvard Divinity Bulletin* 38, no. 1 (2010). https://bulletin.hds.harvard.edu/martin-luther-king-jr-and-the-legacy-of-justice/. Accessed January 27, 2025.

Confucius. *Les Entretiens de Confucius (Lun Yu)*. Translated and annotated by Pierre Ryckmans. Paris: Gallimard, 1987.

Confucius. *The Analects of Confucius.* Translated by Arthur Waley. New York: Vintage Books, 1938.

De Bary, Wm. Theodore, and Irene Bloom, eds. *Sources of Chinese Tradition: From Earliest Times to 1600.* 2nd ed. Vol. 1. New York: Columbia University Press, 1999.

Dickens, Charles. *A Christmas Carol.* London: Chapman & Hall, 1843.

——. *Great Expectations.* London: Chapman & Hall, 1861.

Dostoevsky, Fyodor. *Crime and Punishment.* Translated by Richard Pevear and Larissa Volokhonsky. New York: Vintage Classics, 1993.

Epictetus. *The Art of Living: The Classical Manual on Virtue, Happiness, and Effectiveness.* Translated by Sharon Lebell. New York: HarperOne, 1995.

Federal Trade Commission. "FTC Imposes $5 Billion Penalty and Sweeping New Privacy Restrictions on Facebook." Washington, DC: Federal Trade Commission, 2019. https://www.ftc.gov/news-events/news/press-releases/2019/07/ftc-imposes-5-billion-penalty-sweeping-new-privacy-restrictions-facebook.

Ferrell, O. C.; John Fraedrich; and Linda Ferrell. *Business Ethics: Ethical Decision Making and Cases.* 13th ed. Boston: Cengage Learning, 2020.

Festinger, Leon. *A Theory of Cognitive Dissonance.* Stanford, CA: Stanford University Press, 1957.

Fitzgerald, F. Scott. *The Great Gatsby.* New York: Scribner, 1925.

Frankl, Viktor E. *Man's Search for Meaning.* Boston: Beacon Press, 1946.

——. *The Will to Meaning: Foundations and Applications of Logotherapy.* New York: Meridian, 1988.

Gandhi, M. K. *The Story of My Experiments with Truth: An Autobiography.* Translated by Mahadev Desai. Boston: Beacon Press, 1993.

Garrett, Don, ed. *The Cambridge Companion to Spinoza.* Cambridge, MA: Cambridge University Press, 1996.

Gramsci, Antonio. *Selections from the Prison Notebooks.* Edited and translated by Quintin Hoare and Geoffrey Nowell Smith. New York: International Publishers, 1971.

Han, Byung-Chul. *The Burnout Society.* Translated by Erik Butler. Stanford: Stanford University Press, 2015.

Haugen, Frances, and Bill Cope. *The Power of One: How I Found the Strength to Tell the Truth and Why I Blew the Whistle on Facebook.* London: Little, Brown, 2023.

Henriques, Diana B. *The Wizard of Lies: Bernie Madoff and the Death of Trust.* New York: Times Books, 2011.

Homer. *The Iliad & the Odyssey.* Translated by Samuel Butler. New York: Barnes & Noble Classics, 1996.

Hugo, Victor. *Les Misérables.* Translated by Norman Denny. London: Penguin Classics, 1982.

Isaacson, Walter. *Steve Jobs*. New York: Simon & Schuster, 2011.

Isaak, Jim, and Mina J. Hanna. "User Data Privacy: Facebook, Cambridge Analytica, and Privacy Protection." *Computer* 51, no. 8 (2018): 56-59. https://doi.org/10.1109/MC.2018.3191268.

Jaeger, Werner. *Paideia: The Ideals of Greek Culture*. Translated by Gilbert Highet. Oxford, England: Oxford University Press, 1945.

Josephson, Matthew. *Edison: A Biography*. New York: McGraw-Hill, 1959.

Jung, Carl G. *The Archetypes and the Collective Unconscious*. Translated by R. F. C. Hull. Princeton, NJ: Princeton University Press, 1981.

Kabat-Zinn, Jon. *Full Catastrophe Living: Using the Wisdom of Your Body and Mind to Face Stress, Pain, and Illness*. New York: Bantam Books, 1990.

Kahneman, Daniel. *Thinking, Fast and Slow*. New York: Farrar, Straus and Giroux, 2011.

Kant, Immanuel. *Groundwork of the Metaphysics of Morals*. Translated by Mary Gregor. Cambridge, MA: Cambridge University Press, 1997.

Karen E. Hudson, *Paul R. Williams, Architect: A Legacy of Style*. New York: Rizzoli, 1993.

Keller, Helen. *The Story of My Life*. New York: Doubleday, Page & Co., 1903.

Kierkegaard, Søren. *The Concept of Anxiety: A Simple Psychologically Orienting Deliberation on the Dogmatic Issue of Hereditary Sin*. Translated by Reidar Thomte. Princeton: Princeton University Press, 1980.

———. *The Sickness Unto Death: A Christian Psychological Exposition for Upbuilding and Awakening*. Translated by Alastair Hannay. London: Penguin Books, 1989.

"Kindness Has Ripple Effect." *Smithfield Times*, December 5, 2023. https://www.smithfieldtimes.com/2023/12/05/letter-kindness-has-ripple-effect/.

King Jr., Martin Luther. *A Testament of Hope: The Essential Writings and Speeches*. Edited by James M. Washington. New York: HarperOne, 1991.

———. "I Have a Dream." Delivered August 28, 1963. www.americanrhetoric.com/speeches/mlkihaveadream.htm. Accessed January 27, 2025.

——. *Letter from Birmingham Jail*. April 16, 1963. www.thekingcenter.org/king-philosophy/. Accessed January 27, 2025.

———. *Stride Toward Freedom: The Montgomery Story*. New York: Harper & Brothers, 1958.

Leadbeater, C. W. *The Monad*. Adyar, India: Theosophical Publishing House, 1920

Lao Tzu. *Tao Te Ching*. Translated by Stephen Mitchell. New York: Harper & Row, 1988.

Leo, Alan. *The Art of Synthesis: The Astrological Principles of Success*. London: Modern Astrology Office, 1912.

Lewis, C.S. *The Great Divorce*. New York: HarperOne, 2001.

References

Lippmann, Walter. *Public Opinion*. New York: Harcourt, Brace and Co., 1922.

MacIntyre, Alasdair. After Virtue: A Study in Moral Theory. 3rd ed. Notre Dame, IN: University of Notre Dame Press, 2007

Mandela, Nelson. *Long Walk to Freedom: The Autobiography of Nelson Mandela*. New York: Little, Brown, 1994.

Marshall, Eugene. The Spiritual Automaton: Spinoza's Science of the Mind. Oxford, England: Oxford University Press, 2013

Marty, Peter. "Lucilla Goodman and Other Ordinary Saints." *The Christian Century*, June 16, 2021. https://www.christiancentury.org/article/editorpub lisher/lucilla-goodman-and-other-ordinary-saints.

McLuhan, Marshall. *Understanding Media: The Extensions of Man*. New York: McGraw-Hill, 1964.

Muslim ibn al-Hajjaj. *Sahih Muslim*. Translated by Abdul Hamid Siddiqui. New Delhi, India: Kitab Bhavan, 2000.

Musonius Rufus. *Lectures and Sayings*. Translated by Cynthia King. CreateSpace Independent Publishing Platform, 2011.

Nickerson, Raymond S. "Confirmation Bias: A Ubiquitous Phenomenon in Many Guises." *Review of General Psychology* 2, no. 2 (1998): 175–220.

Nietzsche, Friedrich. *Thus Spoke Zarathustra*. Translated by Walter Kaufmann. New York: Penguin Books, 1978.

Oken, Alan. *Pocket Guide to the Tarot*. Berkeley, CA: The Crossing Press, 1996.

"Parenting in America: Outlook, Worries, Aspirations Are Strongly Linked to Financial Situation." Pew Research Center, December 17, 2015. https://www.pewresearch.org/social-trends/2015/12/17/parenting-in-america/.

Plato. *Apology*. Translated by G. M. A. Grube. Revised by John M. Cooper, in *Plato: Complete Works*, edited by John M. Cooper. Indianapolis, IN: Hackett Publishing, 1997.

——. *The Republic*. Translated by Allan Bloom. New York: Basic Books, 1991.

Postman, Neil. *Amusing Ourselves to Death: Public Discourse in the Age of Show Business*. New York: Penguin Books, 1985.

Purucket, de G. *Occult Glossary: A Compendium of Oriental and Theosophical Terms*. Pasadena, CA: Theosophic University Press, 1972.

Rawls, John. *A Theory of Justice*. Revised ed. Cambridge, MA: Harvard University Press, 1999.

Roberts, Robert C., and W. Jay Wood. *Intellectual Virtues: An Essay in Regulative Epistemology*. Oxford, England: Oxford University Press, 2007.

Ross, Nancy Wilson, ed. *The World of Zen: An East–West Anthology*. New York: Vintage Books, 1960.

Schein, Edgar H. *Process Consultation Volume II: Lessons for Managers and Consultants*. Reading, MA: Addison-Wesley, 1987.

Schuré, Édouard. *Les Grands Initiés*. Paris: Librairie Académique Perrin, 1960.

Schweitzer, Albert. *Reverence for Life: The Ethics of Albert Schweitzer for the Twenty-First Century*. Edited by Marvin Meyer. Syracuse, NY: Syracuse University Press, 2002.

Shakespeare, William. *Julius Caesar*. Edited by David Daniell. London: Arden Shakespeare, 1998.

———. *The Tragedy of Macbeth*. Edited by Stephen Orgel. New York: Penguin Classics, 2000.

Shelley, Mary. *Frankenstein: or The Modern Prometheus*. London: Lackington, Hughes, Harding, Mavor & Jones, 1818.

"Slow Down!" *Christian Minimalism*. October 27, 2018. https://christianminimalism.com/2018/10/27/slow-down/.

Snowden, Edward. *Permanent Record*. New York: Metropolitan Books, 2019.

Spink, Kathryn. *Mother Teresa: A Complete Authorized Biography*. New York: HarperOne, 1997.

Spinoza, Baruch. *L'Éthique*. Translated by Roland Caillois. Paris: Éditions Galimard, 1954

Star, Ély. *Les Mystères de l'Horoscope*. Éditeurs Hector et Henri Durville. Paris: Éditions Hector et Henri Durville, 1888.

Steinbeck, John. *Of Mice and Men*. New York: Covici Friede, 1937.

Teilhard de Chardin, Pierre. *The Divine Milieu: An Essay on the Interior Life*. New York: Harper & Row, 1960.

The Holy Bible: New International Version. Grand Rapids, MI: Zondervan, 2011.

Thera, Nyanatiloka. *The Buddha's Path to Deliverance: A Systemic Exposition in the Words of the Sutta Pitaka*. 2nd ed. Onalaska, WA: Pariyatti Press, 1959.

Tolle, Eckhart. *The Power of Now: A Guide to Spiritual Enlightenment*. Novato, CA: New World Library, 1997.

Vlastos, Gregory, ed. *The Philosophy of Socrates: A Collection of Critical Essays*. Notre Dame, IN: University of Notre Dame Press, 1980.

"What Is the Spiritual Meaning of Dreaming About Water?" Comanifesting.com. https://comanifesting.com/what-is-the-spiritual-meaning-of-dreaming-about-water/.

Wigley, Christian. "Towards a New Envisioning of Ubermensch: A Trans-Nietzschean Response to Nihilism in the Digital Age." Master's thesis, University of Birmingham, June 2017. https://core.ac.uk/download/131163998.pdf

Wilde, Oscar. *The Picture of Dorian Gray*. London: Ward, Lock & Co., 1890.

Zuboff, Shoshana. *The Age of Surveillance Capitalism: The Fight for a Human Future at the New Frontier of Power*. New York: PublicAffairs, 2019.

ABOUT THE AUTHOR

Yvon Milien was born in Port-au-Prince, Haiti, and received a bachelor of science degree in civil engineering from the Institut Supérieur Technique d'Haïti. He earned a bachelor of science degree in mass communications from the State University of Haiti, where he wrote a thesis titled *"Position de la Presse dans la Vie Sociale Haitienne: Recherches sur l'Orientation que Donne le Contenu Educatif de la Presse pour Equilibrer la Vie Sociale"* ("The Press's Position in Haitian Social Life: A Study of the Orientation of the Content of the Media to Sustain Haitian Political and Social Life") for the Department of Human Sciences.

In 1997, he obtained a master of science degree in sociology from Brigham Young University, where he wrote a thesis titled "Haitian Mormon Converts Dwelling in New York City: A Cross-Cultural Perspective in Understanding, Interpreting, and Experiencing the Mormon Subculture."

In 2000, Milien obtained a master's degree in international relations and a master's degree in public administration from Syracuse University, where he wrote a thesis titled "Fostering Democracy and Human Rights in Haiti: An Examination of Haitian Democracy."

In 2004, he earned a master's degree in education from the City University of New York, where he wrote a thesis titled "The Effectiveness of Graphic Organizers and Baxendell's Guiding

Principles for Instructional Practices with Special Needs Students."

www.ingramcontent.com/pod-product-compliance
Lightning Source LLC
Chambersburg PA
CBHW031319120626
46554CB00001BA/476